FREDERICK DOUGLASS

and the

FOURTH *of* JULY

FREDERICK DOUGLASS

and the

FOURTH of JULY

JAMES A. COLAIACO

First published 2006 by
PALGRAVE MACMILLAN™
175 Fifth Avenue, New York, N.Y. 10010 and
Houndmills, Basingstoke, Hampshire, England RG21 6XS.
Companies and representatives throughout the world.

PALGRAVE MACMILLAN is the global academic imprint of the Palgrave
Macmillan division of St. Martin's Press, LLC and of Palgrave Macmillan Ltd.
Macmillan® is a registered trademark in the United States, United Kingdom
and other countries. Palgrave is a registered trademark in the European Union
and other countries.

ISBN 1–4039–7033–5 hardback

Library of Congress Cataloging-in-Publication Data
Frederick Douglass and the Fourth of July / James A. Colaiaco.
    p.   cm.
  Includes bibliographical references and index.
  ISBN 1–4039–7033–5
  1. Douglass, Frederick, 1818–1895.   2. Fourth of July.   3. Constitutional
history—United States.   4. African Americans—Civil rights—History—
19th century   5. Antislavery movements—United States.   I. Title

E449.D75C63   2006
973.7'114'092—dc22

                                                                  2005051520

A catalogue record for this book is available from the British Library.

Design by Letra Libre, Inc.

First edition: February 2006
10 9   8   7   6   5   4   3   2   1

Printed in the United States of America

To Nancy, my kindred spirit

CONTENTS

PROLOGUE

On Monday, July 5, 1852, Frederick Douglass, the former slave, made
his way to majestic Corinthian Hall, located in downtown Rochester,
New York, near the Genesee River.[1] He had been invited to deliver a
speech to celebrate the Fourth of July.[2] For the past few weeks, he had
labored into the night, gathering his thoughts about the urgent message he wanted to give the nation. Arriving at Corinthian Hall, Douglass, the keynote speaker of the day, walked to his seat and faced his
audience. With great dignity and a stern countenance, he surveyed the
assemblage of mostly white people.

Since the early years of the American republic, the Fourth of July
has been the day Americans reaffirm their common identity and purpose in a collective ritual. For Douglass, the day had multiple meanings. It was the anniversary of the birth of the United States of
America, which, he agreed, should be celebrated; the Fourth of July
was the anniversary of the Declaration of Independence, the historic
document that committed the nation to the ideals of liberty and equal
rights for all. But for Douglass, the Fourth of July was also a day to remember that America's ideals remained unfulfilled for blacks enslaved
in the South. Throughout his life, Douglass struggled to resolve the

American dilemma, the contradiction between the ideals professed by the nation's Founders and the practice of denying human rights to black Americans and other minorities.[3]

A self-educated fugitive slave, abolitionist, advocate for women's rights, orator, journalist, and diplomat, Frederick Douglass was the most famous black person of the nineteenth century. He is best known for his three inspiring autobiographies. But his greatest legacy to America is his oratory, forged in the crucible of the battle against slavery in the years prior to the Civil War. With extraordinary courage, he had escaped from his slave master. Having taught himself to read and write while a slave, Douglass is one of the most inspiring examples of the power of literacy. Shortly after attaining his freedom, he came under the influence of the great abolitionist, William Lloyd Garrison, who stirred the nation's conscience by calling for the immediate and complete abolition of slavery. As a member of Garrison's Massachusetts Anti-Slavery Society, Douglass honed his oratorical skills. After publishing his first autobiography in 1845, *Narrative of the Life of Frederick Douglass*, which emphasized the moral evil of slavery, Douglass made the first of two excursions to Great Britain, where he spoke from a variety of platforms, electrifying his audiences. While he initially subscribed to Garrison's rigid views, including denouncing the United States Constitution as pro-slavery, Douglass's careful study led him to embrace the document as the abolitionists' greatest legal weapon.

Having taken his anti-slavery message to Britain in 1847, Douglass had achieved international recognition as a great orator. He emerged as an independent thinker, ready to create his own path. In 1847, as an offensive against slavery, he founded an abolitionist newspaper, the *North Star*, in Rochester, New York. To the dismay of the Garrisonians, by 1851 he had converted not only to the United States Constitution, but also to pragmatic party politics. During the next decade, as tensions over slavery between the North and the South pushed the nation to the brink of civil war, Douglass delivered hundreds of speeches throughout the North calling upon the federal government to abolish slavery in the South. Douglass warned that failing to eradicate the moral evil of slavery would arouse divine retribution.

Despite the valiant efforts of Douglass and others, slavery continued to spread. The antebellum period was dominated by a struggle between the North and the South over whether newly acquired lands would become slave or free states. The outcome would have important political consequences, including control of Congress, the office of the presidency, the composition of the Supreme Court, and ultimately the fate of the nation. In 1850, Congress passed the Fugitive Slave Law, which in effect nationalized slavery by requiring citizens in the North to assist in the return of runaway slaves. Douglass began advocating the abolition of slavery through political means, including support for anti-slavery political parties. When many black reformers, along with anti-slavery whites, believed that the best solution was to free the slaves and ship them out of the United States, Douglass remained a committed integrationist, insisting that blacks should not abandon America and its ideals. He also practiced civil disobedience as a leader in the Underground Railroad movement that assisted hundreds of fugitive slaves in their escape from the South to safe haven in Canada.

In the 1850s, Frederick Douglass and Abraham Lincoln—two giants on the stage of American history—embarked on paths that would converge on the issue of slavery. On June 16, 1858, Lincoln's "House Divided" speech proclaimed that the nation could not survive half slave and half free. While both Douglass and Lincoln, inspired by the ideals of liberty and equality enshrined in the Declaration of Independence, agreed that slavery was immoral, they disagreed on the best method to abolish the institution. Douglass had become convinced that the Constitution was anti-slavery, but Lincoln insisted that the document did not authorize Congress to abolish the institution in the South. The most that the federal government could do, in Lincoln's judgment, was to prevent slavery's extension into new territories. Lincoln hoped that, confined to the South, slavery would die a natural death. While Lincoln was convinced that preserving the Union was more important than abolishing slavery, Douglass believed that a Union with slavery was an unacceptable betrayal of the nation's democratic ideals.

In the years prior to the Civil War, Douglass emerged as a formidable interpreter of the nation's founding documents. Read from an ethical perspective, he argued, the Declaration of Independence and the United States Constitution were essentially abolition documents. The Preamble to the Constitution alone provided sufficient legal basis to eradicate slavery. The Constitution was designed to secure for all persons the inalienable natural rights to life, liberty, and the pursuit of happiness proclaimed in the Declaration. The Supreme Court of the

United States disagreed. Five years after Douglass's July Fourth oration, in the infamous 1857 *Dred Scott* decision, Chief Justice Roger B.
Taney, speaking for a pro-slavery Court, ruled that no black American,
slave or free, was a citizen of the United States. Taney argued that according to the Constitution blacks were property, not human beings.
They were not endowed with inalienable rights. The Chief Justice defended the Court's decision on the grounds that it expressed the original intentions of the nation's Founders. *Dred Scott* essentially denied the
American dilemma and was a devastating blow to the anti-slavery
movement. In the minds of many Americans, the Supreme Court had
definitively settled the slavery question that had plagued the nation
since its inception. Black Americans were unequivocally excluded
from the rights of the Declaration of Independence. Nor were they
among "We the people" who established the Constitution. Blacks were
not citizens of the United States, but aliens. If they were not included
within the body politic in the first place, the nation could not logically
be accused of violating its founding principles.

Dred Scott aroused a storm of protest throughout the North, edging
the nation closer to civil war. The decision radicalized Douglass. He
challenged the Supreme Court, arguing that the decision was based
upon a misreading of the United States Constitution. But the prospect
of repealing *Dred Scott* was bleak. As the battle against slavery by
means of moral persuasion and politics proved to be ineffective, Douglass reluctantly concluded that war against the South was inevitable.
He had always rejected violence in the past, but *Dred Scott* made him
seriously consider the idea of a slave rebellion in the South. When in
1859 the white abolitionist John Brown sought Douglass's support for
his raid on Harpers Ferry, he rejected the venture only because it was
strategically unsound and not because it would be violent. Soon after
Brown's raid was crushed, making Brown a martyr for the abolitionist
cause, Douglass left for Britain, once again bringing the debate over
human rights to an international forum.

Late in life, in his third and final autobiography, composed at his
home in the Anacostia estate of Cedar Hill, Washington, D.C., Douglass reflected upon the issue that consumed him: "I write freely of myself, not from choice, but because I have, by my cause, been morally
forced into thus writing. Time and events have summoned me to stand
forth both as a witness and an advocate for a people long dumb, not al-

lowed to speak for themselves, yet much misunderstood and deeply wronged."[4] The same motive drove his oratory. He spoke at anti-slavery meetings, state black conventions, and ceremonial gatherings. He spoke in halls, churches, auditoriums, courthouses, tents, and open fields. He spoke to give voice to black Americans so that they might be freed from the inhumanity of slavery and from the injustice of racial segregation. He spoke so that blacks might be inspired to stand up for their human rights to liberty and equality.

America took notice. The *New York Tribune* and the *Chicago Tribune* printed full-length accounts of Douglass's many speeches, and they were summarized in the *New York Times*.[5] As early as 1841, one paper observed: "As a speaker [Douglass] has few equals. It is not declamation—but oratory, power of debate. He has wit, arguments, sarcasm, pathos—all that first rate men show in their master efforts."[6] In 1859, the *New York Tribune* included Douglass among the two hundred people of the nation's "Lecturing Fraternity," recognized for their exceptional rhetorical ability. In 1872, the *New York Times* called him "the representative orator of the colored race."[7] The abolition movement had no more inspiring advocate than Douglass. "White men and black men," proclaimed black abolitionist William Wells Brown, "had talked against slavery, but none had ever spoken like Frederick Douglass."[8] In an age when the standards of oratory were much higher than today, many of Douglass's speeches, delivered over a period of more than fifty years, were considered among the best in the American rhetorical tradition.

Two weeks prior to Douglass's July Fourth 1852 address, black orator William G. Allen singled out his fellow abolitionist's unique gifts: "In versatility of oratorical power, I know of no one who can begin to approach the celebrity of Frederick Douglass."[9] Douglass's reputation as a speaker continued unabated throughout the nineteenth century. In 1893, two years before Douglass's death, James Monroe Gregory, professor of classics at Howard University, offered these words of praise: "By whatever standard judged, Mr. Douglass will take high rank as orator and writer." A great orator like Douglass is one who not only delivers great speeches, but also "touches the hearts of his hearers."[10] When Douglass died on February 20, 1895, the reformer Elizabeth Cady Stanton, who knew him since the 1840s and with whom he made common cause supporting women's rights, paid him eloquent tribute in her diary. Stanton never forgot the first time she saw Douglass speak: "He stood there like an African prince, majestic in his wrath. Around him sat the great antislavery orators of the day, earnestly watching the effect of his eloquence on that immense audience, that laughed and wept by turns, completely carried away by the wondrous gifts of his pathos and humor. On this occasion, all the other speakers seemed tame after Frederick Douglass."[11]

Frederick Douglass awakened the conscience of the nation, compelling Americans to confront the gravest moral dilemma in its history. His attack on slavery and defense of human dignity brought him into conflict with the slave states of the South and with the states of the North, where free blacks were segregated and deprived of the full benefits of citizenship. He confronted a nation reluctant to take the necessary steps to abolish slavery. Despite formidable obstacles, he refused to be silenced. Delivering hundreds of speeches on behalf of those condemned to live in slavery, Douglass inspired, converted, and provoked. He mesmerized his audiences. No speaker was more impassioned, more devoted to the advancement of human rights. No person understood better the meaning of the American creed as embodied in the Declaration of Independence and the Preamble to the United States Constitution, and no one was more eloquent in summoning the nation to fulfill this creed for all, regardless of race.

CHAPTER 1

FREDERICK DOUGLASS
AND THE
FOURTH OF JULY

*I do not remember ever to have appeared as a speaker before any as-
sembly more shrinkingly, or with a greater distrust of my ability,
than I do this day.*

—*Frederick Douglass,*
"What to the Slave Is the Fourth of July?"

I

Some five to six hundred people filed into Corinthian Hall in
Rochester, New York on July 5, 1852. They had come to hear the oration by Frederick Douglass celebrating the Fourth of July. By this
time, he had become an esteemed abolitionist and the most famous
black American of his era. Douglass had been invited to speak by the
Rochester Ladies' Anti-Slavery Society.[1] The event had been adver-
tised in the papers and on placards. The Fourth of July is the most important day in what has been called the American "civil religion,"
meaning the unifying beliefs, myths, and rituals shared by citizens of
the United States from the nation's inception. This civil religion has its
sacred scripture—the Declaration of Independence and the Constitu-

tion, including the Bill of Rights; its holidays—the Fourth of July and Memorial Day; its symbols—the Liberty Bell, the American flag, and the Statue of Liberty; and its revered personages—George Washington, Thomas Jefferson, Abraham Lincoln, and Susan B. Anthony. All of these elements have been incorporated in the narrative that Americans use to explain their origins and identity.

In the first part of the nineteenth century, Fourth of July ceremonials were solemn, almost religious occasions, often held in churches and modeled after a Protestant service. Prayers were intoned, hymns were sung, and the Declaration of Independence was recited with piety and fervor. On July Fourth, orators traditionally underscored the belief that America—hailed by New England Puritan John Winthrop as "a city on a hill"—had been chosen by God to fulfill a special mission in the world, to create a moral society. But America, despite its democratic and moral goals, harbored a hideous injustice, the institution of slavery. Most blacks regarded the Fourth of July as a white holiday, a day of mourning rather than celebration.[2] With the expansion of the abolitionist movement in the 1830s and 1840s, Independence Day became an occasion for abolitionists not so much to celebrate the past and preserve tradition, but to remind the nation of its betrayal. The contradiction of a nation tolerating slavery while professing the moral principles of the Declaration of Independence would eventually threaten the survival of the Union.

In the early years of the republic, celebrations of Independence Day were sporadic. But after the victory of the United States over Britain in the War of 1812, renewed patriotism inspired nationwide regular observance of the holiday.[3] The mockery of a nation celebrating freedom while upholding slavery became increasingly obvious. In the North, free blacks and abolitionists often used the Fourth of July to lift their voices in protest, emphasizing the contradiction between the nation's promise and slavery. Because July Fourth fell on a Sunday in 1852, the celebrations in Rochester had been postponed until the next day, July 5. Douglass welcomed the postponement. For years, abolitionists and black Americans often deliberately waited until July 5 as an expression of protest. As Peter Osborne declared at the New Haven African Church in Connecticut on July 5, 1832: "On account of the misfortune of our color, our fourth of July comes on the fifth; but I hope and trust that when the

Declaration of Independence is fully executed, which declared that all men, without respect to person, were born free and equal, we may then have our fourth of July on the fourth."[4] While the nation was celebrating freedom, the southern plantations were filled with slaves. Many blacks in the North refused to partake in the festivities. Even black children from the New York African Free School, including the future black minister Alexander Crummell, vowed not to celebrate the Fourth of July until the abolition of slavery.[5] For the black abolitionist Sojourner Truth, Independence Day symbolized both the promise of freedom and its denial. Her master had pledged to free her on July 4, 1826, but the day came and went without word from him. The following year, on the Fourth of July, she was freed by the State Legislature of New York.[6] Slave rebel Nat Turner had initially intended his ill-fated slave rebellion in Southampton, Virginia to occur on July 4, 1831. The *Weekly Anglo-African* explained on July 23, 1859: "The people generally do not understand why one should celebrate a day that . . . brought freedom to whites and slavery to colored people."[7] Mindful that the liberty and equality principles of the Declaration of Independence had not been applied to slaves, many abolitionists and black protesters chose to recognize the national holiday the day *after*, on July 5.

II

Frederick Douglass was born Frederick Augustus Washington Bailey in Talbot County on the Eastern Shore of Maryland sometime in February 1818. He was the son of Harriet Bailey, a field slave, and a white man believed to be his master, Aaron Anthony, who managed the large plantations of Colonel Edward Lloyd. Douglass was separated from his mother when he was an infant. "I never saw my mother," he related, "more than four or five times in my life, and each of those times was very short in duration, and at night." Douglass's mother, who died when he was about seven years old, had been sent to work twelve miles away. To see her son, Harriet Bailey had to walk twelve miles through the night and make sure she returned to work by dawn, if she wanted to avoid a severe beating. "She would lie down with me," he recalled, "and get me to sleep, but long before I waked she was gone."[8] On the plantation, the child Frederick endured great hardships. He had no clothes other than a linen shirt that reached his knees, and no bed other than a coarse blanket.

Frederick lived with his grandmother, Betsy Bailey, until the age of eight, when his master Aaron Anthony died. Ownership of the young boy passed to Anthony's son-in-law, Thomas Auld. Subsequently, Frederick was sent, by "divine providence," he later wrote, from the plantation in rural Maryland to live in Baltimore with his owner's brother, Hugh Auld, and his wife Sophia. Urban slavery was not as oppressive as that on the plantation, and in the Auld household young Douglass was relatively well treated. Hearing Sophia Auld frequently read the Bible aroused in him a desire to penetrate the "mystery of reading." Upon his request, Sophia began teaching the nine-year-old Frederick the alphabet. Literacy would open the way for Douglass to attain his personhood. When Hugh Auld realized the precocious child's considerable progress, he forbade his wife to further instruct the slave to read. It was not only unlawful, he warned his wife, but also unsafe, for it would make Douglass uncontrollable. "He should know nothing but the will of his master, and learn to obey it." "Learning would spoil the best nigger in the world." "If you teach that nigger . . . how to read the bible, there will be no keeping him." "It would forever unfit him for the duties of a slave." "If you learn him how to read, he'll want to know how to write; and, this accomplished, he'll be running away with himself." His master's words had a profound effect upon young Douglass, who was attentively listening: "His iron sentences, cold and harsh, sunk deep into my heart, and stirred up not only my feelings into a sort of rebellion, but awakened within me a slumbering train of vital thought. It was a new and special revelation, dispelling a painful mystery, against which my youthful understanding had struggled, and struggled in vain, to wit: the *white* man's power to perpetuate the enslavement of the *black* man. 'Very well, thought I;' 'knowledge unfits a child to be a slave.' I instinctively assented to the proposition; and from that moment I understood the direct pathway from slavery to freedom."[9]

The master's words were the spark that ignited the flame. The painful incident was an epiphany for Douglass. He was determined to learn how to read. He secretly taught himself. He perceived the radical difference between himself, a slave, and his master as never before: "The argument which he so warmly urged, against my learning to read, only served to inspire me with a desire and determination to learn."[10] As long as he remained illiterate, his mind subservient to his master, his body could never be free. He would be relegated to a life of silence and invisibility. Douglass defied his master. Seeking to learn the meaning of words, he would ask for the help of any willing white playmate in the streets of Baltimore. *Webster's Spelling Book* became his constant companion. Acquiring literacy was for Douglass a Promethean act of rebellion necessary for the achievement of freedom. Reading gave him access to books, in which he discovered liberating ideas that would sustain him throughout his life as an abolitionist and reformer. Reading newspapers that he picked up in the streets of Baltimore informed him of southern resistance to the abolition movement and the increasing sectional conflict between the North and the South over the issue of slavery. He soon realized that learning to write would enable him to wield the power of the pen on behalf of millions of oppressed people. "With playmates for my teachers, fences and pavements for my copy books, and chalk for my pen and ink," he remembered, "I learned the art of writing."[11] As Henry Louis Gates, Jr. observes: "Nowhere else among the hundred odd slave narratives published by blacks between 1760 and 1865 was the proverbial leap to freedom so inextricably intertwined with literacy."[12]

Douglass also discovered the power of the spoken word. At age thirteen, he purchased with his meager savings a used copy of Caleb Bingham's book, *The Columbian Orator,* a collection of speeches that opened his mind, inspiring him to become a public speaker. Within its pages, Douglass found brief impassioned speeches on human rights by William Pitt the Elder, Charles James Fox, and Richard Sheridan, speeches that Douglass read over and over, absorbing not only their message of freedom but also their rhetorical style. He also studied the oratory of Socrates, Cicero, Cato, George Washington, and Napoleon. As Douglass relates in his autobiographies, these speeches "enabled me to give tongue to many interesting thoughts, which had frequently flashed through my soul, and died away for want of utterance."[13] The speeches articulated what the young Douglass had been feeling since he learned to read—the burning desire to be free. Frederick Douglass the orator was born.

While Douglass avidly studied *The Columbian Orator,* he underwent another life-defining moment. At the age of thirteen or fourteen, as he read the Bible with a devout free black lay preacher named Charles Lawson, Douglass experienced a spiritual awakening. "'The Lord had a great work for me to do,'" Douglass recalled "Uncle" Lawson telling him. He must preach the gospel. Lawson's "words made a deep impression on my mind, and I verily felt that some such work was before me, though I could not see *how* I should ever engage in its performance." But Lawson assured the young boy, "'the good Lord would bring it to pass in his own good time.'" All Douglass had to do was to continue studying the Scriptures. "The advice and the suggestions of Uncle Lawson, were not without their influence upon my character and destiny. . . . He fanned my already intense love of knowledge into a flame, by assuring me that I was to be a useful man in the world. . . . When I told him that 'I was a slave FOR LIFE,' he said, 'the Lord can make you free, my dear. All things are possible with him, only *have faith in God*. Ask, and it shall be given. If you want liberty,' said the good old man, 'ask the Lord for it, *in faith*, AND HE WILL GIVE IT TO YOU.'"[14] Such faith would sustain Douglass not only in the dark days of slavery, but throughout his life. As Lawson prophesied, he would preach the gospel, but his would be the gospel of freedom.

In 1833, at the age of fifteen, Douglass was returned to Thomas Auld and lived in the village of St. Michael's in Maryland's Talbot County. Douglass then secretly organized a Sunday school for slaves and began teaching them to read. After the school was discovered and disbanded, Auld leased the recalcitrant Douglass to Edward Covey, a well-known "nigger-breaker" in 1834. Covey frequently beat Douglass. One day, savagely attacked by Covey, Douglass successfully resisted. The beatings on his back left permanent scars that would serve as reminders of his years in bondage. Empowered by his success against Covey, the sixteen-year-old Douglass resolved to escape slavery as soon as possible. Sent back to Thomas Auld in Baltimore in 1836, Douglass was hired out to a local shipyard and learned to be a caulker. In 1838, disguised as a free black sailor whose identification papers he had acquired, Douglass escaped from slavery and made his way by train and steamship to the North. Arriving in the streets of New York City, he was assisted by the black abolitionist David Ruggles, who hid Douglass in his boarding house. That same year, Douglass married Anna Murray, a free black woman who had been a domestic worker in Baltimore, who assisted him in his escape and later became the mother of their five children, three boys and two girls. Attaining his freedom, Frederick Bailey became "Frederick Douglass," inspired by the name of a heroic Scottish lord in Sir Walter Scott's poem, *Lady of the Lake*. Douglass and his wife first settled in the whaling port of New Bedford, Massachusetts, where he frequently denounced slavery as a lay preacher from the pulpit of the Zion Methodist Church. In 1839, he met the white abolitionist William Lloyd Garrison, who became instrumental in launching his career as the foremost black spokesperson for the abolition of slavery. In *My Bondage and My Freedom*, Douglass relates how as a young fugitive from slavery living in New Bedford, Garrison inspired him. Garrison's *Liberator*, with its moral denunciations of slavery, "took its place with me next to the Bible." Douglass "loved" both the paper and its editor. Garrison became Douglass's surrogate father: "His words were few, full of holy fire, and straight to the heart. Something of a hero worshiper, by nature, here was one, on first sight, to excite my love and reverence." Though their relationship eventually ended in bitter estrangement, Douglass never forgot his first impression of Garrison. Sitting in the back of a hall listening to Garrison's inspiring words, Douglass thought of Garrison: "'You are the man, the Moses raised up by God, to deliver his modern Israel from bondage,' was the spontaneous feeling of my heart."[15]

In 1841, Douglass joined Garrison's Massachusetts Anti-Slavery Society. Within a short time, he became a popular anti-slavery speaker for the society, preaching abolition to mostly white audiences throughout New England, New York, and the Ohio Valley, often traveling with the brilliant orator Wendell Phillips, hailed as the abolition movement's "golden trumpet." Douglass had found his calling. As much as he appreciated the contributions of the white abolitionists, he knew that he could bring to the movement what they could not. Addressing an audience in 1841 in Lynn, Massachusetts, before moving his family there the following year, Douglass declared that although northern white abolitionists can denounce slavery, they "cannot speak as I can from *experience;* they cannot refer you to a back covered with scars, as I can; for I have felt the wounds; I have suffered under the lash without the power of resisting. Yet, my blood has sprung out as the lash embedded itself in my flesh."[16]

Douglass did not initially realize his own oratorical brilliance. His autobiographies reveal a lack of confidence the first time he spoke before a mostly white audience at the Massachusetts Anti-Slavery Society convention on Nantucket Island in 1841, just three years after his escape from slavery. He was asked to testify at this convention, which, like countless others, took on the characteristics of a religious revival meeting. In his first autobiography, *Narrative of the Life of Frederick Douglass, An American Slave, Written By Himself*, published in 1845, he related that he had "felt strongly moved to speak." Yet he regarded the task as "a severe cross" which he took up "reluctantly." He explains: "The truth was, I felt myself a slave."[17] In 1855, Douglass elaborated upon these sentiments in *My Bondage and My Freedom*: "My speech on this occasion is about the only one I ever made, of which I do not remember a single connected sentence. It was with the utmost difficulty that I could stand erect, or that I could command and articulate two words without hesitation and stammering. I trembled in every limb."[18] The Nantucket speech marked Douglass's formal entrance into the public arena, where he would achieve his reputation as one of the nation's greatest advocates of racial justice. Douglass captured the minds and hearts of his listeners. He made an indelible impression upon Garrison, who testified: "I shall never forget his first speech at the convention—the extraordinary emotion it excited in my own mind. . . . I think I never hated slavery so intensely as at that moment. . . . There stood one, in physical proportion and stature commanding and exact—in intellect richly endowed—in natural eloquence a prodigy. As soon as he had taken his seat, filled with hope and admiration, I rose, and declared that PATRICK HENRY, of revolutionary fame, never made a speech more eloquent in the cause of liberty, than the one we had just listened to from the lips of that hunted fugitive. So I believed at that time—such is my belief now."[19]

The life of Frederick Douglass demonstrated that slavery was neither natural nor divinely sanctioned, but the product of the unjust exercise of power by white Americans. As Douglass declared in *My Bondage and My Freedom*: "It was not *color*, but *crime*, not *God*, but *man*, that afforded the true explanation of the existence of slavery; nor was I long in finding out another important truth, viz: what man can make, man can unmake." Having experienced the brutal white supremacist ideology during his years as a slave, Douglass devoted his life to exposing and undermining its symbolic code. Systems of oppression, he had come to understand early, succeed when they inculcate the belief in their victims that subjugation is natural. In a passage Douglass repeated in each of his three autobiographies, he lifts the veil from the pernicious slave system, showing how it penetrated the minds of its victims: "To make a contented slave, you must make a thoughtless one. It is necessary to darken his moral and mental vision, and, as far as possible, to annihilate his power of reason. He must be able to detect no inconsistencies in slavery. The man who takes his earnings must be able to convince him that he has a perfect right to do so. It must not depend upon mere force: the slave must know no higher law than his master's will. The whole relationship must not only demonstrate to his mind its necessity, but its absolute rightfulness."[20]

Continuing his self-education, Douglass discovered the liberal ideas of the Enlightenment that inspired the American Revolution, ideas he later used to combat slavery. He also learned the meaning of a word that, next to freedom, remained the most important word in his life: *abolition.* The white supremacist ideology propagated throughout the South attempted to mask and to legitimate a culture of oppression, leading many Americans to tolerate slavery. But reading and critical thinking had enabled Douglass to see that slavery was not natural, but the product of human corruption. As long as blacks accepted the definitions inculcated in them by the slave system, they could never be free. Addressing an audience in England in May 1846, eight years after he escaped slavery, Douglass offered a penetrating description of the dehumanizing psychological violence that slavery inflicted upon millions of black Americans:

> He is a piece of property—a marketable commodity, in the language of the law, to be bought or sold at the will and caprice of the master who claims him to be his property; he is spoken of, thought of, and treated as property. The will and the wishes of the master are the law of the slave. He is as much a piece of property as a horse. If he is fed, he is fed because he is property. If he is clothed, it is with a view to the increase of his value as property. He is carefully deprived of everything that tends in the slightest degree to detract from his value as property. He is deprived of education. God has given him an intellect; the slaveholder declared it shall not be cultivated. If his moral perception leads him in a course contrary to his value as property, the slaveholder declares he shall

not exercise it. What is to be thought of a nation boasting of its liberty, boasting of its humanity, boasting of its Christianity, boasting of its love of justice and purity, and yet having within its own borders three millions of persons denied by law the right of marriage?[21]

Frederick Douglass used his own story to inspire those who sought to compel the nation to fulfill the promise of its founders. His 1845 autobiographical *Narrative*, with supporting prefaces by William Lloyd Garrison and Wendell Phillips, portrayed an inspirational journey back to recover his past.[22] This journey demanded great courage, for, like that of other slaves, his was a brutal story to tell. Douglass's *Narrative*, the dramatic account of his life as a slave and his quest for identity, was an immediate success. Already known as a magnificent orator, the *Narrative* demonstrated that Douglass was also a gifted writer. The book was greeted by lavish praise. In America, it was sold at anti-slavery lectures and rallies, churches, and bookstalls. Within three years, eleven thousand copies were published in the United States, and French and German translations appeared; the book went through nine editions in Britain.[23] Oppressed by the institution of slavery, deprived of name, birthday, family, and natural rights, Douglass decided to construct in his text the identity that had been denied him. Along with countless other slaves, he never knew the exact year of his birth. The slave system stripped its victims of their human identity. The question of identity preoccupied him throughout his life and largely explains why he wrote his autobiography three times.

The *Narrative* ends with an act of triumph. So devoted was Douglass to the principles of the Declaration of Independence, that, as James Olney points out, the *Narrative*'s coda echoes the rhythms of the Declaration and the commitment of the signatories of the document.[24] The Declaration's conclusion reads: "We the . . . Representatives of the United States of America . . . declare that these United Colonies are, and of Right ought to be, Free and Independent States. . . . And for the support of this Declaration . . . , we mutually pledge to each other our Lives, our Fortunes, and our sacred Honor." The signatures of those who endorsed the document followed. Douglass's *Narrative*, his personal declaration of independence, concludes, "Sincerely and earnestly hoping that this little book may do something toward throwing light on the American slave system, and hastening the glad day of deliverance to the millions of my brethren in bonds, faithfully relying upon the power of truth, love, and justice, for success in my humble efforts, and solemnly pledging myself anew to the sacred cause, I subscribe myself." One imagines Douglass pausing at his writing desk in the study of his home in Lynn, Massachusetts. He has just completed the poignant tale of his journey from bondage to freedom, from chattel slavery to dignified selfhood. He dips his pen one final time into the ink well. Pressing the pen firmly upon the paper, he signs his name: "FREDERICK DOUGLASS."[25]

III

When Douglass was a young man, William Lloyd Garrison dominated the American abolition movement. It grew out of the religious revivalism of the 1830s, known as the Second Great Awakening, which began in New England and spread to upstate New York. Led by preachers such as Lyman Beecher, this religious revival called upon the individual to strive for holiness and to renounce sins such as drunkenness, sexual license, and mistreatment of the defenseless. Spurred by the Puritan doctrine of collective accountability and divine judgment, abolitionists, never more than a minority in America, began a vigorous campaign against the grave sin of slavery. In 1832, Garrison, a Baptist, founded the New England Anti-Slavery Society in Boston. The charismatic Garrison brought the moral fervor of Christian revivalism to the anti-slavery movement. He had been introduced to abolition in 1829 by Benjamin Lundy. The two men edited *The Genius of Universal Emancipation*, a paper published in Baltimore, Maryland, not far from where young Frederick Douglass would work as a slave. Among Garrison's supporters were Wendell Phillips, the poet John Greenleaf Whittier, and women reformers such as Lydia Maria Child, Maria Weston Chapman, and Lucretia Mott. In contrast to other anti-slavery activists, such as the American Colonization Society founded in 1816, which favored gradual emancipation and colonization of blacks to Africa or the Caribbean, the Garrisonians demanded the immediate and unconditional abolition of slavery and integration of blacks into American society. Influenced by the natural law tradition that inspired the American Revolution—the basis for human rights derived from

God's transcendent moral law—abolitionists believed that no person has a right to dominion over another. Garrison and his followers revered the Declaration of Independence as the nation's premier founding document and revolutionary manifesto. Armed with the Declaration's principles of liberty and equality, the abolitionists condemned slavery as violating the ideals of the nation's Founders. The Liberty Bell, one of the nation's greatest symbols, received its name and revered status from the abolitionists.[26] The mission of America is inscribed on the Bell: "Proclaim liberty throughout all the land unto all the inhabitants thereof."[27] Confident that human bondage would be abolished if slave owners were shown the sinfulness of slavery and northerners were awakened to their complicity in the evil institution, the Garrisonians concentrated on moral persuasion alone. Frustrated by organized religion's tolerance of slavery, they advised their supporters not to attend church services. Believing that all forms of coercion, even law, are unjust, these radical abolitionists went so far as to deny the legitimacy of government. The product of sin, they thought government must be supplanted by God's millennial kingdom.

Garrison also dominated the American Anti-Slavery Society as its most effective leader. The society was founded in 1833 in Philadelphia—the city, Garrison proudly proclaimed, where the Declaration of Independence had been signed. Intended to nationalize the abolition movement, the society was the product of two anti-slavery traditions. One was the Garrisonian, whose members stemmed mostly from Puritan New England and Quaker Philadelphia; the other, rooted in evangelical revivalism, was led by the Congregationalists Theodore Dwight Weld from Ohio and the brothers Lewis and Arthur Tappan from New York, and drew its support from western New York and the Old Northwest. At the society's founding, sixty-three delegates from eleven states declared their objectives: the complete abolition of slavery, along with the improvement of "the character and condition of the people of color."[28] Three blacks, James McCrummell and Robert Purvis from Philadelphia, and James G. Barbadoes from Boston, played a role in forming the society.[29] In 1833, black and white women founded the Boston Female Anti-Slavery Society. One year later, the Massachusetts Anti-Slavery Society, successor to the New England Anti-Slavery Society, was organized as an affiliate of the American Anti-Slavery Society.

While united in opposition to slavery, the abolitionists disagreed on strategy. In 1840, a dispute split the movement into two factions: the Garrisonians, who condemned the Constitution as a pro-slavery document and who rejected politics in favor of moral argument; and the political abolitionists, who sought to supplement moral persuasion by political action under the Constitution, especially exercising the ballot and forming abolitionist political parties. Political abolitionists also challenged the wisdom of Garrison's linking of women's rights to abolition, arguing that many supporters would be alienated. Among these political abolitionists who constituted the American and Foreign Anti-Slavery Society were Theodore Dwight Weld, the Tappan brothers, the philanthropist Gerrit Smith, the Reverend Joshua Leavitt, and Ohio journalist and former southern slaveholder James G. Birney. In 1840, the political abolitionists founded the anti-slavery Liberty Party, which nominated Birney for president of the United States the following year. In the North, black Americans were associated with both factions of the abolition movement, although most black leaders favored political action, hoping to build coalitions that might abolish slavery by legislative means. Even the integrated abolitionist movement had its limitations. Some white members relegated black reformers to inferior status, offering them merely token offices in anti-slavery societies. Yet a number of blacks rose to the occasion and achieved prominence.

Throughout the 1830s and 1840s, abolitionists were greeted by much hostility, not only in the South but also in the North, where many working-class whites feared the prospect of hordes of liberated blacks competing with them for employment. In 1831, David Walker, the free black author of the *Appeal to the Coloured Citizens of the World* (1829), a militant call for a massive slave rebellion, was found murdered in Boston's Beacon Hill. Even William Lloyd Garrison was assaulted. Seized by an angry mob in 1835, he was dragged through the streets of Boston before being rescued by local blacks. In dozens of northern cities and towns, abolitionist speakers were attacked and their meetings disrupted. When the mail was used in an attempt to flood the South with anti-slavery literature, post offices were ransacked and abolitionist pamphlets cast into the flames. When local authorities in both the North and the South failed to protect the right of abolitionists to exercise their civil liberties under the Constitution, federal authorities refused to intervene. This strengthened the claim that the national government supported slavery. Moreover, in 1836, the House of Representatives imposed a "gag rule," which prevented debate on the thousands of petitions that had been flooding the federal government to abolish slavery in the District of Columbia. This violation of the First Amendment right to petition the government to redress grievances remained in effect until 1844, when it was repealed largely through the efforts of former President John Quincy Adams, who had vigorously attacked the rule in Congress year after year. In 1837, a pro-slavery mob murdered the abolitionist editor Elijah P. Lovejoy in Alton, Illinois, throwing his printing press into the Mississippi River. In 1838, Pennsylvania Hall, built by abolitionists in Philadelphia, was burned by slavery advocates. Frederick Douglass's speeches frequently resulted in riots and death threats against him. While on an abolitionist speaking tour in 1843, Douglass attempted to protect a white abolitionist from an angry mob in Pendleton, Indiana. Shouting "Kill the nigger, kill the damn nigger," the crowd beat Douglass unconscious, breaking his hand and leaving it permanently damaged.[30] Despite the violence, the abolitionists remained undeterred.

IV

Having disclosed the details of his life in the *Narrative*, Frederick Douglass was vulnerable to capture as a fugitive slave. For his own protection, Douglass left his wife Anna and their four children behind in Lynn, Massachusetts as he embarked on a twenty-one-month speaking tour of Great Britain in 1845. The American anti-slavery movement received inspiration from Britain, which had emancipated 800,000 slaves living in the West Indies on August 1, 1834. From 1845 to 1847, Douglass toured England, Ireland, and Scotland, addressing packed halls and enlisting support for the abolitionist cause. In the summer of 1846, Garrison joined Douglass in Britain, and they shared speakers' platforms. While in Dublin, Douglass listened as the great Irish liberator, Daniel O'Connell, denounced American slavery. Douglass's sojourn in Britain was a defining period in his life. The press treated him as an abolitionist hero. He was even named the "black O'Connell."[31] For the first time, Douglass was regarded as an intellectual, valuable not only for his abolitionist views but also for his support of Irish home rule, the temperance movement, and free trade. He had written to Garrison from Scotland in February 1846: "I cannot allow myself to be insensitive to the wrongs and suffering of any part of the great family of mankind."[32]

In Britain, Douglass experienced a sense of freedom that he had not felt in America. Speaking in Belfast, Ireland in January 1846, he declared: "Persecuted, hunted, outraged in America, I have come to England, and behold the change! A chattel becomes a man. I breathe. I am free."[33] In a letter to Garrison the same month, he confessed: "I seem to have undergone a transformation. I live a new life."[34] In another letter, Douglass wrote: "I feel myself almost a new man—freedom has given me new life. . . . If I should meet you now . . . I am certain—you would see a *great change* in me."[35] He also explained to Garrison that he could not help noting the contrast between the two worlds he had experienced. In the South of the United States, he had been a slave; in the North, he was subjected to racial prejudice and segregation; indeed, he was denied admission to cabins on steamboats, respectable hotels, churches, and public entertainments on equal terms with whites. He was even dragged from white coaches in the North for resisting segregation. When he departed from America for Britain in August 1845, as a black man he was denied a cabin on the *Cambria,* an ocean steamer. In his native land, he was frequently confronted by Americans who cried: "We don't allow niggers in here!"[36]

By the time Douglass returned home to America, he had become an international celebrity and a free man. In December 1846, the British abolitionists Anna and Ellen Richardson purchased Douglass's legal freedom from Hugh Auld, to whom his brother, Thomas Auld, had transferred ownership. Douglass was now secure from capture as a fugitive slave.

V

In 1848, Douglass moved his family to Rochester, New York, where the year before he had founded and began editing the *North Star,* a four-page weekly newspaper providing an independent black voice in the struggle against slavery.[37] After the completion in 1825 of the Erie Canal, joining the Hudson River at Albany with the Great Lakes at Buffalo, Rochester grew from a rural village to a prosperous city of thirty thousand by the 1840s.[38] Along with much of western New

York, Rochester was a center of political abolitionism. As the final destination of the Underground Railroad, a system of routes that led runaway slaves from the South, many slaves fled to Rochester before attaining safety in Canada. Douglass and his family lived in a nine-room, two-story brick house at 4 Alexander Street. Having a fairly large home, Douglass was able to indulge his lifelong passion for books. His library grew to a considerable size. Over years of self-education, his reading included the Bible, the Koran, Shakespeare, Walter Scott, Dickens, Longfellow, Whittier, John Locke, Edmund Burke, Tennyson, Browning, Thackeray, Hugo, and the elder Alexandre Dumas. Douglass also taught himself to read Italian, French, Spanish, and German. Residing in Rochester made it easier for Douglass to launch his independent offensive against slavery.

The *North Star*'s first headquarters was in the basement of the American Methodist Episcopal (AME) Zion Church on Rochester's Favor Street. Douglass later moved his office to the center of the city's downtown, at 25 Buffalo Street (now 25 East Main Street), where he conducted an important part of his mission, writing late into the night the many editorials that galvanized the abolitionist movement during the turbulent years prior to the Civil War.[39] The *North Star*, named after the star that guided fugitive slaves, became one of the most influential abolitionist papers in the country. Settled in Rochester, Douglass looked forward to "wielding my pen, as well as my voice" to change public opinion on slavery.[40]

Douglass's *North Star* did not have to compete with other abolitionist papers for readers. The paper was launched with a bold prospectus: "The object of the *North Star* will be to attack *Slavery* in all its forms and aspects; advocate *Universal Emancipation;* exalt the standard of *Public Morality;* promote the Moral and Intellectual Improvement of the COLORED PEOPLE; and hasten the day of FREEDOM to the Three Millions of our *Enslaved Fellow Countrymen.*"[41] While the autonomy of black abolitionists was important, Douglass continued to stress their common cause with whites. This was demonstrated by the *North Star*'s mission statement: "It is evident we must be our own representatives and advocates, not exclusively . . . , not distinct from, but in connection with our white friends."[42] The plight of free blacks would not be ignored. The paper would combat not only slavery in the South, but also racial prejudice in the North, omitting "no opportunity to gain for the nominally free, complete enfranchisement."[43]

In 1851, having converted from Garrisonian abolitionism to political abolitionism and electoral politics, Douglass changed the name of his newspaper to *Frederick Douglass' Paper*, which he published until 1860. The name of the paper reflected his stature as a leading reformer. His paper would play a vital role in the struggle against slavery. The abolition movement had received a serious setback in 1850 when Congress passed a new Fugitive Slave Law, which practically made slavery legal in the North as well as in the South. Douglass responded by augmenting his oratorical assault upon slavery. As he declared in his final autobiography, *Life and Times of Frederick Douglass* (1881), his most important speeches, writings, and editorial work occurred during this period: "If I have at any time said or written that which is worth remembering or repeating, I must have said such things between the years 1848 and 1860, and my paper was a chronicle of most of what I said during that time."[44]

When he delivered his July Fourth speech at Corinthian Hall in 1852, Douglass had become a titanic figure, arguably slavery's most formidable intellectual foe.

VI

On July 5, 1852, Frederick Douglass presented his vision of America at Rochester's Corinthian Hall. No one more than Douglass understood the power of rhetoric to mold public opinion in a democracy. He wrote to fellow abolitionist Gerrit Smith that he had worked diligently on his speech throughout the last two or three weeks of June. An abolitionist manifesto, Douglass's oration would be the greatest abolition speech of nineteenth-century America. After an opening prayer, the Reverend Robert R. Raymond of Syracuse proceeded to read the Declaration of Independence to honor the great event the entire nation was celebrating.

After Reverend Raymond finished reading the Declaration, with its "self-evident" principles of liberty and equality, the thirty-four-year-old Frederick Douglass rose to speak, the audience quickly hushed, and all eyes became riveted upon him. Standing over six feet tall, with a magnificent mane of hair and a face reflecting iron resolve, he was an imposing figure. According to the poet James Russell Lowell, "the very look and bearing of Douglass are an irresistible logic against the oppression of his race."[45] Douglass paused briefly before beginning. On this Fourth of July, he was well-prepared to address the citizens of Rochester and, by extension, the citizens of America. He had perfected his oratorical skills through the study of great speeches and had matured as a speaker during the years spent as a Garrisonian lecturer advocating the abolitionist cause throughout New England. Speech, Douglass believed, and not written prose was the most effective weapon against slavery, and oral discourse could best move listeners to take effective action.[46] As he proclaimed in an address to the American Anti-Slavery Society in May, 1848: "I am bound to speak, and whenever there is an opportunity to do so, I will speak against slavery."[47]

Douglass possessed all the gifts of a great orator. His magnificent baritone voice had great carrying power. According to one account, his voice "rivaled [Daniel] Webster's in its richness and in the depth and sonorousness of its cadences," making him an orator listeners would "never forget."[48] His knowledge, demonstrated by the many historical, literary, and Biblical allusions that embellished his speeches, was considerable, and his mastery of the art of delivery, employing the appropriate facial expressions and gestures, emphases, and pauses, was virtually unrivaled. His sense of rhythm was impeccable. He could modulate his voice from almost a whisper to a thunderous blast. To amuse his listeners, he also employed humor, wit, satire, and mimicry. He elicited laughter by imitating the voices of slaveholders and southern politicians. His charismatic personality enhanced his powers of persuasion. He easily held the attention of large audiences for hours. Like all great orators, he had the ability to make individual listeners believe that he was speaking directly to them.

Douglass took careful account of his Corinthian Hall listeners as they settled comfortably in their seats. All good speeches involve an interaction between the speaker and the audience, creating a shared meaning and understanding related to the subject addressed. But no audience listening to a masterful speaker can remain neutral. A speech is interpreted and judged in light of the audience's prior knowledge, beliefs, and values. As innumerable cities and towns celebrated the seventy-sixth birthday of the nation's independence in 1852 with the standard ceremonial rhetoric, Douglass's audience had reason to expect that his speech would echo the patriotic sentiments of countless other Fourth of July speeches. Even those who shared his outrage over the persistent American dilemma did not expect the piercing speech he would deliver. Douglass wanted to do more than to inspire his anti-slavery allies in Corinthian Hall. He knew that a speech delivered on the Fourth of July might be regarded as an address to the nation as a whole. He wanted to sting the conscience of America. His July Fourth oration would make brilliant use of the rhetorical device of *apostrophe,* addressing an audience beyond those who were actually present. Douglass hoped to inspire Americans to implement the ideals of the Founders by joining the abolitionists in the battle against slavery and supporting anti-slavery political parties and candidates. He also hoped to move the federal government to reject further compromises with slavery and to take decisive action to abolish the institution in the South. Finally, Douglass intended to attack slave-holding southerners who celebrated the Declaration of Independence while violating its principles of liberty and equality, and who dared to enlist the United States Constitution to support a system of human bondage.

A former slave speaking on the occasion of celebrating the nation's independence had a natural irony. Douglass had been a slave in America for the first twenty-one years of his life. To what extent would he participate in the spirit of jubilation that filled the nation that day? How did he regard a country that permitted such a violation of human rights? What would he say about the Declaration of Independence, the document that inspired the abolition movement? How would he judge the Founders of the republic? Would he denounce the nation for its hypocritical dedication to republicanism and Christianity, both contradicted by the wickedness of slavery?[49] Would he reject the United States Constitution, believed by the Garrisonians to be a pro-slavery document that had incorporated slavery into the fundamental law of the United States? Many Americans held that although slavery was immoral, the institution was nevertheless constitutionally protected in the South as private property.

And what might Douglass say about the 1850 Fugitive Slave Law, one in a series of setbacks for the abolitionist cause? Because the law virtually nationalized slavery in the United States, many of Douglass's Corinthian Hall listeners were on the verge of despair. Fugitive slaves who managed to escape to a free state or territory retained their legal status as slaves. No doubt some listeners would not have been surprised if Douglass used the occasion of the Fourth of July to call for the repeal of this contradiction to the nation's ideals. The Fugitive Slave Law subjected not only runaway slaves but also free blacks to kidnapping and enslavement. Douglass's listeners might have also included some who were suspicious of a black man giving an oration to celebrate freedom. While Rochester deserved its reputation as a center of abolition, many white residents still rejected the idea of full racial equality. Indeed, even though the city contained a significant number of free blacks, they were segregated in the public schools. In his 1850 Rochester lectures on slavery, Douglass referred to evidence from the city's press, pulpit, and his own experience, of the "indifference" to slavery and the "unrighteous spirit of *caste* which prevails in this community."[50] He also argued that "every American citizen" was morally obligated, "by the highest convictions of duty and safety," to work to abolish slavery from the nation.[51]

On the Fourth of July 1852, the abolition movement was in crisis. Using the power of his oratory, Frederick Douglass sought to energize the movement by calling upon the nation to resolve the American dilemma, the contradiction between the ideals of the Founders and the evil practice of slavery.

VII

The Corinthian Hall audience would not be treated to standard Fourth of July rhetoric. In the preparation stage of his speech, what the ancient orators called invention or discovery, Douglass carefully planned his rhetorical strategy. He had decided the persuasive means he would employ and the best arrangement for his arguments. Every word had to be directed toward awakening the nation to the urgency of abolishing slavery. On the day when Americans reflect upon the nation's accomplishments and destiny, Douglass compelled privileged white citizens to look at the nation from the perspective of the free black and the slave. Using the pronoun "your" five times in the opening minutes of his speech, Douglass had established an ominous subtext, a dissonant *basso continuo* that would grow to become his principal message. Douglass's speech is a text composed of many interwoven strands. Sometimes the voices blend together; at other times they collide. There is the voice of the nation's Founders, the voice of succeeding generations who betrayed the promise of the Founders, the voice of the abolitionists, the voice of the free black, and the voice of the slave. There are the voices of America's founding documents, the Declaration of Independence and the Constitution, especially its Preamble. There are the voices of national pride, oppression, suffering, indignation, hope, and liberation.

Douglass's oratory falls within a rhetorical tradition originated by the ancient Greeks, developed by the ancient Romans, and perfected over the centuries. A principal purpose of rhetoric is either to legitimate, shape, or change public beliefs and values. Aristotle defined rhetoric as employing the best available means of persuasion in a given situation. To persuade is to move others to adopt a belief or to act in a certain way. For over two thousand years, throughout the West, knowledge of rhetoric was not only a mark of an educated person but also essential for success in public life. According to Aristotle's classification, there are three basic rhetorical forms — ceremonial, judicial, and political. Ceremonial rhetoric aims to inspire an audience and reinforce communal values. The famous example in antiquity was the funeral oration of Pericles, a celebration of the virtues of democracy delivered to the Athenians early in their war with Sparta. Lincoln's Gettysburg Address is another example of ceremonial rhetoric. Probably the best examples for Americans are the annual July Fourth speeches. Judicial rhetoric, used in the courtroom, is designed to accuse or to defend, securing either a conviction or an acquittal. This form of rhetoric, concerned with justice and injustice, can be extended to include any speech aiming to condemn or defend a person's actions. Finally, political or deliberative rhetoric is designed to persuade an audience either to adopt or to reject a particular policy or piece of legislation. While ostensibly using ceremonial rhetoric, Douglass would take his audience off guard, transforming his July Fourth oration into judicial rhetoric, an abolition speech indicting America for the sin of slavery, and into political rhetoric, demanding the immediate abolition of slavery.

Douglass may not have read Aristotle, but he had an intuitive grasp of the fundamental principles of persuasion. Douglass's study of speeches printed in Caleb Bingham's *Columbian Orator*, in addition to his early exposure to the homiletic style of black slave preachers and to abolition speeches in Massachusetts and Rochester, offered him many models of the art of oratory.[52] Reading Bingham's introduction, "General Instructions for Speaking," Douglass was exposed to the teachings of the Roman rhetoricians Cicero and Quintilian. Many nineteenth-century speakers read Hugh Blair's *Lectures on Rhetoric and Belles Lettres,* published in 1783. Blair had been Regius Professor of Rhetoric at the University of Edinburgh. While Frederick Douglass may not have read Blair, he listened to orators who had done so. A compendium of ancient and modern thinking on rhetoric and literature, Blair's *Lectures* appeared in many American editions and was for decades the most widely used text for the study of rhetoric in the nation's colleges.[53] It was required reading in the courses in rhetoric taken by Edward Everett, one of America's most famous orators, while a student at Harvard College during the early nineteenth century. Douglass also heard some of the greatest orators in America, including Wendell Phillips, Charles Sumner, Ralph Waldo Emerson, William Ellery Channing, Theodore Parker, and Daniel Webster. Having perfected his oratorical skills by addressing countless audiences, both in the United States and Great Britain, Douglass was prepared in 1852 to deliver perhaps his most significant speech.

According to Aristotle, there are three principal means of persuading an audience: ethos, logos, and pathos. Having studied and memorized many great speeches, Douglass had assimilated the best ways to sway an audience. According to Aristotle, the first means is ethos, referring to the character of the speaker as demonstrated by the speech. To be persuasive, a speaker must demonstrate a character of integrity, competence, and credibility. Unless the proper ethos is projected, the necessary trust between a speaker and the audience will be lacking and arguments will be ineffectual. As a former slave and now an abolitionist speaker, Douglass displayed these credentials. His opening disclaimers enhanced his ethos as someone thoroughly versed in the art of rhetoric. He would demonstrate his knowledge of American history, the Bible, and literature. He would also align himself and the abolitionists with the moral ideals of the republic. Logos, or argument, is the second means of persuasion, appealing to the audience's reason or understanding. On the subject of slavery, eliciting the appropriate pathos or emotions would be essential for success. According to Hugh Blair, the highest form of rhetorical art is that which engages an audience's passion. Only passion, he contends, spurs action: "It is the business of the orator to persuade me to act agreeable to it, by engaging my affections on its side. . . . He must address himself to the passions; he must paint to the fancy, and touch the heart. . . ." When a speech arouses the proper passion, "we are not only convinced, but are interested, agitated, and carried along with the speaker; our passions are made to rise together with his; we love, we detest, we resent, according as he inspires us, and are prompted to resolve, or to act, with vigour and warmth."[54] An effective orator appeals not only to the understanding but also to the heart and knows how to stir emotions. Douglass succeeded in arousing anger in his audience toward the slaveholders and shame that America, founded on the ideals of the Declaration of Independence, could not cleanse itself of the abomination of slavery.

Douglass's audience at Corinthian Hall expected a long speech. His speeches averaged two hours in length, and his July Fourth oration totals thirty printed pages.[55] His audiences ranged from a small number to as many as seven thousand.[56] Douglass often spoke extemporaneously, enabling him to adjust his speeches to the reactions of an audience. When the occasion allowed, he relied upon his excellent memory, delivering his speech without notes. He also wrote formal speeches to be read on the lecture circuit. A substantial and important speech such as the July Fourth oration was written and rehearsed and delivered from manuscript.[57] Douglass probably read parts to his audience, reciting some of its more powerful sections from memory. His style was typical of the nineteenth century, the great age of American oratory, when the public was accustomed to hearing speeches lasting from one to four hours. Speeches were a major form of public entertainment, audiences were sophisticated listeners, and the best speakers were great performers. In 1858, crowds listened for hours outdoors as Abraham Lincoln and Stephen A. Douglas debated the issue of slavery during the Illinois senatorial race. In 1863, Lincoln's elegiac 272-word "Gettysburg Address" was an exception for its brevity. Before the president spoke, those gathered at Gettysburg, Pennsylvania sat patiently while Edward Everett delivered a two-hour oration, regaling his audience with rhetorical flourishes and patriotic symbolism.

VIII

Following rhetorical tradition, Frederick Douglass opened his July Fourth speech with a brief exordium or introduction. He had to capture the sympathy of his audience, disposing them to accept his arguments. He employed conventional disclaimers, understating his ability and demonstrating his command of irony. Since the ancient Greeks, speakers had customarily begun speeches with ironic confessions of their meager ability, only to follow with dazzling displays of oratory. Aristotle, whose *Rhetoric* set standards admired in Douglass's day, advised speakers to begin by pleading for their audiences' indulgence in order to elicit sympathy.

Douglass, the orator who had delivered hundreds of speeches over the years since his escape from bondage in 1838, confessed: "A feeling has crept over me, quite unfavorable to the exercise of my limited powers of speech. The task before me is one which requires much previous thought and study for its proper performance."[58] He continues: "The little experience I have had in addressing public meetings, in country school houses, avails me nothing on the present occasion." While conceding that he had often spoken in "this beautiful Hall," and recognized many friends in the audience, Douglass insists that "neither their familiar faces, nor the perfect gage I think I have of Corinthian Hall, seems to free me from embarrassment." He then adverts to his humble background: "The fact is, ladies and gentlemen, the distance between this platform and the slave plantation, from which I escaped, is considerable, and the difficulties to be overcome in getting from the latter to the former, are by no means slight. That I am here today is, to me, a matter of astonishment as well as of gratitude." After apologizing for his lack of "elaborate preparation" and failure to "grace his speech with any high-sounding exordium," he pleads for indulgence. "With little experience and less learning, I have been able to throw my thoughts hastily and imperfectly together."[59]

But Douglass's opening remarks set the stage for a speech that would reveal an orator with extraordinary rhetorical power. What many listeners perceived initially as a lamb quickly became a lion. The initial disclaimers conformed to the standards of declamatory orations.[60] Douglass's mask of subservience — "inexperienced," "embarrassed" — had a further underlying purpose. In order to survive under slavery, many blacks had adopted a deferential persona to protect themselves from their masters, a passivity that reinforced the white southerners' belief in the inferiority of blacks.[61] On July 5, 1852, the deferential mask was discarded. Douglass would channel the outrage of millions living under the contradiction of American slavery. His "perfect gage" of Corinthian Hall would enable him to thunder his message to its rafters. His bold denunciations and blasting reproaches would contradict the notion, perpetuated by southern slave owners, of the contented, passive black, grateful for the honor of addressing a white audience.

Having riveted the attention of his audience with his exordium, Frederick Douglass moved to the main body of his speech, a narrative of America's revolutionary past, its flawed present, and its ominous future.

CHAPTER 2

NARRATING AMERICA'S REVOLUTIONARY PAST

This, for the purpose of this celebration, is the Fourth of July. It is the
birthday of your National Independence, and of your political freedom.
—Frederick Douglass,
"What to the Slave Is the Fourth of July?"

I

Frederick Douglass's July Fourth oration begins with the customary praise, celebrating the Founders and the American Revolution. But he introduces dissonant notes early, foreshadowing the blistering attack to come. While the first-person singular pronoun "I" dominates the opening three paragraphs of the speech, in the next three Douglass distinguishes himself from his audience by using the second-person "your." "This, for the purpose of this celebration, is the Fourth of July. It is the birthday of *your* National Independence, and of *your* political freedom."[1] With his deep baritone voice, Douglass stressed the pronoun "your."[2]

This emphasis would create a dynamic tension between himself and the audience, allowing him to raise fundamental issues related to the nation's present and future that had received insufficient attention.

Douglass refers to his audience ironically as "fellow-citizens," while at the same time using the pronoun "your" to separate himself from their celebration. As a fellow-citizen, he claims the right to address the audience on a vitally important national issue. But as a black man, he was mindful that millions of slaves were not considered citizens. Even "free" blacks in the North, who numbered about one-half million on the eve of the Civil War, were deprived of the full rights of citizenship. Douglass anticipates what W. E. B. Du Bois characterized in 1897 as the "double-consciousness" of black Americans, a "sense of always looking at one's self through the eyes of others." Because of racism, black Americans have from the beginning felt both included and excluded in America. "One ever feels this two-ness,—an American, a Negro," Du Bois explained. "Two souls, two thoughts, two unreconciled strivings; two warring ideals in one dark body, whose dogged strength alone keeps it from being torn asunder."[3] Indeed, Douglass embodied this conflict. With a black slave mother and an unidentified white father, he was the product of the white oppression of blacks. On a personal level, his July Fourth speech would be a dialogue between a black former slave and white America. Douglass's feelings toward his biological father and the Fathers of the republic were ambivalent. He could not suppress a deep sense of betrayal. Appreciative of the ideals proclaimed by the nation's Founders, he could not ignore that they had failed to resolve the problem of slavery.

Douglass considered the day's symbolic significance. Instead of renouncing American values and institutions, he decided to deliver a speech with a dual message. Like the great Hebrew prophet Jeremiah, to whom he is often compared, Douglass would vehemently condemn the nation for its injustice and hypocrisy while at the same time stressing the possibility of redemption. Employing what has been called a rhetorical "strategy of appropriation," Douglass would artfully situate himself within the beliefs and symbols of the Fourth of July, the most important ritual of the nation's civil religion, to underscore the crime against black Americans.[4] He would invoke and interpret the nation's shared cultural tradition and founding documents to include and empower oppressed black people. As a thematic counterpoint, Douglass's resolute "you" and "your," directed at white America, would become a refrain for his speech, emphasizing that the Fourth of July was not a day of celebration for black people.

II

Great as they were, the Founders left the nation a deeply troubling dilemma, slavery in the midst of freedom.[5] This irony, reflected in the title of Douglass's *Narrative* autobiography, written by *"an American Slave,"* tore the nation apart in the mid-nineteenth century. Thomas Jefferson, drafter of the Declaration of Independence, was deeply troubled by what he had done to contribute to the dilemma, owning some two hundred slaves. Although he believed that blacks were intellectually and morally inferior to whites, he feared that slavery might be ended by divine intervention. A nation that tolerated human bondage, he confessed, stood in violation of divinely endowed human rights. "Can the liberties of a nation be thought secure," he asked, "when we have removed their only firm basis, a conviction in the minds of the people that these liberties are the gift of God? That they are not to be violated but with his wrath? Indeed I tremble for my country when I reflect that God is just: that his justice cannot sleep forever."[6] From the nation's inception, abolitionists had pointed out the American dilemma, the contradiction between the Declaration of Independence and the institution of slavery.[7] The bitter frustration of many blacks was reflected in words of the early nineteenth-century black militant David Walker: "See your Declaration [of Independence] Americans!!! Do you understand your own language?"[8] Though Douglass's wrath would be directed at the slave-holding South, the intended principal audience of his 1852 July Fourth oration was the morally complacent North, and those who professed the liberal values of the nation's Founders. Douglass realized that the bulk of the South, which would never hear his speeches, was incorrigible. Southerners had convinced themselves that slavery was a positive good, and rejected the equality principle of the Declaration of Independence. Turning to those who might hear him, Douglass, the nation's leading gadfly, would hold a mirror up to his fellow Americans of the North, stirring them to examine their consciences and see their complicity in the sin of slavery. Stressing America's dilemma, he created a counterdiscourse, mustering the

Founders' liberal values of natural rights and human dignity for the abolitionist cause. The principles invoked by the American revolutionaries of 1776, their cries for justice, their denunciations of tyranny, and their proclamation of equal rights would be turned against the slaveholders. Douglass threw down a gauntlet: the nation must either abolish slavery or continue to betray the human rights promised by the Declaration of Independence.

III

History is more than a record of events. It is a people's creation of its collective memory. Adhering to tradition, Douglass constructed a narrative of the nation's beginnings for his Corinthian Hall audience. He would retell the story of the American Revolution in order to prepare the stage for the dramatic contrast he would draw between the nation's founding ideals and the moral outrage of slavery. At issue for Douglass was the identity of America. Born on July 4, 1776, the new nation had committed itself to a set of moral ideals and principles embodied in the Declaration of Independence and the Constitution. In these documents, Americans are defined not by race, religion, or nationality, but by a creed, a combination of shared values and goals, derived from Lockean liberalism and the Enlightenment, including liberty, democracy, individualism, limited government, and the rule of law under a constitution.

Frederick Douglass believed that as long as these founding principles of liberty and equality were not applied to all persons, the identity of the nation was under question. The nation's identity is determined not only by noble ideals, but more so by the extent to which these ideals are made a living reality for all Americans, regardless of race, creed, or sex. Reminding his audience of the nation's unique destiny, Douglass invoked the Bible, drawing on the archetypal theme of liberation from the Book of Exodus: "Let my people go." The Exodus story was the principal image for the founding of the nation. From its origin, America was regarded as the Promised Land, and the Book of Exodus provided the metaphors used by white orators, preachers, and politicians to help unify the nation. The Puritans believed that they had been summoned by God to undertake an errand in the wilderness to found a Christian commonwealth, a New Jerusalem, in America, ushering in the millennium. During the late eighteenth century, the conception of a people chosen by God to fulfill a divine mission in the world grew to include all Americans, not just the Puritans. Douglass invoked the familiar comparison between the Americans of 1776 and the ancient Hebrews who escaped bondage in Egypt to the Promised Land of freedom. The Fourth of July, marking the birth of the American republic, he proclaimed, "is what the Passover was to the emancipated people of God. It carries your minds back to the day, and to the act of *your* great deliverance; and to the signs, and to the wonders, associated with that act, and that day."[9] In 1776, the American colonists were Israel, the British crown was Pharaoh; now the slaves were Israel, and the slave owners were Pharaoh. Had not God punished the Egyptians for enslaving the Israelites, the chosen people? But now America was the oppressor, and the slaves the chosen people. For the slave, America was not a Promised Land, but a place of bondage, like Egypt.[10] If the colonists were justified in rebelling in 1776, America's slaves were equally justified.

The American Revolution was essential in forming the nation, creating the sense of a unified people with a common belief.[11] Basing their credo upon natural law, the Founders proclaimed that obedience to a government is conditioned by its ability to secure human rights. As the Declaration of Independence reveals, the Founders sought a transcendent source of authority, "the laws of nature and of nature's God," alleging that ultimate sovereignty resides with the Creator, endower of natural rights. Indeed, the Declaration contains four specific references to divinity, enlisting the support of the Creator for the American Revolution and the founding of the republic.[12] Douglass appropriated the ideas of the Revolution, its beliefs, values, and symbols, to make his case on freedom and equality in support of the abolitionist cause.[13] He employed the language of colonial resistance to England to indict American slavery. In his 1852 Fourth of July oration he joined other black Americans, including the internationally known poet Phillis Wheatley, in equating slavery to "British tyranny."[14] Douglass portrayed the abolitionist as the true descendant of the American Revolution and the slave as a glaring symbol of the nation's betrayal of its egalitarian promise.[15] Reflecting on the Revolution, historian Winthrop Jordan observes: "It was perfectly clear that the principles for which Americans had fought required the complete abolition of slavery; the question was not *if*, but *when* and *how*. Although the majority of Americans failed to confront this question, thus effectively answering the *when* with *later*, some men felt that abolition must come soon if not at once."[16]

Before proceeding with his narration of the highlights of the American Revolution of 1776, Douglass declared that America was not beyond redemption. It was not too late for the nation to fulfill its promise. There was hope because "*your* nation is so young. . . . You are, even now, only in the beginning of *your* national career, still lingering in the period of childhood." He continued: "There is hope in the thought, and hope is much needed, under the dark clouds which lower above the horizon. The eye of the reformer is met with angry flashes portending disastrous times; but his heart may well beat lighter at the thought that America is young, and that she is still in the impressionable stage of her existence. May he not hope that high lessons of wisdom, of justice and of truth, will yet give direction to her destiny? Were the nation older, the patriot's heart might be sadder, and the reformer's brow heavier. Its future might be shrouded in gloom, and the hope of its prophets go out in sorrow." Douglass thus tempered his criticism of America with optimism. For true patriots, reformers, and prophets might still be able to steer the nation on the proper course of "wisdom, of justice, and of truth," set by the Founders.[17]

IV

Douglass invoked the rhetoric of the American Revolution for the anti-slavery movement. Recounting the struggle between the Founders, "*your* fathers," he drew an analogy between the revolution against the British Crown and resistance to slavery. The revolutionary generation, he recalled, proclaimed the deeds of Britain "unjust, unreasonable, and oppressive, and altogether such as ought not to be quietly submitted to." Douglass aligned himself with the chorus of July Fourth celebrators in support of the American Revolution. "I scarcely need say, fellow-citizens that my opinion of those measures fully accords with that of *your* fathers." Nevertheless, he argued, it is easy in retrospect, after the colonists won their freedom, to say that America was right and England was wrong. Colonial resistance to home government in 1776 was dangerous. Echoing Thomas Paine's

The Crisis, Douglass affirmed that such resistance "tried men's souls." Creating a parallel between the American Revolution and the current abolitionist movement, Douglass reminded his audience that defenders of human rights in 1776 were condemned as "agitators and rebels." He asserted that being an abolitionist in mid-nineteenth century America was also dangerous. With words applicable to the abolitionists of his day, Douglass declared, using rhetorical antitheses, "To side with the right, against the wrong, with the weak against the strong, and with the oppressed against the oppressor! *Here* lies the merit, and the one which, of all others, seems unfashionable in our day." Douglass concludes with a stinging indictment of those who supported or tolerated slavery: "The cause of liberty may be stabbed by the men who glory in the deeds of *your* fathers."[18]

Douglass recalled for his audience that the numerous petitions and remonstrances of the American colonists for the redress of their grievances, despite being submitted in a "decorous, respectful, and loyal manner," were greeted with "sovereign indifference" by Britain. His perceptive listeners would have understood the parallel with the abolitionists, who had tried every legal means to move the nation to abolish slavery. "The greatest and best of British statesmen" admitted the justice of the colonists' cause. Nevertheless, persisting in its "mad" policies, the British government, like Pharaoh, was ultimately defeated, its armies drowned in the Red Sea. Yet, "we fear," Douglass affirmed, that the lesson of Pharaoh is lost on "our present rulers."

Douglass resumed his narrative of the nation's revolutionary past, appealing to the patriotism of his audience as descendents of the colonists, in order to set the stage for his attack on slavery in mid-nineteenth-century America. He compared the slaves to the colonists. Victims of oppression, the colonists came upon the "startling idea" of rebelling against Britain. Douglass's message was clear: unless the supporters of slavery abolished the hateful institution, they would face armed rebellion. While the cause of the American colonists was just in 1776, many "timid" individuals along with the "prudent" Tories, refused to resist oppression. Likewise in his day, Douglass lamented, many Americans value material comfort more than justice. "They hate all changes," he accused, with biting irony, "but silver, gold and copper change!" He then invoked the inspiring words of the Declaration of Independence, adopted by the Second Continental Congress: "Resolved, that these united colonies are, and ought to be free and Independent States; that they are absolved from all allegiance to the British Crown; and that all political connection between them and the State of Great Britain is, and ought to be, dissolved." Douglass concluded by proclaiming: "Citizens, *your* fathers made good that resolution. They succeeded; and today *you* reap the fruits of their success. The freedom gained is *yours;* and *you,* therefore, may properly celebrate this anniversary. The Fourth of July is the first great fact in *your* nation's history."[19]

V

Douglass could not have chosen a more revered document to support his cause than the Declaration of Independence. The Declaration consecrated liberal ideas: human rights derived from natural law; a contract theory of government; the idea of popular sovereignty; and the right of revolution. Douglass did not have to quote for his Corinthian Hall audience the ringing phrases of the Declaration's first two paragraphs. They contain arguably the most famous phrases in political literature, that "all men are created equal, that they are endowed by their Creator with certain unalienable rights," including the rights to "life, liberty, and the pursuit of happiness." The purpose of government, its just powers being derived from the consent of the governed, is to protect human rights. Whenever any government seeks to destroy these rights, the people have the right, even the duty, to abolish such a government. In the National Archives in Washington, D.C., the Declaration is displayed high above the two other American "charters of freedom," the Constitution and the Bill of Rights.[20]

For Douglass, the Declaration was an abolitionist manifesto. Speaking in Scotland in March 1846, he had proclaimed: "I love the Declaration of Independence, I believe it contains a true doctrine— 'that all men are born equal.' It is, however, because they [Americans] do not carry out these principles that I am here to speak [against slavery]."[21] As America's founding document, the original act of union, the Declaration's second paragraph set forth fundamental principles of government.[22] According to the Founders, the Declaration had constitutional status, laying the basis for binding commitments that the Constitution was supposed to implement. John Hancock, the first signer of the Declaration, wrote on July 5, 1776, that he considered the document "the Ground & Foundation of a future Government." Thomas Jefferson characterized the Declaration as "the fundamental Act of Union of these States."[23] Speaking in the 1830s, John Quincy Adams proclaimed: "The Declaration of Independence comprises and embodies the fundamental elements and principles of American constitutional law. . . . These principles, asserted in the original Declaration of 1776 when the nation came into existence, continue to constitute now . . . the vital essence, the pith, the marrow, and the substance, of our constitutional law."[24] Those who assign primacy to the Declaration of Independence date the nation's founding at 1776, not 1787, when the Constitution was drafted. Indeed, Abraham Lincoln began his Gettysburg Address by proclaiming that the Union, having been founded "fourscore and seven years ago," is older than the Constitution.

The legal prominence of the Declaration of Independence, essential to the thought of Douglass and Lincoln, has been affirmed by the modern legal scholar Charles L. Black, Jr.: "The doctrines of the Declaration should be taken to have the force of *law*—the force *in law* of the general commitments from which *particular* law can be derived. . . . The Declaration as a whole was an act of 'constitution,' a *juristic* act, an act of *law*."[25] Dennis J. Mahoney calls the Declaration "the definitive statement for the American polity of the ends of government, of the necessary conditions for the legitimate exercise of political power, and of the sovereignty of the people who establish the government and, when the circumstances warrant, may alter or abolish it."[26] The fifty-five delegates who gathered at the State House in Philadelphia for the Constitutional Convention in Philadelphia on May 14, 1787, the greatest assemblage in the history of politics, saw no need to discuss the purpose of government, for this had already been established by the Declaration of Independence. Accordingly, the Constitution is ruled by the Declaration, which might be considered its real preamble.[27] Hence, the Declaration is the lens through which the Constitution must be interpreted. In his July Fourth oration, Douglass hailed the Declaration of Independence as the nation's founding document, laying down the ideals and purposes to be implemented by the Constitution.

Employing figurative language, Douglass characterized the Declaration of Independence as the "very Ring-Bolt to the chain of *your* yet undeveloped destiny." Douglass's irony must have stunned his audience. He transmuted a symbol of oppression—a bolt with a ring attached for fitting a rope to it—into a symbol of liberation. The Declaration, the nation's "ring-bolt," will smash the chains of the slaves. It is an abolition tract that bound the nation to certain liberal ideals. "The principles contained in that instrument," Douglass affirmed, "are saving principles. Stand by those principles, be true to them on all occasions, in all places, against all foes, and at whatever cost."[28] Until the slaves were freed and all persons integrated into society on the basis of full equality, the ideals of the Declaration of Independence and the American Revolution would remain unfulfilled.

Douglass's reverence for the Declaration of Independence was rivaled only by that of Abraham Lincoln, who contended that the Founders intended its equality principle to include the black as well as the white race.[29] Spurred to re-enter politics by the Kansas-Nebraska Act of 1854, a victory for the advocates of slavery, Lincoln hailed the Declaration as "the sheet anchor of American republicanism." He went on to challenge the nation: "Let us re-adopt the Declaration of Independence, and with it, the practices, and policy, which harmonize with it. Let north and south—let all Americans—let all lovers of liberty everywhere—join in the great and good work. If we do this, we shall not only have saved the Union; but we shall have so saved it, as to make, and to keep it, forever worthy of saving."[30] Journeying from Illinois to Washington to assume the office of the presidency, Lincoln stopped briefly at Independence Hall in Philadelphia on February 22, 1861. He was like a pilgrim visiting a venerated site. Viewing the Declaration of Independence, he confessed: "I have never had a feeling politically that did not spring from the sentiments embodied in the Declaration of Independence." In the same speech, Lincoln pondered how the Declaration had kept the country unified during the turbulent years of the American Revolution: "It was not the mere matter of the separation of the colonies from the mother land; but something in that Declaration giving liberty, not alone to the people of this country, but hope to the world for all future time. It was that which gave promise that in due time the weights should be lifted from the shoulders of all men, and that *all* should have an equal chance. This is the sentiment embodied in that Declaration of Independence."[31]

On another occasion, shortly after becoming president, Lincoln employed a famous literary analogy, comparing the Declaration, the basis of his political philosophy, to the Constitution, invoking the Book of Proverbs 25:11: "A word fitly spoken is like apples of gold in a setting of silver." Without the Constitution and the Union, the United States could not have attained its present prosperity. Yet they are not "the primary cause of our great prosperity. There is something back of these. That something is the principle of 'Liberty to all,'" incarnated by the Declaration of Independence. "*Without* this, as well as *with* it, we could have declared our independence of Great Britain; but *without* it, we could not, I think, have secured our free government, and consequent prosperity." Lincoln then reflected upon the relationship between the Declaration of Independence, the Constitution, and the Union. The "word fitly spoken" is the Declaration's principle of liberty, "which has proved 'an apple of gold' to us." The Union and the Constitution represent the "picture of silver subsequently framed around it." Lincoln then explained the priority. "The picture," he affirmed, "was made not to conceal, or destroy the apple but to adorn and preserve it. The picture was made for the apple, not the apple for the picture." The Declaration of Independence, especially in its principles of liberty and equality, takes precedence over the legal frame of the Constitution.[32] Setting forth the moral ideals of America, the Declaration deserves primacy, for it established the sovereign people who issued the Constitution's Preamble: "We the people of the United States."

With the nation ravaged by Civil War in 1863, President Lincoln invoked the words of the Declaration at Gettysburg, recalling for his audience a nation "conceived in liberty, and dedicated to the proposition that all men are created equal," and summoning his countrymen to a "new birth of freedom." In the words of the poet Robert Lowell, the Gettysburg Address was "a symbolic and sacramental act."[33] With this speech, Lincoln made equality the essential article of America's political faith. When the Civil War began, Lincoln insisted that its principal purpose was to preserve the Union. But by 1863, his emphasis shifted towards a "new birth of freedom," a freedom that entailed the abolition of slavery.

VI

Like the Founders, Frederick Douglass subscribed to the rich tradition of natural law. Stemming from the ancient Greeks and Romans, and developed by Christian philosophers such as Thomas Aquinas, the significance of natural law in the development of Western civilization can hardly be overestimated. Natural law provided a transcendent, divinely ordained moral standard not only for private individuals, but also for government, laws, and society. The Declaration of Independence, the United States Constitution, and the American republic came into existence at a time in which most people believed in a higher, natural law. According to most American thinkers, natural law was discovered either in God's revelation or by the right use of human reason. The Declaration appeals to "the Laws of Nature and Nature's God." Influenced by philosophers such as John Locke, America's Founders believed that all humans possess equal, God-given rights in the state of nature, which they do not relinquish upon entering civil society. Human rights being antecedent to government, government's purpose is not to bestow but to secure rights.

Adhering to natural law doctrine, Douglass criticized American society from the perspective of the higher moral order, attacking slavery as a violation of human rights. As he proclaimed in an address delivered in Ohio in July 1854, human rights "are supported, maintained and defended, for *all* the human family; because all mankind have the same wants, arising out of a common nature. A diverse origin does not disprove a common nature, nor does it disprove a united destiny." Regardless of a person's color, "his title deed to freedom, his claim to life and to liberty, to knowledge and to civilization, to society and to Christianity, are just and perfect. It is registered in the Courts of Heaven, and is enforced by the eloquence of the God of all the earth."[34] Inspired by the Declaration of Independence, Douglass held that the purpose of government is to protect, not to create, fundamental human rights. Originating from God, the objective universal truths of natural law are eternal. Speaking at Rochester's New Lyceum in January 1854, Douglass insisted that he had nothing new to proclaim. "Indeed, it is scarcely necessary to search for new truths, till the old truths, which have been uttered from the Declaration of Independence until now, shall have become recognized and reduced to practice."[35]

For years, Douglass argued that when the Declaration of Independence proclaimed that "all men are created equal," the principle was not confined to any race or gender.[36] Ever since the American Revolution, abolitionists, black and white, had argued that equality is the fundamental meaning of American democracy. Douglass's interpretation of the Declaration of Independence can be traced back to at least the Jeffersonian Republicans of the 1790s and became increasingly prevalent beginning in the 1820s. While in Rochester in 1847, Douglass allied himself with the burgeoning women's movement. The first issue of the *North Star*—bearing the slogan "right is of no sex" as its masthead—signaled the alliance between the abolitionists and women's rights advocates. Earlier in the century, Angelina and Sarah Grimké, daughters of a South Carolina slave owner, became leading agitators for reform, first as abolitionists, then as members of the movement for women's rights. In July 1848, the thirty-year-old Douglass joined Elizabeth Cady Stanton and Lucretia Mott, both of whom had contributed to the abolition movement, at the women's rights convention held at the Wesleyan Methodist Chapel in Seneca Falls, New York. That month, Douglass proclaimed in a *North Star* editorial that "all political rights" that belong to men belong equally to women: "All that distinguishes man as an intelligent and accountable being, is equally true of woman, and if that government only is just which governs by the free consent of the governed, there can be no reason in the world for denying to woman the exercise of the elective franchise, or a hand in the making and administering the laws of the land."[37]

Douglass knew that women suffered significant civic disadvantages in nineteenth-century America. Not only were they, like blacks, deprived of the right to vote, but married women could not legally own property, make a will, sign a contract, or, if employed, claim ownership of their wages. Douglass would endorse the Seneca Falls rephrasing of the Declaration of Independence: "We hold these truths to be self-evident; that all men *and women* are created equal. The history of mankind is the history of the repeated injuries and usurpations on the part of man *toward woman*, having in the direct object the establishment of absolute tyranny over her. To prove this let the facts be submitted to a candid world." The eloquence of Douglass proved instrumental in the passing of Elizabeth Cady Stanton's controversial resolution at Seneca Falls, declaring that women ought to be free to exercise the right to vote. Douglass realized that women, like blacks, needed the vote in order to achieve their other social goals. Years later, in a speech at the International Council of Women in 1888, Douglass reflected on his contribution to the women's movement: "When I ran away from slavery, it was for my people; but when I stood up for the rights of women, self was out of the question, and I found a little nobility in the act." On the occasion of Douglass's death in 1895, Elizabeth Cady Stanton paid him tribute in a letter to Susan B. Anthony: "He was the only man I ever saw who understood the degradation of the disenfranchisement of women."[38]

VII

While Douglass's 1852 July Fourth oration began with the customary pious invocation of the Founders, it quickly evolved into what is known as a jeremiad, or political sermon. This popular American genre derived its name from the ancient Hebrew prophet Jeremiah, who predicted the Babylonian conquest of Israel and destruction of the temple of Jerusalem as punishment for violating God's covenant. Originating with seventeenth-century New England Puritan religious sermons, the jeremiad became a prevalent revivalist form of exhortation in antebellum Protestant America. Just as the ancient Hebrews were liberated by God from bondage in Egypt, the Puritans escaped oppression in Europe to find freedom in America, where they were charged with a sacred mission to create a New Jerusalem, John Winthrop's shining "city on a hill." The Puritan jeremiad capitalized on the notion that Americans conceived of themselves as a redeemer nation, chosen to fulfill divine justice in this world. Preachers admonished their sinful congregations to repent and fulfill their covenantal promise to obey God's law. The American Revolution imposed upon the nation a further responsibility. To the duty of adhering to Christian values was added that of implementing human rights.[39] An integral part of American culture, the jeremiad's influence spread beyond the confines of institutionalized religion, becoming a ritual mode of public speech that significantly shaped the nation. The American jeremiad observed a standard rhetorical formula. It began with a reference to the nation's promise. Americans, like the Jews of the Book of Exodus, a divinely chosen people, have a moral obligation to fulfill God's covenant. The speaker would then denounce the people for failing to abide by their promise and conclude with a hopeful prophecy that a repentant nation would soon reform.[40] Americans were summoned to reflect upon their shortcomings and rededicate themselves to their special moral mission.

Although the American jeremiad did not originally address the national sin of slavery, the early nineteenth-century abolitionists incorporated it into their rhetoric, creating what has been called the black jeremiad.[41] Adopting the jeremiad formula, black writers and orators, from the antebellum period through the modern civil rights era, condemned slavery as a betrayal of the nation's founding ideals and summoned the American people to reform. Like its Puritan model, the black jeremiad was a sermon of reproach that included a call for renewal. Black Jeremiahs, inspired by their Puritan predecessors, focused on one ideal—the freedom promised by the nation's founding documents—and on one sin—the sin of slavery, a glaring failure to fulfill that ideal. On July 5, 1852, Frederick Douglass became the nation's foremost black Jeremiah. While he extolled the achievements of the Founders, he refused to ignore the nation's moral hypocrisy. Unless the sin of slavery is eradicated, he insisted, God's vengeance will strike. Two months later, he wrote that slavery "involves the whole country in a common guilt and shame, and stands directly in the way of all righteous progress, making true liberty impossible."[42]

A consummate rhetorician, Douglass converted Rochester's Corinthian Hall into a courtroom, indicting the nation for continuing to tolerate the evil of slavery. Douglass pointed to the ominous signs threatening an unrepentant American republic: "From round the top of your ship of state, dark and threatening clouds may be seen. Heavy billows, like mountains in the distance, disclose to the leeward huge forms of flinty rocks! That *bolt* drawn, that *chain* broken, and all is lost. *Cling to this day, cling to it,* and to its principles, with the grasp of a storm-tossed mariner to a spar at midnight."[43] Douglass then urged his fellow Americans to adhere to the eternal principles of the Declaration of Independence. America had reached a crisis in its history, a testing time just as challenging as that faced by the Founders. The generation of the American Revolution, Douglass contended, succeeded in meeting the challenge before them. "*Your* fathers declared for liberty and independence and triumphed." Mindful that many Founders also owned slaves, Douglass told his audience that "the point from which I am compelled to view them is not, certainly, the most favorable." Nevertheless, the Founders who signed the Declaration of Independence deserve praise for establishing the nation on the basis of liberal and humanitarian ideals. They were "statesmen, patriots, and heroes, and for the good they did, and the principles they contended for, I will unite with you to honor their memory." Inspired by the ancient republican tradition, the Founders demonstrated admirable civic virtue, placing the good of the country above their "own private interests." Echoing the ringing per-oration of the Declaration, Douglass lauded the Founders for their courageous commitment: "*Your* fathers staked their lives, their for-tunes, and their sacred honor, on the cause of their country. In their ad-miration of liberty, they lost sight of all other interests."[44]

Douglass paid tribute to the courageous adherence of the nation's Founders to their libertarian principles: "They were peace men; but they preferred revolution to peaceful submission to bondage. They were quiet men; but they did not shrink from agitating against oppres-sion. They showed forbearance; but they knew its limits. They believed in order; but not in the order of tyranny. With them nothing was '*set-tled*,' that was not right." Reflecting on the original intentions of the Constitution, Douglass declared emphatically: "With them, justice, lib-erty and humanity were '*final*,' not slavery and oppression. You may well cherish the memory of such men." The statesmanship of the Founders "looked beyond the passing moment, and stretched away in strength into the distant future. They seized upon eternal principles, and set a glorious example in their defense." Douglass commanded his audience: "Mark them!"[45]

While the Constitution contained unfortunate compromises with slavery, acceded to by the majority of the framers in order to secure support of the southern states for the Union, Douglass believed that the Founders expected slavery to be abolished in the near future as a moral and logical necessity. Yet he knew that they had been tragically mistaken. The cotton engine, or "gin," invented by Eli Whitney in 1793, revolutionized the economy of the South, making slavery more profitable than before. By the mid-nineteenth century, the South pro-duced seventy percent of the world's cotton, supplying the raw mate-rial for the increasing demands of textile mills in Britain and New England. Although Congress abolished the African slave trade as soon as constitutionally possible in 1808, between that year and 1860 the southern slave population tripled, rising to four million on the eve of the Civil War.[46] Conditions in the North above the Mason-Dixon

line—the traditional boundary between the free and the slave states—
were also deplorable. Slavery had been abolished in the North, where
a large supply of free labor made slavery unprofitable. By 1830, about
125,000 free blacks lived in the North, the number swelling to 250,000
by the outbreak of the Civil War.[47] Nevertheless, though nominally
free, blacks in the North and West were denied full citizenship in the
antebellum period. They had no right to vote in Pennsylvania, Connecticut, Indiana, Ohio, Illinois, or Michigan. New York imposed on
blacks a special property qualification for voting.[48] Moreover, free
blacks were subjected to discrimination and legal segregation in public
facilities similar to that which plagued the South from the late nineteenth century.[49]

Douglass concluded the first section of his July Fourth oration by
evoking for his audience the scenes of holiday jubilation replicated in
countless cities and towns throughout America: "Our eyes are met
with demonstrations of joyous enthusiasm. Banners and pennants
wave exaltingly on the breeze. The din of business, too, is hushed.
Even Mammon seems to have quitted his grasp on this day. The ear-
piercing fife and the stirring drum unite their accents with the ascend-
ing peal of a thousand church bells. Prayers are made, hymns are sung,
and sermons are preached in honor of this day; while the quick martial
tramp of a great and multitudinous nation, echoed back by all the hills,
valley and mountains of a vast continent, bespeak the occasion one of
thrilling and universal interest—a nation's jubilee."[50] While the nation
celebrated the Fourth of July with smug complacency, millions of
slaves could only mourn. Douglass would compel those gathered at
Corinthian Hall to look beyond the pomp and circumstance of the
Fourth of July and fix their attention upon how the promise of the nation's Founders remained betrayed.

CHAPTER 3

DENOUNCING AMERICA'S PRESENT

Fellow-citizens, pardon me, allow me to ask, why am I called upon to speak here today? What have I, or those I represent, to do with your national independence?

—Frederick Douglass,
"What to the Slave Is the Fourth of July?"

I

Having narrated the nation's revolutionary past, Douglass focused on the evils of the present. "My business," he declared to his listeners in Corinthian Hall, "if I have any here to-day, is with the present. The accepted time with God and his cause is the ever-living now." Adverting to familiar Scripture, Douglass told his listeners that the ancient Hebrews boasted that Abraham was their father "while they repudiated the deed that made his name great." Similarly, many southerners, aware that George Washington had owned slaves, invoked his name, especially on the Fourth of July, to lend respectability to slavery. But the nation's first president grew to see the immorality of the institution and freed his slaves in his will. Southerners refused to follow the example of Washington's deed and free their own slaves. Douglass exclaimed,

"Washington could not die till he had broken the chains of his slaves. Yet his monument is built up by the price of human blood, and the traders in the bodies and souls of men shout — 'We have Washington [as] *our father.*' Alas! That it should be so; yet so it is." Douglass regretted that Washington, who had done so much for liberty, owned over three hundred slaves. Quoting Shakespeare's *Julius Caesar,* he pointed to the paradox that diminishes the otherwise great legacy of Washington: "The evil that men do lives after them. The good is oft' interred with their bones."[1]

With a series of hammer-like rhetorical questions, Douglass forced the nation to confront its abominable wrongs. Scathing criticism dominates the remainder of his oration. His voice bellowing, his eyes intense, his finger pointing, he cried: "Fellow-citizens, pardon me, allow me to ask, why am I called upon to speak here to-day? What have I, or those I represent, to do with *your* national independence? Are the great principles of political freedom and of natural justice, embodied in the Declaration of Independence, extended to us? Would to God, both for your sakes and ours, that an affirmative answer could be truthfully returned to these questions!" Mindful of the disparity between himself, a black man, and white America, Douglass intentionally used the word "pale," denoting both a boundary and a skin color, to emphasize that the Fourth of July was a white holiday, not a black one: "I am not included within the pale of this glorious anniversary! *Your* high independence only reveals the immeasurable distance between us." Speaking for the almost four million slaves, Douglass stepped from the podium and shook his fist at the audience and, by extension, at all America: "The blessings in which *you,* this day rejoice, are not enjoyed in common. The rich inheritance of justice, liberty, prosperity and independence, bequeathed by *your* fathers, is shared by *you,* not by me. The sunlight that brought life and healing to *you,* has brought stripes and death to me. This Fourth of July is *yours,* not *mine. You* may rejoice, I must mourn. To drag a man in fetters into the grand illuminated temple of liberty, and call upon him to join *you* in joyous anthems, were inhuman mockery and sacrilegious irony." In other words, slavery mocked and violated the sacred liberal principles of the nation's Founders. Then comes the question: "Do *you* mean, citizens, to mock me, by asking me to speak today?" Douglass, the black Jeremiah, issued a solemn admonition, echoing the biblical fate of Babylon: "And let me warn *you* that it is dangerous to copy the example of a nation whose crimes, towering up to heaven, were thrown down by the breath of the Almighty, burying that nation in irrecoverable ruin!'"[2]

Douglass shocked his audience. Instead of congratulating them for having invited a black man to sing praises for the republic, he had them, along with millions of white Americans, bowing their heads in shame for tolerating slavery. Instead of a day of national jubilation, Douglass showed them that the Fourth of July should be a day of national lamentation. Employing familiar evangelical symbolism, Douglass stressed his point by quoting from Psalm 137, reinforcing his parallel between enslaved American blacks and the ancient Hebrews, oppressed during the Babylonian Exile after the destruction of Jerusalem: "By the rivers of Babylon, there we sat down. Yea! We wept when we remembered Zion. . . . For there, they that carried us away captive, required of us a song; and they who wasted us required of us mirth, saying, Sing us one of the songs of Zion. How can we sing the Lord's song in a strange land?" This poignant psalm of lamentation epitomized Douglass's sentiments. A former slave, he had been invited to sing the praises of America, to sing a song of freedom while millions of blacks remained in bondage. They lived like aliens in a strange land. Douglass's plaintive rhetoric soared: "Fellow-citizens, above *your* national, tumultuous joy, I hear the mournful wail of millions, whose chains, heavy and grievous yesterday, are, today, rendered more intolerable by the jubilee shouts that reach them. If I do forget, if I do not faithfully remember those bleeding children of sorrow this day, 'may my right hand forget her cunning, and may my tongue cleave to the roof of my mouth!' To forget them, to pass lightly over their wrongs, and to chime in with the popular theme, would be treason most scandalous and shocking, and would make me a reproach before God and the world."[3]

Looking over the multitude of white faces in the audience, Douglass proclaimed what by then, one-third of the way through his thirty-page speech, was apparent: "My subject, then, fellow-citizens, is American slavery. I shall see, this day, and its popular characteristics, from the slave's point of view." Douglass's listeners must have noted that he said "American slavery," not southern slavery. Slavery was a national offense. The Founders compromised with slavery, subsequent generations of northerners tolerated and bargained with slavery, and the South maintained and defended slavery. Representing the American slave, Douglass judged bitterly: "Standing, there, identified with the American bondsman, making his wrongs mine, I do not hesitate to declare, with all my soul, that the character and conduct of this nation never looked blacker to me than on this Fourth of July." As a black man, his use of the word "blacker" was deliberate and ironic. Douglass condemned the nation's hypocrisy: "Whether we turn to the declarations of the past, or to the professions of the present, the conduct of the nation seems equally hideous and revolting. America is false to the past, false to the present, and solemnly binds herself to be false to the future." As if the divine were speaking through him, Douglass, a black Jeremiah, declaimed: "Standing with God and the crushed and bleeding slave on this occasion, I will, in the name of humanity which is outraged, in the name of liberty which is fettered, in the name of the Constitution and the Bible, which are disregarded and trampled upon, dare to call in question and to denounce, with all the emphasis I can command, everything that serves to perpetuate slavery—the great sin and shame of America!" Douglass concluded by quoting a segment from William Lloyd Garrison's well-known declaration of war on slavery in the first issue of his radical abolition newspaper, *The Liberator:* "I will not equivocate; I will not excuse."[4]

II

In his message to America on July Fourth, 1852, Frederick Douglass did not seek to conciliate the slaveholders. Anticipating objections, he stated: "But I fancy I hear some one of my audience say, 'It is just in this circumstance that you and your brother abolitionists fail to make a favorable impression on the public mind. Would you argue more, and denounce less; would you persuade more, and rebuke less; your cause would be much more likely to succeed.'" Arguments against slavery should not be necessary. "Must I undertake to prove that the slave is a man?" Slaves in the South were legally regarded not as human beings but as chattel, movable personal property, like farm animals. Chattel lack the rational faculty to distinguish between right and wrong. And yet, as Douglass argued, slave owners conceded that slaves were persons by holding them accountable for crimes. "What is this," he inquired, "but the acknowledgment that the slave is a moral, intellectual and responsible being?"[5] Douglass's contemporary, the American philosopher William Ellery Channing, denounced slavery because "all men have the same rational nature and the same power of conscience," which are the foundation of human rights.[6] With a powerful periodic sentence building to a climax, Douglass defended the personhood of blacks by listing their multiple contributions to every aspect of American life:

> Is it not astonishing that, while we are ploughing, planting and reaping, using all kinds of mechanical tools, erecting houses, constructing bridges, building ships, working in metals of brass, iron, copper, silver and gold; that while we are reading, writing and cyphering, acting as clerks, merchants and secretaries, having among us lawyers, doctors, ministers, poets, authors, editors, orators and teachers; that while we are engaged in all manner of enterprises common to other men, digging gold in California, capturing the whale in the Pacific, feeding sheep and cattle on the hill-side, living, moving, acting, thinking, planning, living in families as husbands, wives and children, and, above all, confessing and worshipping the Christian's God, and looking hopefully for life and immortality beyond the grave, we are called to prove that we are men![7]

The last word, "men," received Douglass's emphasis.

Drawing upon the liberal philosophy of thinkers such as John Locke, whose influence can be found in the Declaration of Independence, Douglass concluded that the slave, as the "rightful owner of his body," is entitled to the same "natural right to freedom" as all Americans. "There is not a man beneath the canopy of heaven that does not know that slavery is wrong for *him*." Again, Douglass asked rhetorically: "What, am I to argue that it is wrong to make men brutes, to rob them of their liberty, to work them without wages, to keep them ignorant of their relations with their fellow men, to beat them with sticks, to flay them with the lash, to load their limbs with irons, to hunt them with dogs, to sell them at auction, to sunder their families. . . . Must I argue that a system thus marked with blood, and stained with pollution, is *wrong?* No! I will not." Finally, Douglass decried the religious hypocrisy of those Christians who upheld slavery. He dismissed as "blasphemy" the southern contention that slavery is divinely ordained. "That which is inhuman, cannot be divine!"[8] It was convenient for those who profited by slavery to profess that human bondage reflected divine will. But only human law enslaves a person. Douglass thus declared that slavery was the product not of God, but of the unjust exercise of power. The time for argument was over. It was the time for action.

Two years later, on July 12, 1854, Douglass again confronted the issue of white supremacy. He delivered an address entitled "The Claims of the Negro Ethnologically Considered" at the graduation exercises at Western Reserve College in Hudson, Ohio. He was the first black person to be the principal speaker at a commencement ceremony at an American university. Addressing an audience of nearly three thousand for two hours, he demolished white supremacist pseudoscience that claimed that blacks were a naturally inferior race. Douglass denounced racism and argued in favor of human brotherhood. Slavery will be abolished, he held, when we acknowledge our common humanity and our common human rights. "The relation subsisting between the white and black people of this country," he insisted, "is the vital question of the age."[9] Throughout the antebellum period, racial prejudice and white supremacist views prevailed in both the South and the North, even among many abolitionists. Alleged black inferiority was used to justify slavery, colonizing blacks, and excluding them from the western territories of the United States. Douglass declared: "The oppressor ever finds, in the character of the oppressed, a full justification for his oppression." Slavery subjugates the bodies and the minds of its victims. "Ignorance and depravity, and the inability to rise from degradation to civilization and respectability, are the most usual allegations against the oppressed." The oppressor succeeds only by convincing his victims that slavery is the product of natural inferiority, rather than of social construction. "The evils most fostered by slavery and oppression," Douglass concluded, "are precisely those which slaveholders and oppressors would transfer from their system to the inherent character of their victims. Thus, the very crimes of slavery become slavery's best defense. By making the enslaved a character fit only for slavery, they excuse themselves for refusing to make the slave a freeman."[10]

III

Douglass's 1852 July Fourth oration reached a dramatic crescendo as he reviled the nation for tolerating the systematic dehumanization of its black people. The "dark clouds," "dark and threatening clouds," and "heavy billows" of the first part of his speech now became "thunder." Ever attendant to matters of tone, voice, facial expression, and gestures in delivery, Douglass made a memorable impression upon his audience, especially with his eyes. He had read Cicero's counsel in *The Columbian Orator* that a speaker most effectively expresses emotion through the eyes. Gazing intently at his audience, Douglass vehemently declared: "At a time like this, scorching irony, not convincing argument, is needed." He had provided his audience with both argument and irony. Directing his rebuke beyond Corinthian Hall to the entire United States, he intoned: "O! Had I the ability, and could I reach the nation's ear, I would, to-day, pour out a fiery stream of biting ridicule, blasting reproach, withering sarcasm, and stern rebuke. For it is not light that is needed, but fire, it is not the gentle shower, but thunder. We need the storm, the whirlwind, and the earthquake. The feeling of the nation must be quickened; the conscience of the nation must be roused; the propriety of the nation must be startled; the hypocrisy of the nation must be exposed; and its crimes against God and man must be proclaimed and denounced."[11] The "dark clouds" and the tempest threatening to capsize the ship of state in the opening of Douglass's oration has now been brought to the forefront.

"What, to the American slave, is *your* Fourth of July?" Douglass's roar filled Corinthian Hall. Barely controlling his anger, he revealed what the Fourth of July means to those who have been excluded. Employing a rhetorical device known as *prosopopoeia*, speaking in the voice of someone not present, Douglass expressed the sentiments of the slaves. This July Fourth holiday merely reminded the slave of the unresolved American dilemma. Unleashing his pent-up emotions, Douglass thundered:

> A day that reveals to him, more than all other days in the year, the gross injustice and cruelty to which he is the constant victim. To him, *your* celebration is a sham; *your* boasted liberty, an unholy license; *your* national greatness, swelling vanity; *your*

sounds of rejoicing are empty and heartless; *your* denunciations of tyrants, brass fronted impudence; *your* shouts of liberty and equality, hollow mockery; *your* prayers and hymns, *your* sermons and thanksgivings, with all *your* religious parade, and solemnity, are, to him, mere bombast, fraud, deception, impiety, and hypocrisy—a thin veil to cover up crimes which would disgrace a nation of savages. There is not a nation on the earth guilty of practices, more shocking and bloody, than are the people of these United States, at this very hour.[12]

Having used the pronoun "your" throughout his speech, he continued to emphasize the division between black and white America by using the accusatory "your" in this climactic paragraph.

As the nation's gadfly, Douglass reproached his fellow citizens. His appeal to conscience had been a recurring theme of his oratory prior to his 1852 July Fourth oration. Speaking in Coventry, England, on February 2, 1847, he declared that "the American conscience needs blistering." Addressing an audience in New York City on May 11, 1847, he professed: "I am anxious to irritate the American people on this [slavery] question. . . . The conscience of the American public needs this irritation, and I would *blister it all over from center to circumference,* until it gives signs of a purer and a better life than it is now manifesting to the world."[13] Speaking in Syracuse, New York, on September 24 that same year, Douglass proclaimed: "So long as my voice can be heard on this or the other side of the Atlantic, I will hold up America to the lightning scorn of moral indignation. In doing this, I shall feel myself discharging the duty of a true patriot; for he is a lover of his country who rebukes and does not excuse its sins."[14]

Continuing his moral appeal, Douglass directed the attention of his 1852 Corinthian Hall audience to the internal slave trade. Huge profits, he pointed out, had been amassed from the selling of slaves from the Upper South to cotton planters in the Deep South, where the demand for forced labor was high. Ironically, while the African slave trade, prohibited by Congress after 1808, had been condemned by many Americans as "inhuman," contrary to "the laws of God and of man," the domestic slave trade continued in the South with impunity, supported by American politics and religion. Douglass emblazoned upon the minds of his listeners the horrors of the southern slave trade by painting a graphic picture for them. Such portrayals had become a staple of the slave narrative and of abolition speeches. Douglass repeated this deplorable story many times as an abolitionist speaker. He sought to demolish the myth, encouraged in the South, that the slaves were humanely treated and content with their lot. Douglass depicts the horrors of the New Orleans slave market, compelling his audience to see, hear, and feel the brutality of slavery.

> Here you see men and women reared like swine for the market. . . . Mark the sad procession, as it moves wearily along, and the inhuman wretch who drives them. Hear his savage yells and his blood-chilling oaths, as he hurries on his affrighted captives! . . . Heat and sorrow have nearly consumed their strength; suddenly you hear a quick snap, like the discharge of a rifle; the fetters clank, and the chain rattles simultaneously; your ears are saluted with a scream, that seems to have torn its way to the centre of your soul! The crack you heard, was the sound of the slave-whip; the scream you heard, was from the woman you saw with the babe. . . . Follow this drove to New Orleans. Attend the auction; see men examined like horses; see the forms of women rudely and brutally exposed to the shocking gaze of American slave-buyers.

Douglass knew this nightmare first hand: "I was born amid such sights and scenes. To me the American slave-trade is a terrible reality." He recalled how as a child he would watch the slave ships, "with their cargoes of human flesh," destined for the depot in Baltimore, from which they would be transported to Mobile, or to New Orleans.[15]

IV

Having enabled his audience to experience vicariously the brutality of slavery, Douglass shifted to the Fugitive Slave Law of 1850.[16] As a former fugitive slave, this legislation was particularly disturbing to him. The issue of runaway slaves had been a source of much friction between the North and the South—the South maintained that the Constitution guaranteed the right of slave owners to their runaways as property. Article IV, section 2 of the Constitution, referred to slaves euphemistically as "persons held to service or labor." The Fugitive Slave Law of 1793, designed to implement the fugitive slave clause of the Constitution, made the federal government responsible for enforcing the right of slave owners to recapture their runaways. While northerners could prohibit slavery in their own states, they must also recognize the constitutional right of slavery in the South. But the 1793 law, which referred to fugitives from labor rather than slaves, proved to be largely ineffective. To impede its operation, several northern states enacted personal liberty laws which recognized the right of blacks to due process, including habeas corpus and trial by jury. In 1842, the South secured a significant legal victory when the Supreme Court upheld, in *Prigg v. Pennsylvania,* the constitutionality of the 1793 Fugitive Slave Law and the slaveholder's right to his property. At the same time, the Court left an opening for those opposing slavery when it held that enforcing the Fugitive Slave Law was the responsibility of the federal government and that the states were not obligated to cooperate. Seven northern states responded by passing new liberty laws in the 1840s, forbidding the use of state legal facilities in the recapture of runaways.

The Fugitive Slave Law of 1850 was a product of the growing sectional conflict that continued to divide the country. Ever since the Missouri Compromise of 1820, the South had attempted to gain new land for the extension of slavery. At the same time, the manufacturing and commercial interests of the Northeast and the agricultural concerns of the West sought to contain the growing economic and political power of slavery. Back in 1819, an intense congressional debate ensued when the Missouri territory, a part of the 1803 Louisiana Purchase, sought to enter the Union as a slave state, precipitating the first national crisis over slavery. As Americans moved westward and settled territories petitioned Congress to be admitted to the Union as states, the issue of slavery became increasingly a source of contention. The balance of power in the Senate was determined by whether new states entered the Union as slave or free. In 1819, the nation was evenly divided between eleven free and eleven slave states.[17] Northerners feared that if Missouri entered the Union as a slave state, the new Congress might make slavery legal throughout the entire nation. At the same time, southerners wanted to protect slavery from any future Congress dominated by the free states. The North, whose population continued to grow faster than the South, already had more seats in the House of Representatives. On March 3, 1820, Congress agreed to a compromise, orchestrated by House Speaker Henry Clay, "the Great Pacificator:" Missouri entered the Union as a slave state, but Maine, carved out of northern Massachusetts, entered as a free state. The balance between free and slave states was therefore maintained at twelve each. The compromise also prohibited slavery in the remainder of the Louisiana Purchase territory north of Missouri's southern border, thirty-six degrees and thirty minutes north latitude. While many Americans welcomed the compromise, it turned out to be a mere respite in a spiraling conflict. Douglass later condemned the compromise with disdain, a "covenant with death." "Those who made it had no right to make it; and we who live after them, have no right to keep it. . . . The ground should be distinctly taken that slavery has no rightful existence anywhere—that it is a system of lawless violence."[18]

While the Missouri Compromise diminished sectional conflict between the North and the South for a period of twenty-five years, by the mid-nineteenth century it became clear that the issue of slavery would not go away. At the time of the compromise, former President John Quincy Adams had written prophetically in his diary "that the present question is a mere preamble—a title page to a great tragic volume."[19] American settlers in Texas won their independence from Mexico in 1836, establishing a republic. In 1845, the United States annexed Texas as a slaveholding territory, with the possibility of statehood. As a result of disputes stemming from the annexation of Texas, the United States declared war on Mexico in 1846, which Douglass, like Henry David Thoreau, attacked as an unjust war of conquest to extend slavery. Eager to acquire California and other Mexican provinces, President James K. Polk had provoked the war, which most Americans supported, blinded by the nation's putative "manifest destiny." The hostilities inspired Thoreau to proclaim, "I cannot for an instant recognize that political organization as *my* government which is the *slave's* government also."[20]

Soon after the outbreak of war with Mexico, northern congressmen sought to prevent the extension of slavery into these new lands, while southern congressmen wanted the limitation set by the Missouri Compromise repealed. On August 8, 1846, David Wilmot, antislavery Democratic congressman from Pennsylvania, introduced the

so-called Wilmot Proviso in the House of Representatives, proposing
that "neither slavery nor involuntary servitude shall ever exist" in any
territory won from Mexico. Like many white Americans, Wilmot was
motivated not by humanitarian concern for slaves, but by the prospect
of reserving newly acquired lands for white labor. The proviso received the support of Abraham Lincoln, a member of Congress in
1847–48. Although Douglass believed that the proviso, which aimed
merely at preventing the spread of slavery instead of abolishing the institution altogether, did not go far enough, he viewed it as an important step: "It serves to keep the subject before the people—to deepen
their hatred of the system. . . . To limit slavery where it now is, if it
does not abolish it, will at least fix upon it the nation's reprobation."[21]
As long as Congress succeeded in preventing the spread of slavery in
the western territories, freedom would be national, slavery merely sectional, confined to the South.

But the proponents of slavery countered that Congress had no
right to restrict slavery, a form of private property, from the unorgan-
ized territories. Much was at stake in this conflict. In 1847, John C.
Calhoun of South Carolina, the foremost defender of slavery prior to
the Civil War, rose in the United States Senate to proclaim that the nation teetered on the brink of disaster: "The day that the balance between the two sections of the country—the slaveholding States and the
non-slaveholding States—is destroyed, is a day that will not be far removed from political revolution, anarchy, civil war, and widespread
disaster."[22] Back in 1828, Calhoun strove to protect what he regarded
as the rights of a minority, the southern states, against the "tyranny" of
a northern majority. The residual powers clause of the Tenth Amendment to the Constitution, he argued, protected the rights of states. Calhoun's *South Carolina Exposition and Protest* (1828) held that the
Constitution authorized individual states to veto, or nullify, acts of
Congress that they regarded as exceeding its delegated authority.
Using Calhoun's argument, South Carolina had rejected both the 1828
"Tariff of Abominations," and the compromise tariff of 1832. By the
1840s, Calhoun, the champion of states' rights and secession, was convinced that the North would use its superior political power in the federal government to destroy slavery.

Although the Wilmot Proviso was passed twice in the House of
Representatives, which held a northern majority, it was ultimately de-

feated because of southern power in the Senate. Northerners opposed to slavery cited Article IV, section 3, of the Constitution, which granted Congress the power to "make all needful rules and regulations respecting the territory of the United States," in support of the argument that Congress had the right to prohibit the extension of slavery to the territories. In response, Calhoun held that Congress had no constitutional power to prohibit slavery either in the territories or in the states. As early as 1838, he contended: "Many in the South once believed that slavery was a moral and political evil. That folly and delusion are gone. We see it now in its true light, and regard it as the most safe and stable basis for free institutions in the world."[23] As the mere instrument of the states, Calhoun argued, the federal government must, under the Constitution, protect slavery as much as any other property recognized by state law. In 1848, while Frederick Douglass was summoning America to fulfill the egalitarian promise of the Declaration of Independence, Calhoun, dubbed by Douglass "the great champion of human bondage," emphatically condemned the document for containing what he regarded as subversive teaching.[24] The Declaration's claim that "all men are created equal," he asserted, is "utterly untrue. . . . It was inserted in our Declaration of Independence without any necessity." According to Calhoun, the dangerous effects of the doctrine of equality had become evident: "We now begin to experience the danger of admitting so great an error to have a place in the declaration of our independence. It had a strong hold on the mind of Mr. Jefferson, the author of that document, which caused him to take an utterly false view of the subordinate relation of the black to the white race in the South; and to hold, in consequence, that the former, though utterly unqualified to possess liberty, were as fully entitled to both liberty and equality as the latter; and that to deprive them of it was unjust and immoral."[25] In 1854, George Fitzhugh of Virginia continued the South's assault upon the Declaration of Independence. Alleging that the nation had been founded on erroneous "abstractions," he proclaimed: "Men are not born physically, morally or intellectually equal." Black people are not equal to whites. "Nature has made them slaves." Hence the Declaration was "fallacious."[26]

When the United States defeated Mexico in 1848, Douglass turned a cynical eye upon those who claimed to welcome peace, accusing them of celebrating plunder: "They have succeeded in robbing Mexico of

her territory, and are rejoicing over their success under the hypocritical pretense of a regard for peace."[27] Victory led to the acquisition of
extensive territory in the Southwest, adding almost one million square
miles to the United States. Out of these lands, called the Mexican Cession, would be carved the future states of California, New Mexico, and
Utah, in addition to portions of Arizona, Colorado, Nevada, and
Wyoming. While the majority of Americans rejoiced in their nation's
victory, Ralph Waldo Emerson issued the dire prediction: "Mexico will
poison us."[28] The sectional conflict over slavery intensified as the nation became preoccupied with the question of whether the newly acquired western lands would be slave or free. As the population in the
North continued to grow at a faster pace than that of the South, the
southern states became increasingly concerned about northern domi-
nance of the federal government.

By 1850, it became clear that only major legislation by Congress
could resolve the dispute over slavery in the territories acquired as a
result of the Mexican War. When California adopted an anti-slavery
constitution and sought entrance into the Union as a free state in 1849,
the balance between the free and slave states in Congress was again
threatened. As in the crisis over Missouri years earlier, southerners, led
by John C. Calhoun, feared that if dominated by the North, Congress
would legislate to prohibit the spread of slavery in the territories and
possibly abolish slavery in the South. Once again Henry Clay, now a
senator from Kentucky, devised a compromise. The debate in Congress
was vigorous. Calhoun, now dying, warned that Clay's compromise
would end the Union. Daniel Webster delivered what would be his
final oration in the Senate: "I wish to speak today, not as a Massachusetts man, nor as a Northern man, but as an American. . . . I speak
today for the preservation of the Union."[29]

The Compromise of 1850, ushered through Congress by Stephen
A. Douglas, Democratic senator from Illinois, provided that California
be admitted to the Union as a free state, while the regions of New
Mexico and Utah—the remainder of the Mexican Cession—were organized as territories. Once attaining the requisite population, these
territories would be admitted as states "with or without slavery, as
their constitutions may prescribe" at the time of admission.[30] In other
words, the status of slavery in the remaining territories of the Mexican
Cession would be determined by popular sovereignty. As part of the

Compromise, the slave trade, but not slavery itself, was also terminated in the District of Columbia, the nation's capital. Perhaps the most infuriating part of the Compromise, from the perspective of Frederick Douglass and all opponents of slavery, was the more stringent Fugitive Slave Law, enacted to mollify the slave states. Many southerners, frustrated by liberty laws passed by northern states to assist runaway slaves, clamored for a more effective fugitive slave law as a necessary protection for their chattel property. At the time of the compromise, there were about thirty thousand fugitive slaves in the North.

The Compromise of 1850, including the new Fugitive Slave Law, was passed by a majority in the Senate and the House of Representatives and signed into law by President Millard Fillmore. The Fugitive Slave Law, passed on September 18, 1850, explicitly made the federal government responsible for capturing fugitive slaves anywhere in the United States, overriding the wishes of local police and courts. Federal marshals were dispatched to assist in the capture of runaway slaves. Under the law, northerners had to consider the runaway slave a criminal and support the slave owner's constitutional right to recovery. According to one provision, "all good citizens are hereby commanded to aid and assist in the prompt and efficient execution of this law, whenever their services may be required."[31] Because the law was retroactive, slaves who had fled to the North prior to 1850 and who may have been living as free persons for years could be apprehended and returned the South by bounty hunters. Fugitive slaves were denied the right to a jury trial, to summon witnesses, or to testify on their own behalf, impelling several thousand black men, women, and children to flee to Canada. All citizens were also compelled by law to assist in the capture of fugitives, and severe penalties were imposed upon those who aided their escape. Southern slave owners rejoiced that the new law supported their property rights as guaranteed by the Constitution. More fugitives were seized in one year after the passage of the law than in the previous sixty years.[32] Even Abraham Lincoln supported the law's enforcement. Although morally opposed to slavery, he regretted that it was legally protected by the Constitution.

While Frederick Douglass directed most of his criticism against the Fugitive Slave Law provision of the 1850 Compromise, he viewed Henry Clay's entire plan as a transparent attempt to bolster the institution of slavery. "The plan which Mr. Clay proposes, like all Southern compromises, gives everything to Liberty, *in words*, and secures every-thing to Slavery, *in deeds*," wrote Douglass in a February 8, 1850 *North Star* editorial. An infuriated Douglass lashed out at the insidious prospect of extending slavery in the territories on the basis that it is a "right:" "The impudence of slaveholders exceeds everything! They talk about *the rights* (!!) of slavery, just as if it were possible for slavery to have rights. The *right* to introduce it into the territories! . . . Slavery has no RIGHTS. It is a foul and damning outrage upon all rights, and has no right to exist anywhere, in or out of the territories."[33] William H. Seward, United States Senator from New York, shared Douglass's sentiments, attacking the Compromise as essentially a violation of God's law, which superseded even the Constitution. In his famous "Higher Law" address on March 11, 1850, Seward decreed: "All meas-ures which fortify slavery, or extend it, tend to the consummation of vi-olence; all that check its extension and abate its strength tend to its peaceful extirpation." The Compromise of 1850 was therefore "radi-cally wrong and essentially vicious." Extending slavery into the west-ern territories not only violated the Constitution, "but there is a higher law than the Constitution," the eternal law of God, according to which, all men are free and equal. Southerners, fearing Seward's higher law doctrine, assailed it as "monstrous and diabolical." Despite the contro-versy provoked, most people greeted the compromise as the best possi-ble solution, given the political circumstances. President Millard Fillmore pronounced it "a final and irrevocable settlement."[34]

The new Fugitive Slave Law aroused the fiercest opposition north of the Mason-Dixon line. Throughout the 1850s, the law became the major target of the abolitionists, who condemned it as yet another shameful conciliation to slavery, worse than the Fugitive Slave Law of 1793.[35] On October 2, 1850, some fifteen hundred blacks crowded into New York City's Zion Chapel to decry the law as a violation of the let-ter and the spirit of the Declaration of Independence. The following year, blacks assembled in Albany to repudiate the legislation as con-trary to both the Declaration and the Constitution.[36] Northerners who had never opposed slavery vocally were inspired by the legislation to join the chorus of denunciation. Abolitionist Harriet Beecher Stowe was inspired to write *Uncle Tom's Cabin*, acclaimed by Douglass as a hammer blow against slavery. The abolitionist novel, which initially ap-peared in serial form before publication as a book in 1852 — the year of

Douglass's July Fourth oration—selling a million copies in the United States in the next seven years, presented a vivid picture of the brutality of slavery. "The word of Mrs. Stowe," Douglass declared, "is addressed to the soul of universal humanity.... *God bless her for that word.*"[37] The novel quickly became a literary sensation, capturing the minds and sentiments of countless northerners who directed their indignation against the South.

Some famous northerners responded dramatically to the Fugitive Slave Law. At a meeting of the Massachusetts Anti-Slavery Society in Framingham, Massachusetts, on the Fourth of July 1854, William Lloyd Garrison, after praising the Declaration of Independence, publicly burned the Fugitive Slave Law, along with the United States Constitution. Raising the Constitution aloft, he shouted: "And let the people say, Amen." The people responded, "Amen." Condemning the Fugitive Slave Law as a violation of higher natural law, abolitionists and their supporters committed civil disobedience as a matter of conscience. The Massachusetts Anti-Slavery Society urged that the new law be "resisted, disobeyed, and trampled under foot, at all hazards." The poet John Greenleaf Whittier protested that he would face death rather than obey "that wicked law."[38] Ralph Waldo Emerson, the "sage of Concord," shared this rebellious sentiment, writing in his journal: "By God, I will not obey it!"[39] And Henry David Thoreau, speaking at the 1854 anti-slavery meeting in Framingham, Massachusetts, called upon his fellow citizens to violate the Fugitive Slave Law on the basis of conscience. "They are the lovers of law and order, who observe the law when the government breaks it."[40]

Under the provisions of the Fugitive Slave Law, black Americans who had escaped to the North were no longer secure. Free people, white and black, were now legally obligated to assist in the capture of runaway slaves. Even free blacks felt vulnerable to kidnapping, since alleged fugitives were deprived of the right to a defense or a jury trial.[41] The law did not go unviolated. Even while the legislation was pending, Douglass helped draft a resolution for a protest meeting held at Corinthian Hall on April 5, 1850: "Resolved, compromise or no compromise, constitution or no constitution, no testimony short of a bill of sale from Almighty God can establish the title of the master to his slave, or induce us to lift a finger to aid in his return to the house of bondage."[42] Many argued that the Fugitive Slave Law was unconstitutional. Blacks held protest meetings throughout the North. Some responded by committing civil disobedience. In one famous case, a fugitive from Virginia named Shadrach Minkins—the first runaway to be arrested in New England under the Fugitive Slave Law of 1850—was rescued from a Boston courthouse in 1851 and ushered off to freedom in Canada. The same year, in Syracuse, New York, abolitionists rescued an arrested fugitive from Missouri known as Jerry, delivering him to Canada.[43] Three years later, another notable case occurred when Anthony Burns, a fugitive slave from Virginia, was captured in Boston. The arrest of Burns led to such an uproar that two thousand federal troops were required to escort him to the ship that returned him to slavery in the South.[44]

The activity of the Underground Railroad also increased, as white and black abolitionists aided runaway slaves. In 1852, the year Douglass delivered his July Fourth speech, abolitionists boasted that a fugitive slave could be whisked from a border state to Canada in as little as forty-eight hours.[45] Three years after the passage of the Fugitive Slave Law, some three thousand blacks had found refuge in Canada, and within another year, according to one historian, the number increased to possibly ten thousand.[46] Blacks played an instrumental role in the Underground Railroad. Douglass was a valuable superintendent in Rochester. Fees raised by his abolition lectures went to assist many slaves in their flight to freedom. On many mornings Douglass found runaways sitting on the steps of the *North Star* office on Buffalo Street in Rochester. He hid them until evening, when he would dispatch them to Canada. In addition to Douglass, other black leaders, including Reverend J. W. Loguen and Samuel Ringgold Ward in Syracuse, Robert Purvis and William Still in Philadelphia, and Lewis Hayden in Boston, assisted fugitive slaves.[47] Among the most famous contributors to the Underground Railroad was Harriet Tubman. Having escaped slavery from Maryland to New York in 1849, she worked indefatigably for the Underground Railroad, making nineteen trips back to the South to lead more than three hundred fugitive slaves to freedom. Hailing Tubman as "the Moses of her people," Douglass paid her moving tribute: "You . . . have labored in a private way. I have wrought in the day—you in the night. I have had the applause of the crowd and the satisfaction that comes of being approved by the multitude, while the most that you have done has been witnessed by the few trembling, scarred, and foot-sore bondmen and women, whom you have led out of the house of bondage. . . . The midnight sky and the silent stars have been the witnesses of your devotion to freedom and of your heroism."[48]

Despite the indignation it aroused, the Fugitive Slave Law was generally enforced. As Douglass argued in his 1852 July Fourth oration, no place in America was now safe from slavery: "Slavery has been nationalized in its most horrible and revolting form. By that act, Mason and Dixon's line has been obliterated; New York has become Virginia; and the power to hold, hunt, and sell men, women, and children as slaves remains no longer a mere state institution, but is now an institution of the whole United States." Douglass indicted both the federal government — "*your* President, *your* Secretary of State" — and "American Christianity," for supporting the Fugitive Slave Law. He also condemned the judiciary for sanctioning injustice. "The minister of American justice is bound by the law to hear but *one* side; and *that* side, is the side of the oppressor."[49] Speaking in Ithaca, New York on October 14, 1852, Douglass assailed the Fugitive Slave Law as a violation of the due process clause of the Fifth Amendment. The law upheld slavery as an American institution: "Wherever the star-spangled banner waves, there may men hold men as slaves."[50]

V

Moving toward the conclusion of his July Fourth oration, Douglass focused on another source of consternation: The failure of America's white churches, not only in the South but also in the North, to denounce and combat slavery. While Douglass commended the Church of England, vigorously active in the anti-slavery movement and instrumental in the abolition of slavery throughout the British Empire in 1833, he rebuked the American churches for their un-Christian hypocrisy. As early as his autobiographical *Narrative,* Douglass attacked slave masters who professed Christianity while participating in the sinful institution of human bondage. This theme appeared in many of Douglass's speeches throughout the antebellum period. Appealing to the Christian sentiments of his Corinthian Hall audience, he insisted that the Church was morally obligated to condemn the Fugitive Slave Law, "one of the grossest infringements of Christian Liberty." Yet the Church continued to be indifferent to the evils of slavery. "At the very moment that they are thanking God for the enjoyment of civil and religious liberty, and for the right to worship God according to the dictates of their own consciences, they are utterly silent in respect to a law which robs religion of its chief significance, and makes it utterly worthless to a world lying in wickedness." Instead of regarding religion as a "vital principle, requiring active benevolence, justice, and good will toward men," the church regards it as "simply a form of worship, an empty ceremony." While conceding exceptions, such as Henry Ward Beecher, Douglass alleged that the vast majority of American clergymen were what the Bible calls hypocrites. Even more painful, the Church was not only indifferent to slavery's evils, it also sided with oppression: "Many of its most eminent Divines, who stand as the very lights of the church, have shamelessly given the sanction of religion and the Bible to the whole slave system. They have taught that man may, properly, be a slave; that the relation of master and slave is ordained by God." Douglass's vehemence grew: "For my part, I would say, welcome infidelity! Welcome atheism! Welcome anything! In preference to the gospel, *as preached by those Divines!* They convert the very name of religion into an engine of tyranny." According to Douglass, southern white preachers who defended slavery mocked the teachings of the Christian Gospel. They were the infidels; they were the atheists. Invoking the words of the Hebrew prophet Isaiah, Douglass declared: "Your hands are full of blood."[51]

Finally, Douglass assailed the nation's hypocritical foreign policy. While supporting resistance to tyranny in Europe and welcoming refugees to its shores, America continued to tolerate the tyranny of slavery at home and to hunt down its fugitives. Returning to the parallel he had drawn earlier in his speech between the abolition of slavery and the American Revolution, Douglass quoted the second paragraph of the Declaration of Independence, again using the pronoun "you" to enforce his accusation: "*You* declare, before the world . . . that *you 'hold these truths to be self-evident, that all men are created equal; and are endowed by their Creator with certain inalienable rights; and that among these are, life, liberty, and the pursuit of happiness;'* and yet, you hold securely, in bondage which, according to Thomas Jefferson, '*is worse than ages of that which your fathers rose in rebellion to oppose,*' a *seventh* part of the inhabitants of your country."[52] Douglass concluded by unleashing a torrential rebuke: "Fellow-citizens! I will not enlarge further on *your* national inconsistencies. The existence of slavery in this country brands *your* republicanism as a sham, *your* humanity as a base pretense, and *your* Christianity as a lie. It destroys *your* moral power abroad; it corrupts *your* politicians at home. It fetters *your* progress; it is the enemy of improvement, the deadly foe of education; it fosters pride; it breeds insolence; it promotes vice; it shelters crime; it is a curse to the earth that supports it; and yet, *you* cling to it, as if it were the sheet anchor of all *your* hopes." Douglass's words reverberated throughout Corinthian Hall. He brought his foreboding periodic sentence to a shattering climax: "Oh! Be warned! Be warned! A horrible reptile is coiled up in your nation's bosom; the venomous creature is nursing at the tender breast of your youthful republic; *for the love of God, tear away* and fling from you the hideous monster, *and let the weight of twenty millions crush and destroy it forever!*"[53] Here Douglass, the black Jeremiah, reflected the millennial expectations of many abolitionists prior to the Civil War. A nation, unrepentant and unreformed, will call upon itself divine vengeance.[54]

But the nation neither repented nor reformed. Although regarded by many Founders as a necessary but temporary evil in 1787, slavery continued, defended by prominent politicians, such as John C. Calhoun, and many southerners as a positive moral good and a social necessity. The South realized that admitting that slavery is evil would make them defenseless as soon as a majority in Congress moved to abolish the institution.[55] Slaveholders were determined to thwart the expectation held by the framers of the Constitution that slavery would pass into oblivion. The acrimonious debate in the Senate over the Wilmot Proviso reflected the intense sectional rivalry that gripped the nation. The Compromise of 1850, while designed to settle the growing sectional strife, merely postponed the ultimate crisis. The efforts to stop the spread of slavery in the territories had failed, and the stringent Fugitive Slave Law left no part of the nation free of the stigma of slavery. Twenty years of preaching nonviolence and moral revolution had led to meager victories, while slavery spread into the western territories and the number of slaves increased by over four hundred thousand.[56] Douglass's reevaluation of the efficacy of moral argument and party politics led him to conclude that violence might be a necessary abolitionist tool, a position highlighted by his association with the militant white abolitionist John Brown. Speech and the pen must now be supported by the sword.

CHAPTER 4

CONVERTING TO THE UNITED STATES CONSTITUTION

*Interpreted as it ought to be interpreted, the Constitution is a GLO-
RIOUS LIBERTY DOCUMENT.*

> —*Frederick Douglass,*
> *"What to the Slave Is the Fourth of July?"*

I

Having arrived at the central question of his 1852 oration, "What, to the
American slave, is *your* Fourth of July?," Frederick Douglass pro-
ceeded to address the vexing issue that divided the nation: Was the
United States Constitution a pro-slavery or an anti-slavery document?
For years, Douglass had agreed with William Lloyd Garrison that the
Constitution supported slavery. Garrison and his followers assailed the
Constitution as a "covenant with Death, and an agreement with hell."
Speaking in London on March 30, 1847, Douglass lamented that the
same individuals who drew up the great Declaration of Independence,
asserting the rights of man, also framed the Constitution "trafficking in
the blood and souls of their fellow men."[1] The leading Garrisonian

Wendell Phillips sought to demonstrate in *The Constitution: A Pro-Slavery Compact* (1844) that the nation's charter gave unequivocal protection to slavery. Phillips pointed to parts of the Constitution that he claimed supported his position: the three-fifths compromise in Article I, section 2, which increased the political power of the slave states; the authorization of the federal government to suppress slave rebellions in Article I, section 8; the slave trade clause in Article I, section 9, which allowed the South to augment its slave population for at least twenty years, until 1808; and the fugitive slave clause in Article IV, section 2, which legally obligated all citizens to assist in the return of runaways. When James Madison's records of the debates of the 1787 Constitutional Convention, which included the extensive discussion on slavery, were published posthumously in 1840, Garrison's *Liberator* declared that the framers' malevolent intentions were now revealed.[2]

While a Garrisonian, Douglass believed that the federal Union established by the Constitution must be dissolved. The free North should separate from the slave South. Garrison's *Liberator* bore the following slogan as its masthead—"No Union With Slaveholders!" In a speech delivered in 1847 at New York City's Market Hall, Douglass proclaimed: "I welcome the bolt, either from the North or the South, which shall shatter this Union." Like the Garrisonians, Douglass also denounced the political process. Holding political office and voting, he believed, implied sanction of a pro-slavery Constitution, making one as guilty as the slave owners. Office holders, he declared, who "swear to support that Constitution and execute its provisions," are "responsible for all the outrages committed on the millions of our brethren now in bonds."[3] Indeed, Douglass vowed that he would "rather that my right hand should wither by my side than cast a ballot under the Constitution of the United States."[4]

Believing that the intent of the framers was pro-slavery, Douglass could not view the Constitution as anti-slavery. "I now hold," he explained, "as I have ever done, that the original intent and meaning of the Constitution (the one given to it by the men who framed it, those who adopted it, and the one given to it by the Supreme Court of the United States) makes it a pro-slavery instrument," which, "I cannot bring myself to vote under, or swear to support."[5] At this time, Douglass assumed that the original intent of the framers could be inferred from evidence extraneous to the text of the Constitution itself. As long as Douglass assumed that the framers' intentions were pro-slavery, he adhered to Garrison's reading of the Constitution. On May 11, 1849, Douglass defended his early pro-slavery view of the document in a public debate in New York City with abolitionist Samuel Ringgold Ward.[6]

II

Douglass's move to Rochester was a major step in developing his intellectual independence. Along with much of western New York, Rochester became fertile ground for an abolition movement that dissented from Garrison's. Douglass's contact with abolitionists in Rochester contributed to his transformation. Unlike the Garrisonians, they saw the Constitution and the political process as invaluable instruments for the abolition of slavery. During the 1840s and 1850s, many abolitionists, including James Birney, and Arthur and Lewis Tappan, had become frustrated by the failure of Garrison's method of moral persuasion to eradicate slavery. They turned to politics to achieve their anti-slavery goals.[7] Henceforth, politically minded abolitionists, who constituted the majority, would support political parties—the Liberty, Free Soil, and Republican parties—that opposed the spread of slavery. Rejecting the rigid stance of the Garrisonians, two black national conventions, in 1853 and 1855, vowed to support politics and the Constitution.[8]

The conflict between the North and the South over slavery reflected opposing visions of America based upon two incompatible interpretations of the Constitution. If the nation's charter supported slavery, it would not be possible to abolish the institution legally. The South would continue to hold that slavery was consistent with the intentions of the Constitution's framers. Both sides in the slavery controversy pointed to the text to support their positions. The interpretation of the Constitution that prevailed would settle the question of slavery in America once and for all. As a written document, indeed the first modern written constitution for a nation, the Constitution contains ambiguities that require interpretation.[9] The Founders agreed on the content of the Constitution, but not on its meaning. James Madison, the Father of the Constitution, anticipated the difficulty in assigning a definitive meaning to the document when he acknowledged the inadequacy of human language to communicate ideas with precision and clarity. Even the Bible, he felt, needs interpretation: "When the Almighty himself condescends to address mankind in their own language," he observed in *Federalist* No. 37, "his meaning luminous as it must be, is rendered dim and doubtful by the cloudy medium through which it is communicated."[10]

By the early 1850s, after intense critical reading and reflection, Douglass had evolved to a radical anti-slavery interpretation of the Constitution. Struggling with the correct way to read the document, Douglass would capitalize on its ambiguous language. In a February 1849 issue of the *North Star* he conceded that the Constitution, "construed according to its reading"—the words themselves—opposed slavery.[11] Just as modern interpreters have read rights such as the presumption of innocence into the Constitution on the basis of the values stated in its Preamble, Douglass joined other abolitionists in reading slavery, a deprivation of rights, out of the Constitution. As historian Donald G. Nieman observes, "Black leaders understood that the general language of the Constitution made it a malleable document whose meaning was subject to redefinition through political and legal processes, that the polity was, in a sense, an ongoing constitutional convention."[12] Douglass employed his oratory to influence more Americans to perceive the anti-slavery potential of the Constitution. He waged an interpretative battle on two fronts, not only against southern supporters of slavery, but also against the Garrisonians. Both groups, albeit for different reasons, interpreted the document as supporting slavery. If the pro-slavery reading of the Constitution prevailed, there was no American dilemma, for the framers never intended to include black people within the document's legal protections. As Douglass asserted in his 1852 July Fourth oration, if the Constitution guarantees and sanctions slavery and "the right to hold and to hunt slaves," the inevitable conclusion is that the Fathers of this Republic, "instead of being the honest men I have before declared them to be," were great "imposters." But Douglass differed from "those who charge this baseness on the framers of the Constitution of the United States." To interpret the Constitution as supporting slavery, he affirmed, is to perpetrate "a slander upon the memory" of the framers.[13]

The Liberty, Free Soil, and Republican parties, who merely opposed the extension of slavery in the newly acquired territories of the United States, while tolerating the institution where it already existed, could not be called abolitionists. Their motto, Douglass observed, was "No Slavery Outside the Slave States."[14] As the *New York Tribune* clarified in 1856, most northern opponents of slavery wanted to "secure the new Territories for Free White Labor, with little or no regard for the interest of Negroes, free or slave."[15] They were motivated neither by moral opposition to slavery nor by belief in equal rights for blacks, but by the threat of the economic competition from newly freed slave labor in the territories. For Republicans, "free soil" meant that the territories should be reserved for the labor of the white race.[16] In stark contrast, Douglass and political abolitionists argued that the Constitution prohibited slavery anywhere in the nation and empowered the federal government to abolish the institution immediately, completely, and unconditionally in the South.

Douglass joined the political abolitionists in seeking to mobilize the vote for political parties that had the potential to achieve the destruction of slavery. His acceptance of the political process was not opportunism, as the Garrisonians charged. Douglass never abandoned his moral goals. He merely altered the means by which they might be implemented. He explained: "There is a place in the world for individual action, and a place for political party action. In the field of moral action, a man may place his standard as high as he pleases. In this field, one man with the right and the true is the majority. He may invoke his standard of religious perfection. . . . But in politics a man to be of any practical use to his country or the world, must work with the multitude."[17] Douglass realized that Garrison's aim to disband the Union was a reckless and futile strategy.

The Garrisonian denunciation of the Constitution, the Union, and the political process provoked resentment in the North and hurt the anti-slavery cause. Their pro-slavery reading of the Constitution, moreover, lent credence to the southern contention that abolishing slavery would be unconstitutional. Addressing the Rochester Ladies' Anti-Slavery Society in 1855, Douglass charged that Garrison's popular slogan, "no union with slaveholders," while a good reflection of anti-slavery sentiment, nevertheless "expressed no intelligible principle of action, and throws no light on the pathway of duty. . . . No less shocking is the sentiment of the leader of the disunion forces, when he says, that if one vote of his would emancipate every slave in this country, he would not cast that vote. . . . The freedom of the whole slave population would be sacrificed."[18] Douglass had come to see that dissolving the Union as a means to defeat slavery "is about as wise as it would be to burn up this city, in order to get the thieves out of it. The Union, under the Constitution, requires me to do nothing which is wrong, and gives me many facilities for doing good."[19]

III

By 1851, Frederick Douglass had found his own voice. The *North Star* had become the most successful black newspaper of its day. Despite the difficulty of editing the paper, he later confessed that "under the circumstances, it was the best school possible for me. It obliged me to think and read, it taught me to express my thoughts clearly, and was perhaps better than any other course I could have adopted." Most importantly, it enabled him to become an abolitionist leader, "a principal, and not an agent."[20] William Lloyd Garrison opposed Douglass's decision to establish his own abolitionist newspaper. The Garrisonians set forth a number of plausible objections to convince Douglass that the venture would inevitably fail. Another abolitionist paper was not needed; with the *Liberator*, the *Anti-Slavery Bugle*, the *Anti-Slavery Standard*, and the *Pennsylvania Freeman* already established, the competition for readers would be stiff. Moreover, the time-consuming work of editing a paper would interfere with his work as a lecturer. For a short time, Douglass accepted the judgment of the Garrisonians, but he eventually forged ahead. While Garrison and other white abolitionists contributed much to the anti-slavery movement, Douglass believed that black Americans must assume the responsibility of combating slavery with their own organizations and press.

Douglass's break from Garrison was inevitable. The seeds of his intellectual independence were evident during his first year as an abolitionist speaker for Garrison's Massachusetts Anti-Slavery Society. As a lecturer, he was expected to recite countless times his suffering under slavery, with its horrors and indignities. During his Garrisonian years, Douglass helped to spread the abolitionist message throughout New England, New York, and the Ohio Valley. He recalled that after his first abolitionist speech in Nantucket during the summer of 1841, "Garrison followed me, taking me as his text." Like the slave he had once been, he was treated as an object, something to be commented on, rather than as a person capable of independent thought. He was introduced as a *"chattel,"* a *"thing"*—a "piece of southern *property*—the chairman assuring the audience that *it* could speak." He was not expected to interpret the oppressive slave system he had escaped. "Give us the facts," his abolitionist mentors insisted, "we will take care of the philosophy." Yet, Douglass confessed: "I could not always obey, for I was now reading and thinking. New views of the subject were presented to my mind. It did not entirely satisfy me to *narrate* wrongs; I felt like *denouncing* them."[21] Douglass was already emerging as an independent thinker. He felt stifled as a mere symbol. He did not want to be taken merely as someone's "text." The title of his second autobiography, *My Bondage and My Freedom,* echoing the theme of the Book of Exodus, symbolized his declaration of intellectual independence.

Spurred by his new political abolitionist friends in western New York during the late 1840s, Douglass undertook a protracted study of the Constitution. Reflecting upon his early views in *My Bondage and My Freedom,* he remembered that his first exposure to the anti-slavery movement was through Garrison and the radical abolitionists. Finding their reading of the Constitution "supported by the united and entire history of every department of government, it is not strange that I assumed the constitution to be just what their interpretation made it." The young Douglass deferred to the reputed superior knowledge and interpretations of his mentors, especially as he had "no means of showing their unsoundness."[22] But once his mind grasped the possibilities of the Constitution to support the abolition of slavery, he was compelled to convert to the document. By the time he stepped before his Corinthian Hall audience on July 5, 1852, he revered the Constitution as the slave's best hope for liberty.

IV

The Constitution has been characterized as a bundle of compromises. The framers created a document expressing principles that, once fully implemented, would spell the end of slavery. As law professor George Anastaplo observes, the compromises with slavery "left the Constitution

deeply flawed, but not without hope of eventual redemption."[23] The relationship between the original Constitution and slavery continues to stim-
ulate debate today. Most contemporary scholars take a neo-Garrisonian
position, casting blame upon the Constitution's framers for striking a
bargain with slavery.[24] The original Constitution contains several clauses
reflecting a necessary compromise between advocates and opponents of
slavery. According to James Madison, "the real difference of interests"
at the Philadelphia Convention "lay, not between the large and small, but
between the Northern and Southern states. The institution of slavery
and its consequences formed the line of demarcation."[25]

Slavery existed in the United States since the first colonial settlement in 1607, and had become an integral part of American society.
Most framers of the Constitution consented to protect slavery not because they believed in the institution, but because they felt compelled to
do so, given the stand taken by the Deep South. The delegates to the
1787 Philadelphia Convention had the responsibility to create a national government that would make the American experiment in republicanism politically and economically viable. When Shays's Rebellion, a
consequence of severe economic distress, broke out in 1786, many
feared that the new nation would not survive. Many wondered whether
America could earn respect among the nations of the world. The
Philadelphia delegates faced the challenge of creating a republic in
which sovereign power was divided between the national government
and state governments. They had to deal with rivalries between large
and small states, in addition to conflicts of interest between states that
depended economically upon slavery and those that did not. As consummate practical politicians, they understood that without compromise, there would have been no Constitution and no Union. It would
have to be either one nation with slavery or two nations, one with and
one without slavery. They chose one nation, many framers hoping that,
if confined to the South, slavery would eventually disappear.

By the time of the Philadelphia Convention, the total population of
the nation included two slaves for every nine free persons in the North,
and two slaves for every four free persons in the South, where slavery
had become the basis of the economy.[26] Historian Joseph Ellis observes that, although the Constitution's final draft was "conspicuously
silent on slavery," Madison's published notes on the Convention reveal
that "the subject itself haunted the closed-door debates." Neither the

North nor the South could claim total victory at Philadelphia. While the Constitution did not abolish slavery, the institution did not receive permanent sanction. As Ellis observes, the Constitution was "neither a 'contract with abolition' nor a 'covenant with death,' but rather a prudent exercise in ambiguity."[27] For Garrison, the sworn enemy of the Constitution, Madison's *Notes* on the Philadelphia Convention, whose sessions had been secret, merely confirmed what he had said all along: "They demonstrate that the slave population were sacrificed on the altar of political expediency—with some tinges of conscience, it is true, but nevertheless sacrificed—on the maxim that the end sanctified the means, and that it is right to do evil that good may come."[28] But others, including Abraham Lincoln, interpreted the work of the Founders more positively. On October 16, 1854, Lincoln reflected on the Constitution and slavery: "[Slavery] is hid away, in the constitution, just as an afflicted man hides away a wen or a cancer, which he dares not cut out at once, lest he bleed to death; with the promise, nevertheless, that the cutting may begin at the end of a given time. Less than this our fathers COULD not do; and MORE they WOULD not do. Necessity drove them so far, and further, they would not go . . . . Thus we see, the plain unmistakable spirit of that age, towards slavery, was hostility to the PRINCIPLE, and toleration, ONLY BY NECESSITY."[29] According to Lincoln, the absence of explicit mention of slavery in the Constitution reflected not only the framers' moral disapproval of the institution, but also their hope that it would soon expire.[30]

The fifty-five men who gathered for the 1787 Philadelphia Constitutional Convention, eight of whom had been signers of the Declaration of Independence, did not perceive their primary task as resolving the problem of slavery. They were responding instead to the threat to the rights of all Americans posed by the weak national government under the Articles of Confederation.[31] The preceding years had demonstrated that the nation could not survive without a strong Union. Preservation of liberty within the context of a strong federal Union, therefore, took precedence over abolishing slavery. The framers recognized that the Constitution, designed to create "a more perfect Union," could not have been ratified without making concessions to the slave holding interests of the southern states. By incorporating the South into the Union, slavery could at least be regulated. If the nation had instead been divided into two separate confederations, the North and the South, slavery would have been abolished in the North, but further entrenched in the South, free from northern abolitionist agitation, and from the political power exerted by the northern states within the federal system.[32]

V

One of the largest influences upon Douglass's new reading of the Constitution was the white abolitionist Gerrit Smith. A wealthy Peterboro, New York landowner, Smith had helped found the abolitionist Liberty Party in 1840, and was its presidential candidate in the election of 1848. A portrait of Gerrit Smith, along with one of Wendell Phillips, hung on the wall of Douglass's home on South Avenue, Rochester. Knowing Douglass's ambivalence about the Constitution, Smith wrote to him in 1849 that he remained hopeful that he was "on the eve of wielding the Federal Constitution for the Abolition of American Slavery."[33] The two men became close shortly after Douglass moved with his family to Rochester. Historian David Blight observes: "If William Lloyd Garrison was a fatherly figure in Douglass's life, then Gerrit Smith was his mentor."[34]

More than any other person, Gerrit Smith enabled Douglass to see the virtues of political activism. For some time in Rochester, Douglass remained troubled by an apparent contradiction in the Constitution between liberty and slavery. Writing in the *North Star* on April 5, 1850, he declared, in true Garrisonian fashion, that the "the whole framework of the American government is radically at fault; that it is founded on a gross and scandalous fraud; that in it are comprised two distinct and hostile elements; and that no Jesuitism can ever reconcile and render them consistent." According to Douglass: "Liberty and Slavery—opposite as Heaven and Hell—are both in the Constitution; and an oath to support the latter, is an oath to perform that which God has made impossible. . . . This fundamental contradiction in the Constitution is the real cause of the present storm-tossed condition of the public mind." The contradiction enabled both the North and the South to find support for their positions while ignoring the merits of the opposing side. "The South have [*sic*] looked to the Constitution, from the ramparts of Slavery, and have seen in it their highest power of defense. Slaveholders have sworn to support it as such, and have never sworn to support the whole Constitution. On the other hand, northern men have recognized in the instrument the principles of liberty and justice; and have scarcely observed the pro-slavery principle cunningly wrought into the instrument." Initially, Douglass could not in conscience take an oath to support the Constitution: "We must continue to hold, for the present, that the Constitution, being at war with itself, cannot be lived up to, and what we cannot do, we ought not swear to do; and that, therefore, the platform for us to occupy, is outside that piece of parchment."[35]

Douglass's conversion to the United States Constitution did not come easily. His correspondence reveals his turmoil. In a January 21, 1851 letter to Gerrit Smith, Douglass revealed a modification in his interpretation of the document. "Although I cannot yet see that instrument in the same light in which you view it, I am so much impressed by your reasoning that I have about decided to let Slaveholders and their Northern abettors have the Laboring *oar* in putting a proslavery interpretation upon the Constitution."[36] While still believing that the intent of the framers favored slavery, Douglass confessed that he was "sick and tired of arguing on the slaveholders' side of this question." In the same letter, Douglass conceded that Smith's adherence to a strictly textual interpretation, disregarding the personal intentions of the Constitution's framers, had begun to sway him. "But these intentions you fling to the winds. Your legal rules of interpretation override all speculations as to the opinions of the Constitution makers and these *rules* may be sound and I confess I know not how to meet or refute them on *legal* grounds. You may say that I have conceded all that you require, and it may be so."[37] Although on the verge of revising his pro-slavery reading of the Constitution, Douglass was not yet fully confident about Smith's conclusions. Could he derive the intent of the document exclusively from the words of the text itself while disregarding the intent of its authors? He confessed his moral quandary to Smith: "But there is a consideration which is of much importance between us. It is this: may we avail ourselves of legal rules which enable us to defeat even the wicked intentions of our Constitution makers? It is this question which puzzles me more than all others involved in the subject. Is it good morality to take advantage of a legal flaw and put a meaning upon a legal instrument the very opposite of what we have good reason to believe was the intention of the men who framed it?

Just here is the question of difficulty with me. I know well enough that slavery is an outrage, contrary to all ideas of justice, and therefore cannot be law according to [William] Blackstone. But may it not be law according to American legal authority?"[38]

Douglass could not deny that the framers had incorporated compromises with slavery in the Constitution. He pondered the ethics of a purely textual reading that disregarded any extrinsic intentions the framers might have had on the issue of slavery.[39] Natural law philosophy would provide Douglass with an ethical solution. According to natural law, slavery is morally wrong, a violation of human rights. Sir William Blackstone, the great English jurist, provided a definition of natural law widely cited by Americans during the early years of the republic. He declared in his *Commentaries on the Laws of England* (1765): "This law of nature, being coeval with mankind and dictated by God himself, is of course superior in obligation to any other. It is binding over all the globe in all countries, and at all times: no human laws are of any validity, if contrary to this; and such of them as are valid derive all their force, and all their authority, mediately or immediately, from this origin."[40] Holding all persons, all laws, and all governments to a higher, divinely ordained objective standard, the natural law tradition could be used to refute slavery. As Garrison argued at the 1833 American Anti-Slavery Convention: "All those laws which are now in force, admitting the right of slavery, are therefore before God utterly null and void."[41] This view of a law transcending state law, otherwise known as positive law, was adopted by anti-slavery advocates even prior to the American Revolution and became central to the abolitionist philosophy.[42] Indeed, in 1777, Massachusetts blacks drafted a petition for freedom based on the doctrine of natural law enshrined by the American Revolution.[43]

American abolitionists cited the opinion of England's Lord Mansfield, Chief Justice of the King's Bench, who argued in *Somerset v. Stewart* (1772) that slavery violated natural law. James Somerset was a Jamaican slave who escaped when his master brought him to England. When Somerset was captured, British abolitionists intervened to bring him by a writ of habeas corpus before the King's Bench. Lord Mansfield ruled that Somerset was free because he had lived in England, where slavery was not recognized. With words that would inspire American abolitionists, Mansfield declared that slavery is "so odious," and so contrary to natural law, "that nothing can be suffered to support it but positive [state] law."[44] In accord with the Somerset doctrine, radical constitutional theorists such as Lysander Spooner and William Goodell argued that slavery, even when supported by statute law, violated natural law and human rights. Read from the perspective of natural law, the Constitution, like the Declaration of Independence, is opposed to slavery.

As a political abolitionist, Douglass had come to believe that natural law doctrine justified a moral, aspirational reading of the Constitution, overriding the extrinsic intentions of the framers.[45] Like the radical constitutional theorists, he refused to interpret the Constitution divorced from its higher natural law foundation.[46] Even if the framers had intended to establish slavery, they had no right to do so, because slavery violates human rights. Douglass's new interpretation of the Constitution as anti-slavery, based upon his study of constitutional theory, armed him with a powerful legal argument against slavery. Writing to Gerrit Smith on May 1, 1851, he revealed that he was now "prepared to contend for those rules of interpretation which when applied to the Constitution make its details harmonize with its declared objects in its preamble. I am satisfied on those points, and my heart is strong." After "months of thought and investigation," Douglass had ceased to waver. He had completely converted to the United States Constitution.[47]

VI

Having developed what has been called "a constitutional faith," Douglass embraced the United States Constitution as a sacred document of America's civil religion.[48] Henceforth he would argue that the Constitution had established the institutional framework to implement the natural rights proclaimed in the Declaration of Independence. Adhering to his ethical conception of the Constitution, Douglass argued that the document enshrined fundamental values, derived from natural law, offering abolitionists powerful legal leverage against slavery. The Constitution, especially its Preamble, embodies the framers' vision of a good society.[49] Concentrating upon the document's ideals helped Douglass to understand that the compromises with slavery struck by the framers in 1787 could be viewed as mere temporary expedients made under necessity. In no way do they vitiate the ethical potential of the

Constitution. Douglass concluded that the compromises with slavery were only a means (the "scaffolding") to preserve the Union. Most of the influential delegates at the Philadelphia Convention viewed slavery to be a dying institution.[50] As Herbert J. Storing concludes, "Slavery was an evil to be tolerated, allowed to enter the Constitution only by the back door, grudgingly, unacknowledged, on the presumption that the house would be truly fit to live in only when it was gone, and that it would ultimately be gone."[51] Armed with his ethical reading of the Constitution, Douglass would seek to demonstrate that slavery was not only immoral, but also unconstitutional. Garrison's "covenant with death" was now interpreted by Douglass as the bulwark of liberty and equality. His vision of the Constitution as a potent weapon against slavery anticipated the legal strategy of the NAACP and Martin Luther King, Jr. in the struggle to overturn segregation in the South in mid-twentieth-century America.[52]

According to Douglass, the Constitution empowered the federal government to abolish slavery, not only in the federal territories and the District of Columbia, but also in the states. As early as the 1840s, political abolitionists, including Liberty Party members Lysander Spooner, William Goodell, Gerrit Smith, and Joel Tiffany, amplifying the views of Alvan Stewart, leader of the New York State Anti-Slavery Society, argued that the due process clause of the Fifth Amendment to the Constitution empowered the federal government to eliminate slavery anywhere in the nation.[53] For slaves, acknowledged as "persons" in the Constitution, were deprived of liberty without due process of law. Arguments like these encouraged Douglass. Abolitionists also referred to Article I, section 8, clause 18 of the Constitution: Congress shall have power "to make all Laws which shall be necessary and proper for carrying into Execution the foregoing Powers, and all other Powers vested by this Constitution in the Government of the United States, or in any Department or Officer thereof." While Douglass agreed that the framers were concerned to limit the powers of the federal government, reserving certain powers to the states, he nevertheless held that the federal government is "not so limited as to prevent it from performing what it is expressly required to perform." Specifically, he argued, the federal government is empowered to implement the objectives of the Constitution's Preamble.[54]

Many framers of the Constitution expected that slavery, if confined to the South, would meet an early death. The language of the Constitution had been carefully constructed so as not to lend moral sanction to slavery. While slavery existed in the South, it had not been established by the national government. The framers isolated slavery, accepting it only as a matter of state rather than national law. Douglass believed that the majority of the Founders expected slavery to end during the early years of the republic. "The patriots of the American Revolution clearly saw," he explained in a lecture to the Rochester Ladies' Anti-Slavery Society in January 1855, "and with all their inconsistency, they had the grace to confess the abhorrent character of slavery, and to hopefully predict its overthrow and complete extirpation. Washington and Jefferson, Patrick Henry and Luther Martin, Franklin and Adams, Madison and Monroe, and a host of earlier statesmen, jurists, scholars, and divines of the country, were among those who looked forward to this happy consummation."[55]

Douglass believed that the Constitution, read correctly, did not need to be amended to abolish slavery. Speaking at a mass meeting in Philadelphia on July 6, 1863, in the midst of the Civil War, Douglass proclaimed: "I hold that the Federal Government was never, in its essence, anything but an anti-slavery government. Abolish slavery tomorrow, and not a sentence or syllable of the Constitution need be altered. It was purposely so framed as to give no claim, no sanction to the claim, of property in man. If in its origin slavery had any relation to the government, it was only as the scaffolding to the magnificent structure, to be removed as soon as the building was completed."[56]

No one appreciated the dilemma of the Constitution's framers on the slavery issue more than Abraham Lincoln. In the course of his 1858 Illinois senatorial debates with Democrat Stephen A. Douglas, the future president argued that although the Constitution acknowledges slavery's existence in the republic, the framers' "covert language" reflected an intention to ultimately abolish the institution. Lincoln believed that the framers hoped that when the document "should be read by intelligent and patriotic men, after the institution of slavery had passed from among us—there should be nothing on the face of the great charter of liberty suggesting that such a thing as negro slavery had ever existed among us. The fathers of the Government expected and intended the institution of slavery to come to an end. They expected and intended that it should be in the course of ultimate extinction."[57]

Lincoln knew that unless the slavery controversy was soon resolved, the nation would be torn apart. In his "House Divided" speech, delivered in Springfield, Illinois on June 16, 1858, Lincoln, recently nominated by the Republican Party for the United States Senate, declared: "'A house divided against itself cannot stand.' I believe this government cannot endure, permanently half *slave* and half *free*."[58] Six weeks later, Frederick Douglass quoted Lincoln's ominous words in a speech in Poughkeepsie, adding: "Well and wisely said. One system or the other must prevail. Liberty or Slavery must become the law of the land."[59] Lincoln agreed with Douglass that the Constitution's framers regarded slavery as a temporary feature of American society that would be abolished in the near future.[60] Speaking at New York City's Cooper Institute on February 27, 1860, Lincoln reminded his audience of the absence of the words "slave" and "slavery" from the Constitution. Delivered during a decisive election year, Lincoln's speech, designed to appeal to the eastern political establishment, would launch him toward the Republican nomination for the presidency. The first part of his speech was devoted to demonstrating that the framers of the Constitution sought to prevent the spread of slavery, expecting that if curtailed, the institution would eventually become extinct. Adverting to *Dred Scott*, Lincoln argued that Taney's claim that "the right of property in a slave is distinctly and expressly affirmed in the Constitution" could not be substantiated by the language of the text. While Lincoln would not go as far as Douglass in reading the Constitution as an abolition document, he concluded that the framers deliberately avoided explicit allusion to slaves and slavery in order to "exclude from the Constitution the idea that there could be property in man." With words that would become famous, Lincoln concluded by urging fellow Republicans to refuse to compromise between right and wrong: "LET US HAVE FAITH THAT RIGHT MAKES MIGHT, AND IN THAT FAITH, LET US, TO THE END, DARE TO DO OUR DUTY AS WE UNDERSTAND IT."[61]

Despite his opposition to slavery as a moral evil, Lincoln was not an abolitionist. Indeed, he assured the South in his First Inaugural Address, on March 4, 1861, that he believed his oath of office bound him to enforce the Fugitive Slave Law on the grounds that the property rights of southern slaveholders were protected by the Constitution. While Lincoln remained committed to preventing the extension of slavery into the territories, he nevertheless declared, with words that angered Douglass: "I have no purpose, directly or indirectly, to interfere with the institution of slavery in the States where it exists. I believe I have no lawful right to do so, and I have no inclination to do so." Lincoln supported the 1860 Republican Party platform, which resolved that "the maintenance inviolate of the rights of the States, and especially the right of each State to order and control its own domestic institutions according to its own judgment exclusively, is essential to that balance of power on which the perfection and endurance of our political fabric depend."[62] Lincoln therefore pledged himself and the Republican Party not to attempt to eradicate slavery in the South. While Douglass was seeking to demonstrate that slavery was unconstitutional, Lincoln upheld the right of southerners to own slaves, hoping that, if confined to the South, the institution of slavery would in time simply fade away.

According to Douglass, any reading of the Constitution that sanctioned slavery was incorrect. Unlike Lincoln, he insisted that the Constitution must be interpreted according to the express goals stated in its Preamble, which incorporates ethical values antithetical to slavery, such as justice, liberty, and the general welfare. As an interpretive device, he employed what is known as a hermeneutic circle, based upon the reciprocal relationship between the parts and the whole of a text. His reading of the Constitution as an interrelated system, interpreting the clauses allegedly dealing with slavery in light of the Preamble, resembles the modern structuralist view of Charles L. Black, Jr. Black demonstrates the importance of interpreting the Constitution based on "inference from the structures and relationships created by the constitution in all its parts or in some principal part."[63] For Douglass, the Constitution's Preamble was no mere rhetorical flourish, but the basis of fundamental principles that infused the entire document. As Madison advised in *Federalist* No. 40: "There are two rules of construction, dictated by plain reason, as well as founded on legal axioms. The one is, that every part of the expression ought, if possible, be made to conspire to some common end. The other is, that where the several parts cannot be made to coincide, the less important should give way to the more important part; the means should be sacrificed to the end, rather than the end to the means."[64] Reading the clauses allegedly supporting slavery in the context of the entire document, especially the Preamble, Douglass argued that the Constitution opposed slavery. "The great principles," he affirmed, "which they [the framers] laid down as the fundamental objects of the Government and the completeness with which they have excluded every word sanctioning the right of property in man, is no slight testimony in proof of the intention to make the Constitution a permanent liberty document."[65]

The language of the Constitution, Douglass argued, is our best guide to its interpretation. Instead of "slave" and "slavery," the document refers to "other persons" in the apportionment clause, "such persons" in the slave-trade clause, and "persons held to servitude or labor" in the fugitive slave clause. One could not tell from the explicit language of the original Constitution that slavery existed in the United States prior to the Civil War. Ironically, the word "slavery" did not expressly enter the language of the Constitution until after the Civil War when the Thirteenth Amendment abolished "slavery" in 1865. The framers referred to slaves euphemistically as "persons" in those clauses dealing with the three-fifths compromise, the fugitive slave clause, and the prohibition against Congress interfering with the African slave trade until 1808. Such ambiguous language, Douglass contended, reflected the anti-slavery intentions of most framers. If the majority of the framers intended to establish slavery in the United States, they would have spelled it out in the Constitution.

Other opponents of slavery joined Douglass in emphasizing that the Constitution nowhere expressly acknowledges slavery. In 1850, James Fenimore Cooper exclaimed: "They say that the Constitution requires slavery. I should like to see in what clause."[66] Ralph Waldo Emerson noted in 1854 that the Constitution "has not the word slave in it, and very good argument has shown that it would not warrant the crimes that are done under it. That with provisions so vague, for an object *not named*, and which would not be suffered to claim a barrel of sugar or a bushel of corn, the robbing of a man and all his posterity, — is effected."[67] Since many of the delegates to the Philadelphia Convention were competent lawyers, we must attribute the absence of the word "slavery" in the document's language to deliberate calculation. The record of their debates reveals that the issue of slavery was much discussed. With the world looking on, the delegates would not have inadvertently left serious ambiguities in the Constitution. Luther Martin, delegate from Maryland, confessed that his fellow delegates "anxiously sought to avoid the admissions of expressions [i.e., slavery] which might be odious to the ears of Americans." Nevertheless, he conceded, the framers were "willing to admit into their system those *things* which the *expressions signified*."[68] James Madison divulged that the Philadelphia Convention "thought it wrong to admit in the Constitution the idea that there could be property in men."[69] John Quincy Adams, reflecting on the work of the framers, observed: "The words slave and slavery are studiously excluded from the Constitution. Circumlocutions are the fig-leaves under which these parts of the body politic are decently concealed."[70]

VII

By 1851, Frederick Douglass had become one of the foremost advocates for the United States Constitution. His new understanding of the document had to be put into political practice. As he explained in *My Bondage and My Freedom:* "Here was a radical change in my opinions and in the action logically resulting from that change." With new faith in the Constitution, Douglass encouraged others to participate in the political process sanctioned by the document. The experience of editing the *North Star,* complemented by his discussions with the political abolitionists of western New York, "compelled me to rethink the whole subject" of political action, "and to study, with some care, not only the just and proper rules of legal interpretation, but the origin, design, nature, rights, powers, and duties of civil government, and also the relations which human beings sustain to it."[71] Douglass's extensive readings on American government, constitutional law, and political philosophy led him to see the value of both the Union and politics. He summarized his new creed: "I became convinced that there was no necessity for dissolving the 'union between the Northern and Southern states;' that to seek this dissolution was no part of my duty as an abolitionist; that to abstain from voting, was to refuse to exercise a legitimate and powerful means for abolishing slavery; and that the Constitution of the United States not only contained no guarantees in favor of slavery, but, on the contrary, it is, in its letter and spirit, an anti-slavery instrument, demanding the abolition of slavery as a condition of its own existence, as the supreme law of the land."[72] Dissolving the Union would mean the end of the American republic.

Garrison's fundamental flaw, Douglass concluded, was his unyielding righteousness: "He revolted at halfness."[73] In a eulogy for Garrison, delivered at the Fifteenth Street Presbyterian Church in Washington, D.C., on June 2, 1879, Douglass acknowledged the friction that had developed between them years before: "By one principle he tried all men, all parties, and all sects. They that were not for him were against him."[74] In contrast to Garrison's dogmatism, a self-righteousness that led him to burn the United States Constitution, denounce the federal Union, and withdraw from the democratic political process, Douglass perceived that the moral goal of abolishing slavery had to be achieved by pragmatic political means.

Douglass recognized that in the public realm morality and expediency do not necessarily conflict. Failure to consider what the situation realistically allows, refusing to accept a lesser evil to avoid a greater one, can actually thwart the achievement of one's ethical goals. Failing to make necessary compromises "would make party action, or combined effort impossible, by requiring an identity of opinion." It does not necessarily follow "that what is *morally* right is, at all times, politically possible." Douglass explained his philosophy of electoral politics: "We can vote for a man who affirms, and will carry our one important truth, even though he should be totally blind in respect to others that we might deem important, provided, of course, he does not require us to deny any part of the truth which we hold; or, in other words, we can affirm his truths just so far and so long as he does not require us to negative [*sic*] ours. It seems to us, there can be no valid objection against this rule of action, or the philosophy by which it is sustained, especially when it is remembered that, often the very best way of promoting one cause, is by promoting the triumph of another."[75]

Unlike Garrison, Douglass learned that success in the political realm demands a prudential morality that carefully weighs the consequences of actions. To abolish slavery, the intractable Garrison would have gone as far as dissolving the Union, leaving two nations, one slave and one free. Preserving the Union enabled the North, especially the abolitionists, to combat slavery politically. If the South were to become a separate nation, such political efforts would not be possible. Dissolving the Union by a secession of the North would be an unconscionable flight from moral responsibility, for it would leave the slaves of the South at the mercy of the slave owners. Forsaking the Union and the Constitution would deprive abolitionists of the only means, short of civil war, of ending slavery in the United States. The abolition movement would end in travesty. "It started to free the slave," Douglass told a Rochester audience in 1855: "It ends by leaving the slave to free himself."[76]

VIII

Douglass's ethical interpretation of the Constitution, based upon the document's fundamental liberal principles, made possible political action consistent with the demands of conscience. "Men should not," Douglass wrote to Gerrit Smith, in 1852, "under the guidance of a false philosophy, be led to fling from them such powerful instrumentalities against Slavery as the Constitution and the ballot."[77] By means of the ballot, Douglass asserted, candidates can be elected to office who will use their political power to abolish slavery and a strong anti-slavery party might bring about what the Democratic and Whig parties would not. Steering his own abolitionist course, Douglass told an audience of Garrisonians in Salem, Ohio, on August 23, 1852, that he would forego no weapon in the battle against slavery: "I am going to be a man. A free man. Free to adopt any views, any instrumentalities, which I think will advance the good cause, and although I vote, I believe that the great instrumentality after all, is the 'foolishness of preaching.' The work is to be done by exposing the damning deeds of Slavery, the abominations of the church, in short agitation. Agitate, *agitate*."[78] David Blight observes that throughout the 1850s Douglass "yearned for any means to link the cause of black liberation more closely with the national government."[79] As early as 1847, Douglass threw his support behind various anti-slavery political parties—the Liberty Party, the Free Soil Party, and eventually the Republican Party. "Our rule of political action is this," Douglass declared shortly before the 1852 presidential election, "the voter ought to see to it that his vote shall secure the highest good possible, at the same time that it does no harm."[80] Douglass was disappointed when Democrat Franklin Pierce, a staunch foe of abolition, was elected president, carrying the majority of the free and the slave states.

Douglass put his pragmatism into practice. For national elections, he did everything in his power to advance the cause of freedom by supporting the platform of the Liberty Party, later known as the Radical Abolitionist Party, calling for the immediate abolition of slavery everywhere in the United States. But once the election drew near, recognizing that an abolitionist victory was unlikely, he prudently switched his support to those political parties, such as the Free Soil Party, and subsequently to the Republican Party, which had better chances of success. Even though the Free Soil Party sought merely to contain rather than abolish slavery, Douglass believed that partial victories were better than no victories. Hence, he supported the Free Soil presidential ticket in 1852; and in 1856, he endorsed the Republican John C. Frémont for President. After backing abolitionist Gerrit Smith in the 1860 presidential election, Douglass eventually supported the Republican Abraham Lincoln, even though Lincoln's party aimed not to abolish slavery in the South, but merely to prevent its spread in the territories.[81] In an address on the presidential campaign of 1860, Douglass conceded that a Republican victory, while not meeting the ultimate demands of abolition, would still be a blow to slavery. "I would gladly have a party openly combined to put down slavery at the South. In the absence of such a party, I am glad to see a party in the field against which all that is slave-holding, malignant and Negro-hating, both at the North and the South, is combined."[82] In the face of staunch opposition, it is better to secure partial victories than receive total losses. The fight against slavery should not fall prey to a foolish rigidity. "Right Anti-Slavery action," Douglass insisted, "is that which deals the severest deadliest blow upon Slavery that can be given at that particular time. Such action is always consistent, however different may be the forms through which it expresses itself."[83]

Although Douglass's conversion to politics and the Constitution had been germinating since 1847, he did not make it public until 1851. At the eighteenth annual meeting of the American Anti-Slavery Society, held in Syracuse, New York in May of that year, Douglass stunned the Garrisonians by rejecting a proposal that the society would refuse to endorse any newspaper that did not view the Constitution as proslavery. An 1851 *North Star* editorial made the conversion official. Douglass declared that he had "arrived at the firm conviction that the Constitution, construed in the light of well-established rules of legal interpretation, might be made consistent in its details with the noble purposes in its preamble." Henceforth, he affirmed, "we should insist upon the application of such rules to that instrument, and demand that it be wielded in behalf of emancipation." This view of the Constitution, he assured his readers, "has not been hastily arrived at," but stemmed from "a careful study of the writings of Lysander Spooner, of Gerrit Smith, and of William Goodell." Declaring that slavery was a system of "lawless violence," a flagrant violation of the Constitution, Douglass insisted that every American citizen must in conscience "use his *political* as well as his *moral* power for its overthrow."[84]

Infuriated by Douglass's defection, Garrison retaliated by exclaiming, "there is roguery somewhere" and moved to have the *North Star* withdrawn from the list of papers endorsed by the American Anti-Slavery Society. The convention acquiesced to this demand.[85] Garrison's slander hurt Douglass deeply. He never expected Garrison, whom he greatly respected, to impugn his motives. In September 1852, Douglass wrote about Garrison to Senator Charles Sumner: "I stand in relation to him something like that of a parent to a child." Although Douglass conceded that Garrison's school possessed "many good qualities," he charged that it was nevertheless "too narrow in its philosophy and too bigoted in spirit to any who venture to differ from it."[86] While Garrison's moral indignation inspired many, "his righteousness," observes historian Benjamin Quarles, "led him to assume that because his own motives were honest, those of his opponents were the reverse."[87]

IX

Douglass's declaration of intellectual autonomy was not without personal consequences. Garrison and his followers vilified him as an "enemy," citing his new favorable view of the Constitution and his advocacy of political abolitionism.[88] Douglass responded that his "apostasy" was not from the anti-slavery movement, but from "Garrisonianism."[89] In June 1851, Douglass's financially strapped *North Star* received much needed monetary support from the wealthy philanthropist Gerrit Smith and merged with the *Liberty Party Paper,* creating a new weekly, *Frederick Douglass' Paper.* Endorsing political abolitionism, its motto was "All Rights for All." The Garrisonians charged that Douglass's support for the abolitionist Liberty Party as well as his favorable view of the Constitution stemmed from ulterior motives.[90] Douglass, they alleged, had betrayed his principles in exchange for substantial financial assistance from the political abolitionist Gerrit Smith. This accusation demeaned Douglass's capacity for independent thought and reflected the paternalistic white supremacist views of many Garrisonians toward black abolitionists.[91]

The Garrisonians continued to disparage Douglass's character. They went so far as to suggest publicly that he was involved romantically with Julia Griffiths.[92] A white English abolitionist, Griffiths was the daughter of a friend of the great British abolitionist, William Wilberforce. She and Douglass had met in her home in Newcastle upon Tyne, England during his 1845–1847 lecture tour of Britain. In May 1849, Griffiths came to assist Douglass in Rochester, moving in with his family on 4 Alexander Street. She helped Douglass edit the *North Star* and later became business manager of *Frederick Douglass' Paper.* Her editorial and fund-raising skills sustained Douglass's journalistic efforts. While Douglass's wife, Anna Murray, was instrumental in his escape from slavery, Julia Griffiths was instrumental in his achieving an independent literary voice.[93] Douglass and Griffiths spent much time together, fueling speculation that their relationship was more than professional. They shared intellectual interests that Douglass could not share with his wife Anna, who remained illiterate her entire life.

The Garrisonians refused to relent. At the annual meeting of the American Anti-Slavery Society, held in Rochester from May 11 to 13, 1852, less than two months before his July Fourth address, Douglass was attacked by Wendell Phillips, and the black abolitionist Charles Lenox Remond, along with other Garrisonians for his apostasy on the Constitution, his defense of the Union, and his advocacy of party politics.[94] In December 1852, Wendell Phillips wrote that "Douglass is entirely estranged from us." Six months later, Phillips confessed to Garrison, "With Douglass, the die seems to be cast."[95] Yet, Douglass had defenders. After a long discussion with Douglass in 1853, Harriet Beecher Stowe wrote to Garrison: "I am satisfied that his change of sentiments was not a mere political one but a genuine growth of his own conviction." She was impressed by Douglass's intellect. "He holds no opinion which he cannot defend, with a variety and richness of thought and expression and an aptness of illustration which shows it to be a growth from the soil of his own mind."[96]

X

In his 1852 July Fourth address, Douglass told his audience that his very reading of the Constitution as an abolition document came after studying the works of Lysander Spooner and William Goodell, whose articles appeared in the pages of *Frederick Douglass' Paper*. Reading the arguments of these radical constitutionalists, Douglass had learned the principles and rules of interpreting legal instruments. Viewing the Constitution in light of natural law principles, Spooner and Goodell concluded that if the document protected slavery, it would be egregiously inconsistent. Slavery, they argued, is not only unconstitutional but also violates the equality doctrine of the Declaration of Independence, which they regarded as integral to constitutional law.[97] Inspired by his new reading of the Constitution, Douglass proclaimed to his 1852 Corinthian Hall listeners: "Interpreted as it *ought* to be interpreted, the Constitution is a GLORIOUS LIBERTY DOCUMENT." Having summoned the nation to fulfill the promise of the Declaration of Independence, Douglass now declared that the United States Constitution, read correctly, was an abolitionist Constitution. "Read its preamble, consider its purposes. Is slavery among them? Is it at the gateway? Or is it in the temple? It is neither." Because a July Fourth oration was not a suitable forum for a detailed textual analysis, Douglass did not elaborate on his new anti-slavery interpretation of the Constitution. But he did affirm the right of every American citizen "to form an opinion of the constitution, and to propagate that opinion, and to use all honorable means to make his opinion the prevailing one."[98]

During the 1850s, Douglass took to the lecture circuit arguing that the Constitution authorized the federal government to abolish slavery throughout the nation. Speaking before the Rochester Ladies' Anti-Slavery Society in 1855, he criticized the Republican Party for merely seeking to prevent the spread, instead of calling for the outright abolition, of slavery: "It aims to limit and denationalize slavery, and to relieve the Federal Government from all responsibility for slavery. Its motto is, '*Slavery Local—Liberty National.*' The objection to this movement is the same as that against the American Anti-Slavery Society. It leaves the slave in his fetters—in the undisturbed possession of his master, and does not grapple with the question of emancipation in the States." In contrast to the Republicans, New York's Liberty Party, representing radical constitutional abolitionism, is "the *only* abolition-ist organization in the country, except a few local organizations. It makes a clean sweep of slavery everywhere. It denies that slavery is, or *can* be legalized. It denies that the Constitution of the United States is a pro-slavery instrument, and asserts the power and duty of the Federal Government to abolish slavery in every State of the Union."[99]

When Douglass read the Constitution, he rejected the historical or "originalist" view that attempted to interpret the document by divining the alleged original intentions of its framers and ratifiers. There were no stenographic records of the Philadelphia Convention. Even *The Federalist* (1788), an analysis and defense of the Constitution written by Madison, Hamilton, and John Jay, provides little evidence of the framers' aims. Publication in 1849 of James Madison's *Notes* on the Convention, the only substantial record of its proceedings, sparked a vigorous debate about the intentions of the framers and what weight these should have in interpreting the Constitution. Madison himself was skeptical of the value of interpreting the document according to "original intent." He wrote that he had postponed publishing his notes because "as a guide in expounding and applying the provisions of the Constitution, the debates and incidental decisions of the Convention can have no authoritative character."[100] Throughout the early years of the republic, the Supreme Court, Congress, and presidents construed the Constitution without the benefit of a published record of the proceedings of the Philadelphia Convention. Many modern scholars find the search for "original intent" fruitless and misleading. Leonard Levy argues that the framers did not believe that "the original understanding at Philadelphia" was of much importance. "What mattered to them was the text of the Constitution, construed in the light of conventional rules of interpretation, the ratification debates, and other contemporary expositions."[101] Searching for the original intentions of the Constitution's framers is plagued by insurmountable difficulties.[102] According to Lawrence H. Tribe: "There is little to commend the frequent practice of seeking to unearth the actual views of those who helped to draft" the Constitution.[103] Reflecting on judges who claim fidelity to the alleged "intentions of the framers," Supreme Court Justice William J. Brennan, Jr. argues that such deference "is little more than arrogance cloaked as humility. It is arrogant to pretend that from our vantage we can gauge accurately the intent of the Framers on application of principle to specific, contemporary questions."[104]

A principal obstacle confronting those who seek to interpret the
Constitution according to "original intent" is identifying whose intentions should count—the framers, the nearly sixteen hundred ratifiers in
the states, or "we the people." As Douglass understood, because those
who voted for the Constitution acted from a variety of motives, it is not
possible to find a common denominator among their divergent positions. Hence, the supposed "original intent" of those who framed or
ratified the Constitution is a mere abstraction, allowing interpreters to
impose their subjective views and philosophy on the document in the
guise of an objective reading. Even while Douglass subscribed to Garrison's pro-slavery interpretation of the Constitution, as early as 1849,
we have noted, he admitted that the document's ambiguous phrasing
left it open to an anti-slavery construction, especially in light of the
purposes expressed in the Preamble.[105] Douglass remarked that if people from different nations, with no knowledge of American history or
institutions, were to read the Constitution, they would be unaware of
slavery's existence.[106] Expressing his new literalist perspective, he
wrote to Gerrit Smith on May 21, 1851: "I am only in reason and in
conscience bound to learn the intentions of those who framed the Constitution *in the Constitution itself.*"[107] If the Constitution, Douglass
claimed, is to be regarded as law, its language must be regarded as
paramount in its interpretation.[108]

Douglass considered, therefore, only those intentions found expressly in the document's language, not in the alleged designs of the
drafters. In the mid–1840s, political abolitionist Lysander Spooner had
written on the question of intent. While reconsidering his views on the
Constitution, Douglass read Lysander Spooner's pages discussing how,
failing to find explicit sanction for human bondage in the Constitution,
defenders of slavery resorted to the purported intentions of its framers,
divined through external circumstances and historical evidence. But
this, Spooner argued, is to substitute erroneously the intentions of
"those who drafted the constitution for the intentions of the constitution
itself." As a written legal instrument, the Constitution must have a legal
meaning, which must be found in the letter of the instrument, clearly
and distinctly expressed, not from exterior evidence and imputations of
original intent. The Constitution's "intentions are no guide to its legal

meaning . . . , but its legal meaning is the sole guide to its intentions."[109] By 1851, therefore, Douglass concluded that interpreters should not be bound by intentions not expressly found in the Constitution.

The framers, ratifiers, and early interpreters of the United States Constitution relied upon a rich hermeneutic tradition found in English common law. In 1611, Chief Justice Thomas Fleming of the King's Bench declared: "As touching construction of words, they shall be taken according to the . . . intent of parties." Ascertaining the intent is the challenge. According to the seventeenth-century English jurist John Selden, the "one true sense" of a document is that which "the Author meant when he [wrote] it." The court, he argued, must determine "the intention of the King" on the basis of the words of the law alone, and not from extratextual sources. In 1790, John Joseph Powell argued in his treatise on contract law that the intent of the parties to a contract must be derived from their words, from "that which, in common presumption, may be taken to be their intent." Contract law considers pertinent "external expression," not "internal sentiments." According to common law standards, therefore, the intent of a maker of a legal document is inseparable from the intent of the words of the document itself. Americans applied these interpretive canons from common law to the Constitution. H. Jefferson Powell explains: "The Philadelphia framers' primary expectation regarding constitutional interpretation was that the Constitution, like any other legal document, would be interpreted in accord with its express language. . . . Debates over the language of the document were abundant, yet in none of them did any delegate suggest that future interpreters could avoid misconstruing the text by consulting evidence of the intentions articulated at the convention."[110] The meaning of the Constitution, therefore, should be determined only by what it says.

This interpretive canon was essential to the jurisprudence of Chief Justice John Marshall. Lysander Spooner cited Marshall's opinion in *Ogden v. Saunders* (1827), where the Chief Justice argued that in construing the Constitution, "the intention of the instrument must prevail; that this intention must be collected from the words; that its words are to be understood in that sense in which they are *generally used* by those for whom the instrument was intended."[111] The Marshall Court articulated the same principle in *Gibbons v. Ogden* (1824): "As men whose intentions require no concealment, generally employ the words which most directly and aptly express the ideas they intend to convey, the enlightened patriots who framed our constitution, and the people who adopted it, must be understood to have employed words in their natural sense, and to have intended what they have said."[112] According to Marshall, and this is the mode of interpretation Douglass adopted, the framers' intentions must be ascertained not from extrinsic historical sources such as their debates, speeches, essays or letters during the drafting and ratification of the Constitution, but from the words of the document itself. This was the traditional common law method of interpreting legal instruments. Just as one discerns the intentions of a testator from the words of his will, one must discern the intention of a constitution or statute from its words.[113]

Political abolitionist William Goodell, another influence upon Douglass, also advocated a strict literal construction of the Constitution, which "allows no reference to past or passing events, for a key to the meaning of the document. It insists that the *words* of the instrument, the *literal words*, and *nothing but* the words shall be allowed to tell us the meaning of the Constitution. It rules the Historian and the New Journalist out of the witness-box, and installs the Grammarian and the Lexicographer in their stead."[114] Spooner and Goodell taught Douglass that in reading legal documents, especially the Constitution, what counts is the text, not the context. This rule of interpretation made possible Douglass's new anti-slavery view of the Constitution. As he argued on July 24, 1851: "The Constitution is the record of its own intention." Looking beyond the document for its meaning is futile, "because outside that instrument we shall find conflicting and irreconcilable intentions. One state may have adopted the Constitution, intending that it should subserve one end; while another may have adopted it intending that it serve another and quite different end."[115] Douglass's strict constructionist reading of the Constitution, clinging to the literal text, became the basis for a radical reading of the Constitution, one that extended full human rights to black Americans.

XI

Douglass had to prove to the American people that Congress had the legal power to abolish slavery. At the same time, he had to answer the Free Soil and Republican parties, including the future president,

Abraham Lincoln, who held that slavery was constitutionally protected in the South and that the federal government could do no more
legally than prevent the spread of slavery in the western territories. To
the Garrisonians, he would argue: Do you not realize that in condemning the Constitution, you are forsaking a vital legal weapon
against slavery? To the southern slaveholders, he would argue: Do
you not realize that slavery violates the republican ideas of the
Founders? To the Free Soilers and Republicans, he would argue: Do
you not realize that the Constitution authorizes the federal government to abolish slavery not merely in its branches in the territories,
but also at its roots, the southern states?

The only way to defeat slavery legally was to demonstrate its unconstitutionality. As Douglass argued in an August 1855 editorial, "If
one half of the time, talent and money, which has been spent in at-
tempts to fix upon the Constitution of the United States, a pro-slavery
interpretation, had been devoted to showing its anti-slavery character,
and in pointing out the duty of the citizen and the statesman to abolish
slavery under the Constitution, the anti-slavery cause would be in a far
more hopeful condition than it is now."[116] In 1857, the Supreme Court,
on the basis of what it assumed to be the original intent of the framers,
ruled in the *Dred Scott* case that black people were not citizens of the
United States. Consequently, they were not entitled to the freedoms
guaranteed by the Constitution. The Civil War, which tore the fabric of
the Union, was fought over two conflicting interpretations of the Constitution on the subject of slavery. In 1861, eleven southern states seceded from the Union in the belief that the Constitution not only
protected but also permitted the extension of slavery. The seceding
states claimed that slavery was consistent with the original intent of the
Founders. The Civil War would decide the question of whether the republic would continue half slave and half free.

Properly and strictly construed, Douglass contended, the original
unamended Constitution guaranteed liberty and equality for all. He
would use his ethical reading of the Declaration of Independence and
the Constitution to argue that the Founders had created the basis for a
multiracial democracy.[117] According to Douglass's vision of the future,
black people would occupy an integral place in American society.
When the nation was ravaged by Civil War, he would proclaim in a
May 1863 address on "The Present and Future of the Colored Race in

America," delivered in the Church of the Puritans, in New York City: "I shall advocate for the Negro, his most full and complete adoption into the great national family of America. I shall demand for him the most perfect civil and political equality, and that he shall enjoy all the rights, privileges and immunities enjoyed by any other members of the body politic. I weigh my words and I mean all I say, when I contend as I do contend, that this is the *only solid, and final solution* to the problem before us." The destiny of black Americans was crucial to the resolution of the American dilemma. "It is demanded not less by the terrible exigencies of the nation, than by the Negro himself for the Negro and the nation, are to rise or fall, be killed or cured, save or lost together. Save the Negro and you save the nation, destroy the Negro and you destroy the nation, and to save both you must have but one great law of Liberty, Equality and Fraternity for all Americans without respect to color."[118] If the framers chose to grace the Constitution with a Preamble expressing their aspiration that the blessings of liberty and equality be granted to all, without explicitly excluding the black race, Douglass would hold them to their words. The burden of proof fell upon those who, departing from the strict language of the text itself, introduced other meanings, especially meanings inconsistent with human rights. The nation had been established upon objective moral principles applicable to all humanity, even if not all of the Founders grasped their full import. Douglass considered the Preamble, like the Declaration of Independence, as part of the nation's fundamental law. For him, the key to interpreting all sections and clauses of the Constitution lay in comprehending its purpose in light of the language of the Preamble, which reveals the moral aspirations of the framers.

When confronted with passages euphemistically referring to slavery, Douglass interpreted the document according to the values expressed in the Preamble.[119] It outlines the color-blind objects of the government created by the Constitution—to "establish Justice," to "promote the general Welfare," and to "secure the Blessings of Liberty to ourselves and our Posterity."[120] As Constitution scholar Dennis J. Mahoney explains, "The purposes listed in the Preamble are consistent with what the Declaration of Independence asserts to be the end of all governments instituted among men, namely to secure the equal and inalienable natural rights of all to life, liberty, and the pursuit of happiness."[121] When the happiness of some is pursued to the detriment of others, the general welfare standard of the Preamble is violated.

Douglass's reverence for the Preamble echoed that of the anti-slavery Supreme Court Justice Joseph Story, author of a famous mid-nineteenth-century exposition of the United States Constitution. Story argued that the Preamble is important for ascertaining the purposes of the Constitution and it is the best guide for its interpretation.[122] Since, according to Douglass, the intent of a legal document must be ascertained from its language, slavery should be abolished on the basis of the Preamble. The Thirteenth Amendment should not have been necessary. Curiously, while the courts have sometimes invoked the Preamble in support of particular constitutional interpretations, it has not been recognized as law.[123] Nevertheless, the moral ideals of the Preamble highlight the American dilemma. Slavery violated both the letter and the spirit of the Constitution. Interpreted in light of the principles of the Declaration of Independence and the ethical purposes stated in the Preamble, the Constitution, Douglass insisted, must be "wielded in behalf of emancipation."[124] He continued to read the Preamble through the lens of natural law.

Douglass's anti-slavery reading of the Constitution relied upon a moral mode of legal interpretation stemming as far back as Aristotle. Considering Sophocles' *Antigone*, which dramatizes a conflict between human law and the higher universal natural law, Aristotle suggests that a speaker might interpret the law in the interest of justice: "It is clear that, if the written law is adverse to your case, [the speaker] must appeal to the universal law, and to the principles of equity as representing a higher order of justice." When two laws conflict with each other, Aristotle advises that the speaker "turn it and see which construction lends itself to justice, which to expediency."[125] While it is not known whether Douglass was familiar with this passage from Aristotle's *Rhetoric*, his oratory on the Constitution after 1849 reveals an interpretive strategy similar to that suggested by the Greek philosopher. Lysander Spooner had grown impatient with the Garrisonians for failing to perceive the advantage of using the Constitution on behalf of the abolitionist cause. He saw the importance of adhering to the Constitution's ethical basis: "If they have the Constitution in their hands," he wrote of his fellow abolitionists in 1847, "why, in heaven's name do they not out with it, and use it?"[126]

In a debate on the Constitution and slavery held in New York City in May 1857, Douglass argued: "If the language of any part of the Constitution could be tortured into a doubt whether Slavery were favored or not, we had a right to take advantage of that dubious language, and construe it on the virtuous side."[127] He felt justified in concluding that where the words of the framers are ambiguous, they must have intended ambiguity. If the words "slave" and "slavery" are absent from the original Constitution, the framers must have intended the omission, expecting the eventual demise of slavery. Refusing to give slavery explicit recognition or moral sanction, the framers left an opening for the abolition of what they regarded as a decadent institution, contrary to republican principles. As historian Bernard Bailyn observes: "What is significant in the historical context of the time is not that the liberty-loving Revolutionaries allowed slavery to survive, but that they—even those who profited directly from the institution—went so far in condemning it, confining it, and setting in motion the forces that would ultimately destroy it. For they were practical and moderate men, though idealistic and hopeful of human progress."[128]

XII

As Frederick Douglass concluded his 1852 July Fourth oration at Corinthian Hall, he followed the tradition of the jeremiad, tempering his warnings with a message of optimism.[129] "Allow me to say," he confessed, "notwithstanding the dark picture I have this day presented of the state of the nation, I do not despair of this country. There are forces in operation, which must inevitably work the downfall of slavery. . . . I therefore leave off where I began, with hope. While drawing encouragement from the Declaration of Independence, the great principles it contains, and the genius of American institutions, my spirit is also cheered by the obvious tendencies of the age."[130] Douglass's oration contains the same combination of stinging rebuke and hope for spiritual renewal that characterized his oratory throughout most of the 1850s.[131] Stemming from a providential view of human history and his conviction that America held a special place in the fulfillment of the divine plan, Douglass concluded his oration with a vision of a nation redeemed. In the first part of his July Fourth oration, he had identified the slave with the ancient Hebrews, a suffering people awaiting salvation. Inspired by the archetypal liberation theme of the Book of Exodus, he expressed confidence that enslaved black Americans would ultimately triumph over Pharaoh in the South. Quoting the prophet Isaiah, ("the arm of the Lord is not shortened"), Douglass insisted that "the doom of slavery is certain." Drawing upon a prevalent idea in African American literature—the link between apocalypse and freedom—he invoked Psalm 68:31: "Africa must rise and put on her yet unwoven garment. 'Ethiopia shall soon stretch out her hands unto God.'"[132] Douglass brought his July Fourth oration to a close with a victorious note, quoting William Lloyd Garrison's poem, "The Triumph of Freedom." Garrison's verse reflects Douglass's own belief and commitment: "God speed the year of jubilee. . . . That year will come, and freedom's reign, to man his plundered rights again restore. . . . Until that year, day, hour, arrive, with head, and heart, and hand I'll strive . . . and never from my chosen post, whate'er the peril or the cost, be driven."[133] With or without the cooperation of white America, the slave will be free.

When Douglass ended his speech at Rochester's Corinthian Hall, he continued to gaze at his audience as they sat silently, absorbing the impact of his powerful words. He had delivered one of the most electrifying speeches in American history, summoning his listeners to reflect upon the nation's destiny. He had transformed a conventional July Fourth speech into an indictment of America for the injustice of slavery. Marshaling a series of compelling arguments, he had projected a character of dignity, knowledge, and credibility. He had constructed a narrative of the nation's revolutionary past, emphasizing its founding moral principles and values. He had paid respect to the nation's architects and the course upon which they had set America in 1776. But he had also underscored the American dilemma, the contradiction between the republic's ideals, as stated in the Declaration of Independence and the Preamble to the Constitution, and slavery. He had condemned the nation for its hypocrisy, its claim to represent the cause of freedom before the world while forcing millions of its own people to live under the degradation of slavery. He had defended the Constitution, using the document's explicit words to demonstrate its opposition to slavery. And he had denounced the American church for professing Christian love while tolerating the dehumanization of slaves.

Having spoken for more than two hours, Douglass indelibly etched his emotionally charged message on the minds of his listeners. As he gathered the pages of his speech and returned to his seat on the rostrum, the audience broke the silence with a "universal burst of applause."[134] His message would spread beyond the confines of Corinthian Hall, inspiring all those who sought the abolition of slavery. The text of his 1852 oration was published first in the July 9 issue of *Frederick Douglass' Paper.* A week later, a slightly revised version appeared as a pamphlet. The speech was then excerpted in an appendix to Douglass's *My Bondage and My Freedom.* His urgent plea to resolve the contradiction between freedom and slavery was a call for action. He was hopeful that if the federal government could be compelled by moral argument and political necessity to fulfill the libertarian principles of the Declaration of Independence and the Preamble to the Constitution, slavery would be abolished everywhere in the United States. But the ensuing years would increasingly dampen Frederick Douglass's optimism as America, refusing to confront the evil of slavery, proceeded on its ominous path toward civil war.

CHAPTER 5

THE OMINOUS FUTURE

A NATION ON THE BRINK

I do not despair of this country. The doom of slavery is certain.
                                        —*Frederick Douglass,*
                        "What to the Slave Is the Fourth of July?"

I

The Frederick Douglass who delivered the 1852 July Fourth oration had come of age. His transformation is evident when we compare the introductions to his first two autobiographies. The *Narrative* of 1845 is preceded by Garrison's challenge to the reader to embrace the banner: "No compromise with slavery! No Union with slaveholders!" The story of Douglass's life was intended to arouse the moral indignation of readers and encourage them to denounce the Constitution and the Union. But his second autobiography, *My Bondage and My Freedom,* published in 1855, three years after his speech at Corinthian Hall, is dedicated to abolitionist-philanthropist Gerrit Smith, the person most influential in Douglass's conversion to political abolitionism. *My*

Bondage and My Freedom may be regarded as Douglass's own "declaration of independence."[1] Within two months, fifteen thousand copies of the book were sold. Whereas the *Narrative* declared his independence from slavery, *My Bondage and My Freedom* declared his intellectual independence from Garrison. As we have noted, the theme of identity preoccupied Douglass his entire life. As a slave he had been deprived of knowledge of anything to do with his personhood, facts as basic as knowing his birthday and his father. Having seized his freedom from slavery and having discovered the power of the word, Douglass refused to have an identity imposed upon him by slave society. He alone would interpret his life. The three versions of his autobiography were a crucible that enabled him to shape his public identity. Whereas the early *Narrative* portrays the hero's journey from slavery to freedom, *My Bondage and My Freedom,* which is more than three times longer, reveals an emerging political activist, an independent thinker who attained prominence as a public figure. No mere expansion of his first autobiography, his second considers more political themes, especially the persistent American dilemma, and reflects Douglass's serious reconsideration of the meaning of his life.[2]

By this time, oratory had become Douglass's most potent weapon against slavery. Having perfected the skills of rhetoric, he saw his speeches as inseparable from his life and individuality. Douglass's second autobiography contains seven speeches exposing and denouncing the destructive physical and psychological consequences of slavery and predicting ultimate victory for the abolition movement. Significantly, the dedication of *My Bondage and My Freedom* to Gerrit Smith, lauding Smith's refusal to grant either "a legal or constitutional existence to slavery," reveals Douglass's new reverence for the Constitution. *My Bondage and My Freedom* also reflects the new direction in Douglass's abolitionism. Whereas the *Narrative* concludes with a Garrisonian Douglass devoted to moral suasion alone, pledging to combat slavery by "faithfully relying upon the power of truth, love and justice," *My Bondage and My Freedom* concludes with Douglass committing himself never to refuse "to use my voice, my pen, or *my vote,* to advocate the great and primary work of the universal and unconditional emancipation of my entire race."[3] Unlike Garrison, the mature Douglass refused to forsake politics, the Constitution, or the Union. He remained hopeful that Congress could be persuaded to legislate slavery out of existence.

Douglass's oratory and writing throughout the antebellum period reflects his commitment to the liberal natural rights tradition that inspired the American Revolution. Speaking in Boston, Massachusetts, on February 8, 1855, he proclaimed the existence of eternal truth: "Such is the truth of man's right to liberty. He was born with it. It entered into the very idea of man's creation. It was his before he comprehended it. It is written upon all the powers and faculties of his soul. The title deed is in his own breast; the record of it is in the heart of God. No compacts, no agreements, no covenants, no constitutions which man may make can abrogate nor in any way impair or destroy this right. It is a right to be asserted rather than to be argued. Your fathers held it to be a self-evident truth." Emphasizing the American dilemma, he concluded: "The great difficulty with the American people, in considering the subject of slavery, is to apply the same rules and maxims to the condition of the slaves of this country that will apply to the cases of other men."[4]

In *My Bondage and My Freedom*, Douglass tells of the profound effect that natural rights arguments had upon him when he first perused *The Columbian Orator* as a young slave boy. The mature Douglass reprises in his second autobiography the pages of his *Narrative*, recalling how speeches by great eighteenth-century British orators on behalf of human rights had inspired him. Once awakened to the power of knowledge, the word "liberty" assumed magical status for Douglass: "Liberty! The inestimable birthright of every man, had, for me, converted every object into an asserter of this great right. It was heard in every sound, and beheld in every object. It was ever present, to torment me with a sense of my wretched condition."[5] According to Eric Sundquist, *My Bondage and My Freedom* transformed Douglass's first autobiography, the *Narrative*, into "a text of revolution."[6] This revolution would have universal significance. In a prefatory letter to *My Bondage and My Freedom*, Douglass declares that the system of slavery was "at the bar of public opinion—not only of this country, but of the whole civilized world."[7] As his speeches and writings of the 1850s testify, Douglass had assimilated America's liberal values and was committed to exercising his rhetorical skills to exploit the republican tradition to expose the American dilemma to the entire world.

Whereas the *Narrative* made Douglass significant as an ex-slave, *My Bondage and My Freedom* made him significant as an American. In addition to telling Douglass's representative story, *My Bondage and My Freedom* is, in the words of Eric Sundquist, "the key to interpreting his rise to self-possession and to historical greatness. Douglass's very revision of his own life is the central element of his entry into America's revolutionary tradition of liberal individualism and the sign of his embrace of the principles of autonomy, property, and equal rights."[8] Opening the book, the reader finds an introduction by James M'Cune Smith, black physician, abolitionist, and staunch opponent of the Garrisonians. By elevating himself from slavery to freedom, Smith proclaimed, Douglass had become "a burning and shining light," a "Representative American man — the type of his countrymen," bearing "upon his person and upon his soul everything that is American." For Smith, as for Ralph Waldo Emerson, "representative" meant the ideal; Douglass set a standard to which all Americans, black and white, should aspire. *My Bondage and My Freedom*, Smith concluded, is "an American book, for Americans, in the fullest sense of the idea."[9]

My Bondage and My Freedom is Douglass's testament of hope, urging black Americans to unite in their struggle for freedom. Progress could be made only with black solidarity. He wanted his second autobiography to inspire blacks to discover an inner strength, as he had, to take steps toward self-elevation. With this in mind, Douglass sought to create opportunities for blacks to become educated. In March 1853, he traveled from Rochester to Andover, Massachusetts to visit Harriet Beecher Stowe, the author of *Uncle Tom's Cabin*. He gained her support for his idea to establish an industrial college to train free black artisans. In a subsequent letter to Stowe, Douglass explained the importance of his plan: "The most telling, the most killing refutation of slavery, is the presentation of an industrious, enterprising, thrifty, and intelligent free black population. Such a population I believe would rise in the Northern states under the fostering care of such a college as that supposed."[10] Douglass encouraged black Americans to demonstrate what they could accomplish with freedom. In an editorial published in *Frederick Douglass' Paper*, written in 1855 when the prospect of abolishing slavery seemed gloomy, he proclaimed: "Every day brings with it renewed evidence of the truthfulness of the sentiment, now, in various quarters, gaining the confidence and sympathy of our oppressed People. THAT OUR ELEVATION AS A RACE IS ALMOST WHOLLY DEPEN-

DENT UPON OUR OWN EXERTIONS."[11] One of Douglass's most popular lectures, delivered many times throughout the United States and Great Britain over a period of thirty-five years beginning in 1859, was entitled "The Self-Made Man," in which he championed the importance of self-help, hard work, and ethical conduct. Insofar as Douglass stood for what any person, black or white, could accomplish, his humanistic goals placed him solidly in the mainstream.

II

Few critics equaled Douglass's ability to situate himself within the discourse of liberal democracy in order to accentuate its contradictions and failings. By the time he addressed his Corinthian Hall audience in 1852, there was already a tradition of slave rebels invoking the principles of the American Revolution to justify their violent resistance. In August 1831—the same year Garrison began publishing *The Liberator*—the slave Nat Turner, fired by religious zeal, led a band of some fifteen slaves on a violent rampage in Southampton County, Virginia, slaying some sixty whites before he and his followers were captured, tried, and executed. Turner declared that he was to "slay my enemies with their own weapons."[12] Douglass was ready to do the same; his weapon of choice, however, was not the bullet but the ideas of the American Revolution. In *My Bondage and My Freedom*, Douglass invokes the nation's revolutionary tradition to support armed self-defense against slavery: "The slaveholder, kind or cruel, is a slaveholder still— the every hour violator of the just and inalienable rights of man; and he is, therefore, every hour silently whetting the knife of vengeance for his own throat. He never lisps a syllable in commendation of the fathers of this republic, nor denounces any accepted oppression of himself, without inviting the knife to his own throat, and asserting the rights of rebellion for his own slaves."[13] Violence committed against the slaveholder is violence committed to enforce the law, which consists of not only the Constitution—interpreted by Douglass and the abolitionists as an antislavery document—but also the higher moral law.

Douglass's appropriation of the American revolutionary tradition found expression in a speech delivered at the annual meeting of the American and Foreign Anti-Slavery Society in New York City in May 1853. "Aliens are we in our native land," he thundered. Black Americans had been denied the liberty and equality that they were entitled to as human beings: "The fundamental principles of the republic, to which the humblest white man, whether born here or elsewhere, may appeal with confidence in the hope of awakening a favorable response are held to be inapplicable to us. The glorious doctrines of your revolutionary fathers, and the more glorious teachings of the Son of God, are construed and applied against us. We are literally scourged beyond the beneficent range of both authorities, human and divine. We plead for our rights, in the name of the immortal Declaration of Independence, and of the written constitution of the government, and we are answered with imprecations and curses."[14]

Two months later, Douglass reiterated these themes in an "Address to the People of the United States," delivered at the Black National Convention, held in Rochester, New York, in July 1853. In contrast to his 1852 July Fourth Corinthian Hall oration, delivered from the perspective of those who had been unjustly excluded from "your" national independence, Douglass now stressed that the motives, ideas, and goals of black Americans conformed to the nation's fundamental liberal values, established by the Founders. All Americans, white and black, share a common cause. Black Americans, Douglass insisted, protest slavery and racial discrimination on the basis of the Declaration of Independence and the Preamble to the United States Constitution. Addressing his predominantly white audience, Douglass declared: "The great truths of moral and political science, upon which we rely, and which we press upon your consideration, have been evolved and enunciated by you. We point to your principles, your wisdom, and to your great example as the full justification of our course this day." Douglass then enunciated the nation's republican principles, the principles celebrated each Fourth of July: "That 'all men are created equal'; that 'life, liberty, and the pursuit of happiness' are the right of all . . . that governments are to protect, not to destroy, the rights of mankind; that the Constitution of the United States was formed to establish justice, promote the general welfare, and secure the blessings of liberty to all the people of this country; that resistance to tyrants is obedience to God — are American principles and maxims, and together they form and constitute the constructive elements of the American government." Douglass concluded: "From this elevated platform, provided by the Republic for us, and for all the children of men, we address you."[15]

Black Americans, Douglass continued, must be accorded the rights of full citizenship, including equality before the law, equal access to public facilities, and the right to vote. These demands were presented not from the perspective of aliens, the "other," but from Americans to Americans. "We are Americans," he proclaimed, "and as Americans, we would speak to Americans. We address you not as aliens nor as exiles . . . but we address you as American citizens asserting their rights on their own native soil. . . . By birth, we are American citizens; by the principles of the Declaration of Independence, we are American citizens; within the meaning of the Constitution, we are American citizens; by the facts of history, and the admissions of American statesmen, we are American citizens."[16] Employing the rhetorical device of epistrophe, ending a series of clauses with the refrain, "we are American citizens," for emphasis, Douglass compelled his listeners to confront the nation's unjust treatment of so many of its citizens.

Despite years of bitter frustration, Douglass never lost faith in the essential republican values of America. Unlike the black abolitionists Henry Highland Garnet, Alexander Crummell, Martin R. Delany, and Samuel Ringgold Ward, who encouraged blacks to exile themselves, Douglass believed America to be their rightful home. He was one of the most outspoken opponents of black emigration, an objective of the American Colonization Society (ACS), founded in 1816. Douglass once contrasted himself with Martin R. Delany, the Harvard-educated physician who had assisted him as co-editor of the *North Star* from 1847 to 1849: "I thank God for making me a man simply, but Delany always thanks him for making him a *black* man."[17] Throughout his life, Douglass opposed plans to colonize freed blacks outside the United States. When Henry Clay delivered a speech before the American Colonization Society in January 1848, arguing that the slaves, once freed, should be shipped to Africa, their real home, Douglass was provoked to respond that Clay's proposals damaged blacks by teaching them that their efforts at self improvement were futile. "It is an insult, an insolent and tyrannical assumption on the part of Clay, or anyone else, to tell us, or any part of the Colored people of this country, that he wishes us to go anywhere. . . . Our right to stay here is as good as that of Mr. Clay, or any man-stealer in this land; and God helping us, we will maintain this right before all the world."[18] Douglass's sentiment would be reiterated many times over the years. In 1859, he declared: "No one idea has given rise to more oppression and persecution toward the colored people of this country, than that which makes Africa, not America, their home. It is that wolfish idea that elbows us off the side walk, and denies us the rights of citizenship."[19] As an opponent of black separatism, Douglass affirmed that American democracy must include all races. Black Americans may be enslaved in the South and discriminated against in the North, but he would not have them embark on the suicidal path of forsaking the values and political structures that made full citizenship in the nation of their birth possible.[20] He felt a moral obligation to remain in America, making every possible effort to turn the country, whose ideals he loved, away from the sin of slavery. "Love for America," he avowed, "was not inconsistent with the strongest rebuke of its crimes."[21]

III

Appended to *My Bondage and My Freedom* is Douglass's famous open letter "To My Old Master, Thomas Auld," composed in England in 1848 on the tenth anniversary of his emancipation. Douglass began by raising the question of whether he was justified in exposing Auld's name to the public in an unfavorable light. Acknowledging that some might believe him to have invaded Auld's privacy, Douglass, using the rhetoric of the American Revolution, affirmed the priority of "rights which are personal and essential." Defending his escape from slavery, Douglass proclaimed his equal personhood: "We are distinct persons, and are each equally provided with faculties necessary to our individual existence."[22] Douglass's letter to Auld, written to dramatize his resurrection from the depths of slavery at the hands of an oppressive master, closed with a revelation that sheds light upon the rhetorical strategy of his 1852 July Fourth speech. Insisting that he harbored no personal malice toward Auld, he nevertheless revealed: "I intend to make use of you as a weapon with which to assail the system of slavery—as a means of concentrating public attention on the system."[23] Douglass's treatment as a slave under Auld would be employed to emphasize the evils of slavery. Not only did Douglass take advantage of his own life story as a weapon against slavery, his July Fourth oration also shows that he had appropriated the democratic rhetoric of America's Founding Fathers to underscore the contradiction of a slaveholding republic.[24]

My Bondage and My Freedom reflects another transition in Douglass's thinking during the early 1850s. In the book's conclusion, he related that he became more aware of white prejudice against free blacks in the North. When he first joined the abolition movement in New England and began his lecture tours, he witnessed much discrimination against blacks. The abolitionists were not entirely free of the prejudice that pervaded the white community, and many treated Douglass with benign condescension. He recalled in *My Bondage and My Freedom* that when traveling by railroad during the early 1840s, he had frequently been ordered to move to the "Jim Crow" car. Refusing to obey, Douglass was more than once dragged from his seat and beaten by conductors and brakemen. Nor could Douglass forget that when he first moved to Rochester, New York, a reputed abolitionist stronghold, his daughter was prohibited from attending an all-white school. He would lead the fight against the city's public schools, achieving a victory by leading a boycott in 1857. This experience would induce him to broaden his goals beyond the abolition of slavery in the South to include combating racial discrimination in the North. "I shall labor in the future," Douglass solemnly pledged, "as I have labored in the past, to promote the moral, social, religious, and intellectual elevation of the free colored people."[25]

Meanwhile, the conflict between the North and the South over slavery continued to intensify throughout the 1850s, severely testing Douglass's hope that civil war could be averted by moral persuasion and politics.

IV

The Compromise of 1850, which produced a more stringent Fugitive Slave Law, was regarded as a major defeat for abolition. After the Kansas-Nebraska Act of 1854 and the Supreme Court's 1857 decision in *Dred Scott*, abolitionists feared that slavery would spread to the entire nation. Although Douglass drew a parallel in his 1852 July Fourth speech between the abolitionist and the revolutionary of 1776, both opposed to tyranny, and both acting on behalf of human rights, he stopped short of calling for offensive violence against the South. A Jeremiah is always hopeful that the sinner will reform. Addressing the London Peace Society on May 19, 1846, the audience cheered when

Douglass declared: "Were I asked the question as to whether I would have my emancipation by the shedding of one single drop of blood, my answer would be in the negative."[26] Nevertheless, beginning in the 1840s, and through the early 1850s, Douglass became increasingly aware that violence might be inevitable. As Douglass converted to political realism, he understood that the South would not cooperate in dismantling an institution that defined its political, social, and economic life. Faced with the seemingly invincible power of the slaveholders, many abolitionists concluded that slavery could be defeated only by violence.

The call for violence was not new to the anti-slavery movement. As we have seen, David Walker's 1829 *Appeal,* the most revolutionary abolitionist tract of the antebellum years, summoned blacks to overthrow the system of slavery. Nat Turner's 1831 rebellion sent shock waves throughout the South. In 1843, black abolitionist Henry Highland Garnet delivered his militant "Address to the Slaves of the United States" to the National Convention of Colored Citizens of America, held in Buffalo, New York. As inspirational revolutionary forebears, Garnet cited, in addition to Nat Turner, the names of Toussaint L'Ouverture, leader of the successful slave rebellion in Haiti in 1793, establishing the western hemisphere's first independent black nation; Denmark Vesey, leader of an aborted massive slave rebellion in South Carolina in 1822; Joseph Cinque, leader of the mutiny aboard the slave ship the *Amistad* in 1839; and Madison Washington, leader of the mutiny aboard the slave ship the *Creole* in 1841. Garnet issued a clarion call for America's slaves to strike a violent blow for freedom. "Brethren, arise, arise. Strike for your lives and liberties. Now is the day and hour. Let every slave throughout the land do this and the days of slavery are numbered. *Rather die free-men than live to be slaves.* Remember that you are four millions. . . . Awake, awake; millions of voices are calling you! Your dead fathers speak to you from their graves. . . . Let your motto be resistance! Resistance! RESISTANCE."[27] Garnet's speech was the most incendiary indictment of slavery delivered by a black person since David Walker's *Appeal.* Frederick Douglass, then adhering to Garrison's principle of nonviolence and moral persuasion, repudiated Garnet's volatile address, alleging that "there was too much physical force." Instead, he counseled "trying the moral means a little longer."[28] But by the late 1840s, Douglass had changed his position, reluctantly concluding that violent slave resistance would be necessary in the South. When Douglass addressed an 1847 anti-slavery convention in Salem, Ohio, and declared that slavery could be destroyed only by bloodshed, he was interrupted by Sojourner Truth, the black woman abolitionist, lecturer and advocate of nonviolent resistance: "'Frederick, is God dead?'" Douglass retorted: "'No, and because God is not dead, slavery can only end in blood.'"[29]

Douglass became increasingly militant in his public pronouncements. In the winter of 1849, he defended the right of slaves to kill slaveholders: "Slaveholders have no more rights than any other thief or pirate. They have forfeited even the right to live, and if the slave should put every one of them to the sword to-morrow, who dares pronounce the penalty disproportionate to the crime, or say that the criminals deserved less than death at the hands of their long-abused chattels?"[30] This was strong language from a former supporter of Garrisonian nonviolence. Speaking at Boston's Faneuil Hall, on June 8, 1849, Douglass again compared oppressive slavery in the South with the condition of the American colonies in 1776. As the colonists resorted to justifiable violence to secure their rights against Britain, the slaves of the South would be justified in rebelling against their masters. Douglass stunned his Faneuil Hall audience when he declared that he would welcome news "that the slaves had risen in the South, and that the sable arms which had been engaged in beautifying and adorning the South were engaged in spreading death and devastation there."[31]

Throughout the 1840s, Douglass had opposed violence for prudential reasons. He realized that for slaves to rebel against the overwhelming military strength of the southern states would be sheer folly. The slaves apparently also recognized the futility of violence. Between the 1831 Nat Turner revolt and the Civil War, no major slave rebellion occurred on American soil. Open slave violence was, therefore, the exception in the antebellum South.[32] Yet Douglass viewed slave violence, at least on an individual level, as important in achieving self-dignity. In 1833, at the age of sixteen, Douglass had been returned to his master, Thomas Auld. One of the best-known incidents in his early life occurred when Auld rented him as a fieldhand to Edward Covey, the well-known "nigger-breaker." When Douglass began to teach reading at a small Sunday school for blacks, Auld became alarmed that his slave might become "another Nat Turner."[33] The strong-willed Douglass,

Auld concluded, had to be tamed; he had to be psychologically broken. Covey would symbolize for Douglass the most dehumanizing aspects of slavery. Douglass told the story of his confrontation with Covey as a rite of passage, foreshadowed by what is perhaps the *Narrative's* best-known sentence: "You have seen how a man was made a slave; you shall see how a slave was made a man."[34]

Expanding on the story in *My Bondage and My Freedom*, Douglass remembered that during the first six months of Covey's brutal domination and whippings, he was virtually defeated: "I was broken in body, soul and spirit. My natural elasticity was crushed; my intellect languished; the disposition to read departed; . . . the dark night of slavery closed in upon me; and behold a man transformed into a brute! I suffered bodily as well as mentally. . . . The overwork, and the brutal chastisements of which I was the victim, combined with that ever-gnawing and soul-devouring thought, *'I am a slave—a slave for life—a slave with no rational ground to hope for freedom,'* rendered me a living embodiment of mental and physical wretchedness."[35] It was the lowest point in his life. Yet he rose like a phoenix from the ashes. *"I was resolved to fight."* And fight he did, resisting Covey's attempt to beat him again, grabbing his antagonist by the throat. But Douglass insisted that his action was "strictly on the *defensive,* preventing him from injuring me, rather than trying to injure him." Nevertheless, the fight was not bloodless. "I held him so firmly by the throat, that his blood followed my nails. He held me, and I held him." At last, Douglass got the better of Covey. "I *did mean to resist, come what might,"* he told his defeated opponent. Having been "treated like a *brute,* during the last six months," he would "stand it *no longer."* Douglass persisted in claiming that his violent act was purely defensive: "My aim had not been to injure him, but to prevent his injuring me."[36] After this incident, Covey never again attempted to beat Douglass.

The battle with Covey was, according to Douglass, "the turning point in my *life as a slave*. . . . I was a changed being after that fight. I was *nothing* before. I WAS A MAN NOW. It recalled to life my crushed self-respect and my self-confidence, and inspired me with a renewed determination to be a FREEMAN."[37] Violent self-defense enabled Douglass to seize for himself what slavery had systematically denied him. "A man, without force, is without the essential dignity of humanity. Human nature is so constituted, that it cannot *honor* a helpless man, although it can pity him; and even this it cannot do long, if the signs of power do not arise."[38] The twentieth-century revolutionary theorist Frantz Fanon saw psychological benefit in native populations resorting to violence in overcoming oppression. This effect can be seen in Douglass: "At the level of individuals," wrote Fanon, "violence is a cleansing force. It frees the native from his inferiority complex and from his despair and inaction; it makes him fearless and restores his self-respect."[39] Douglass used violence to seize his humanity. After resisting the "tyrant" Covey, Douglass "felt as I never felt before. It was a glorious resurrection from the tomb of slavery, to the heaven of freedom. My long-crushed spirit rose, cowardice departed, bold defiance took its place." Douglass was determined that "however long I might remain a slave in form, the day had passed forever when I could be a slave in fact."[40] He had made the decision that any white man who dared whip him would have to kill him. After defeating Covey, Douglass became consumed by the desire to escape from bondage. "I hated slavery, always, and the desire for freedom only needed a favorable breeze, to fan it into a blaze, at any moment. The thought of only being a creature of the *present* and the *past*, troubled me, and I longed to have a *future*—a future with a hope in it. To be shut up entirely to the past and present, is abhorrent to the human mind; it is to the soul—whose life and happiness is unceasing progress—what prison is to the body, . . . a hell of horrors."[41] Having overcome the mental prison of slavery, he would now claim his right to a future.

V

The comparison Douglass made in his 1852 July Fourth oration between the rebelling slaves and the heroes of the American Revolution was dramatized in his sixty-five-page novella, "The Heroic Slave" (1853), depicting the mutiny aboard the slave ship *Creole* in November 1841. This work of historical fiction was published in *Autographs for Freedom*, an anti-slavery anthology created by Julia Griffiths to raise funds for *Frederick Douglass' Paper*. As William Andrews observes, Douglass's "'The Heroic Slave' is recognized today as the first work of fiction in African-American literature."[42] The story's protagonist is the leader of the *Creole* mutiny, the slave Madison Washington, whom Douglass described as a true hero, "a man who loved liberty as well as did Patrick Henry—who deserved it as much as Thomas Jefferson."[43] Beginning in the mid–1840s, Douglass began to praise Madison Washington, for him a hero akin to George Washington, in a number of speeches.[44] In the preface to "The Heroic Slave," Douglass revealed his intention to raise Madison Washington from "undeserved obscurity" to a militant defender of justice in the tradition of the American Revolution. Douglass aimed to fill out for his readers Madison Washington's character, giving him a heroic voice appropriate to his heroic deeds.[45]

Oppressed by slavery, Douglass's Madison Washington is determined to be free: "Liberty I will have, or die in the attempt to gain it." Echoing the language of America's Founders and the American Revolution, Douglass's Madison Washington proclaims: "Liberty, the inalienable right of every man, precious and priceless, will be mine. My resolution is fixed. *I shall be free.*" Like other slave rebels, he appealed to the tradition of the American Revolution. In 1800, the Virginia self-taught slave Gabriel Prosser cited the Declaration of Independence to justify his failed plan to attack Richmond. In 1822, black radical Denmark Vesey, a former slave, quoted the Declaration while conspiring to attack Charleston, Virginia. Madison Washington fled slavery to Canada, leaving his wife and children behind in Virginia. Returning to rescue them, he was captured and placed aboard the *Creole,* bound for New Orleans with 134 slaves. On the eleventh day of the voyage from Hampton, Virginia, 19 slaves, led by Washington, mutinied, wounding the captain, overpowering the crew, killing one white man, and altering the brig's course to the British territory of Nassau. Criticized for using violence against his white oppressors on the *Creole,* Douglass's fictionalized Washington responds: "You call me a *black murderer.* I am not a murderer, God is my witness that LIBERTY, not *malice,* is the motive for this night's work." Arriving in Nassau, the British government freed all the slaves except the 19 who were involved in the mutiny. In 1842, the mutineers were freed. In Douglass's account, Washington gives eloquent voice to all slaves who, like the heroes of the American Revolution, fight for their freedom. Washington cries triumphantly: "We have struck for our freedom, and if a true man's heart be in you, you will honor us for the deed. We have done that which you applaud your fathers for doing, and if we are murderers, *so were they.*"[46]

Madison Washington was for Douglass a symbol of violent slave resistance, as were other rebellious black heroes, including Joseph Cinque, Nat Turner, and Toussaint L'Ouverture. Speaking at an anti-colonization meeting in New York City on April 23, 1849, four years prior to the publication of "The Heroic Slave," Douglass advised that, instead of emigrating to Africa, blacks should remain in America and "imitate the example of our fathers of '76." While opposed to unnecessary violence, he regretted that bloodshed would be inevitable "if the nation shall persevere in the enslavement of the coloured people." Believing that "*a state of war*" existed in the South, Douglass told his New York City audience: "Sir, I want to alarm the slaveholders, and not to alarm them by mere declamation or by mere bold assertions, but to show them that there is really danger in persisting in the crime of continuing Slavery in this land. I want them to know that there are some Madison Washingtons in this country."[47] The time for moral argument was over. It was now time for militant action.

VI

Douglass's growing militancy was profoundly influenced by his relationship with the white abolitionist revolutionary John Brown, an intense, Bible-quoting man who believed that God had sent him on a mission to destroy slavery.[48] Their friendship began in 1848, when Douglass visited Brown's home in Springfield, Massachusetts. According to Douglass, Brown, a subscriber to the *North Star*, made "a very deep impression upon my mind and heart." Douglass was struck not only by Brown's sincere hatred of slavery, but also by his charismatic personality. His eyes "full of light and fire," Brown was "one of the most marked characters and greatest heroes known to American fame." Brown reinforced Douglass's growing skepticism about the efficacy of moral suasion and political action.

Invoking a God of vengeance rather than unconditional love, Brown insisted that only violence could overturn slavery. Believing himself to be God's avenging angel, Brown's favorite New Testament passage was from Hebrews: "Without shedding of blood there is no remission of sin."[49] Douglass relates that Brown declared that he was "not averse to the shedding of blood." He listened intently as Brown outlined a plan to organize a slave rebellion in the South and create a separate black state in the Appalachian Mountains. Arguing that "slaveholders had forfeited their right to live," Brown held that slaves were justified in attaining their freedom by any means necessary. "No people," he insisted, "could have self-respect, or be respected, who would not fight for their freedom." He then unfolded a map of the United States before Douglass and pointed to the Alleghenies, stretching from the borders of New York into the South. These mountains, with their natural hiding places, would provide the fort for his assault upon slavery. He expected to take about twenty-five armed recruits into the mountains, from where they would induce the slaves in the nearby plantations to rise in rebellion. Escaping slaves would seek refuge in the guarded mountain hideaways. Brown's purpose was "to destroy the money value of slave property; and that can only be done by rendering such property insecure." Brown's passionate commitment haunted Douglass. He undoubtedly recalled his early days as a slave in Baltimore, when only his violent resistance to Covey, the "nigger-breaker," enabled him to discover his selfhood. Listening to Brown's plan to arm slaves to fight their masters, Douglass must have empathized with his black brothers and sisters yearning to seize their freedom. After spending the night with Brown in Springfield, Massachusetts, Douglass confessed: "While I continued to write and speak against slavery, I became all the same less hopeful of its peaceful abolition. My utterances became more and more tinged by the color of this man's strong impressions."[50]

VII

Douglass's 1852 July Fourth oration stops short of calling for violence. The Fourth of July, Douglass judged, was not a day on which to explicitly incite a slave rebellion. Nevertheless, at a convention held at the City Hall in Syracuse, New York, in January 1851, he had explained that the 1850 Fugitive Slave Law led him to abandon any hope that slavery would succumb peacefully: "I am a peace man," he insisted. "I am opposed to the shedding of blood in all cases where it can be avoided. But this Convention ought to say to Slaveholders that they are in danger of bodily harm if they come here, and attempt to carry men off into bondage. . . . The slaveholder has no right to live."[51] In

June 1854, an editorial appeared in *Frederick Douglass' Paper* entitled "Is it Right and Wise to Kill a Kidnapper?" Douglass affirmed the right of fugitive slaves to kill in defense of their liberty. "Every slave-hunter who meets a bloody death in his infernal business," he proclaimed, "is an argument in favor of the manhood of our race. Resistance is, therefore, wise as well as just."[52] On August 11, 1852, Douglass had underscored his militancy in an address to the National Free Soil Convention in Pittsburgh. He endorsed Gerrit Smith's invocation of the revolutionary principles of 1776: "I am proud to be one of the disciples of Gerrit Smith, and this is his doctrine; and he only utters what all law writers have said who have risen to any eminence. Human government is for the protection of rights; and when human government destroys human rights, it ceases to be government, and becomes a foul and blasting conspiracy; and is entitled to no respect whatever." Douglass proclaimed: "Slavery has no rightful existence anywhere. The slaveholders not only forfeit their right to liberty, but to life itself. The only way to make the Fugitive Slave Law a dead letter is to make half a dozen or more dead kidnappers." The audience broke into applause. Douglass refused to restrain his wrath: "I believe that the lines of eternal justice are sometimes so obliterated by a course of long continued oppression that it is necessary to revive them by deepening their traces with the blood of a tyrant." Slaves who seize their right to freedom have eternal justice on their side. No majority can deprive a person of natural rights. "The man who is right is a majority. He who has God and conscience on his side, has a majority against the universe. Though he does not represent the present state, he represents the future state."[53] More applause followed.

Two years later, Douglass supported defensive violence to prevent the recapture of runaway slaves. When James Batchelder, a Boston truckman serving as a deputy marshal, was killed while attempting to prevent an angry crowd from releasing the fugitive slave Anthony Burns from court, Douglass defended the action. Batchelder, he affirmed, "had forfeited his right to live, . . . his death was necessary, as a warning to others liable to pursue a like course." Douglass concluded by equating those who violently resist slavery with the American revolutionaries. "It was glorious for Patrick Henry to say, *Give me liberty or give me death!* It was glorious for Americans to drench the soil, and crimson the sea with blood, *to escape the payment of a three-penny tax upon tea;* but it is a crime to shoot down a monster in defence of the liberty of a black man and to save him from a bondage 'one hour of which (in the language of Jefferson) is worse than ages of that which our fathers rose in rebellion to oppose.'"[54] Many Americans applauded the civil disobedience of 1776 while condemning those who refused to obey the unjust Fugitive Slave Law. Many Americans were quick to celebrate the violence of those who founded the republic but reluctant to accept violence committed in support of fugitive slaves seeking republican liberty.

VIII

The 1850 Fugitive Slave Law underscored the American dilemma. In a speech in Chatham, Canada West on August 3, 1854, an angry Douglass called America "a land of inconsistencies and contradiction — aspiring to be honest, and yet a nation of liars." While she proclaims "all men equal" in the Declaration of Independence, "the gateway of her Constitution," three and a half million of her subjects are held in bondage, "robbed of every right, deprived of every privilege, and sold and bought like the beasts that perish."[55] Focusing on the Fugitive Slave Law at a meeting of the National Council of Colored People on May 11, 1855, Douglass professed: "I would have you fight for your liberty when assailed by the slave hunter. This will gain you some respect. . . . Fear inculcates respect. I would rather see insurrection for the next six months in the South than that slavery should exist there for [the] next six years."[56] In *My Bondage and My Freedom,* Douglass took a more philosophical stand, arguing that because slavery is a system of lawless violence, "slaveholders have made it almost impossible for the slave to commit any crime, known either to the laws of God or to the laws of men." In exercising the natural right to self-defense, the resisting slave acts within the American revolutionary tradition. "If he steals, he takes his own; if he kills his master, he imitates only the heroes of the revolution."[57]

Even the political abolitionist Gerrit Smith shared Douglass's despair that slavery could be defeated by political means: "Hitherto," wrote Smith, "I have opposed the bloody abolition of slavery. But now, when it begins to march its conquering bands into the Free States, I

and ten thousand other peace men are not only ready to have it re-
pulsed with violence, but pursued even unto death, with violence."[58] In
1856, Douglass declared that although bound "to use all our powers of
persuasion and argument," as well as "every instrumentality that promises to peacefully destroy" slavery, such methods have failed, and "its
peaceful annihilation is almost hopeless." Accordingly, "the slaves'
right to revolt is perfect, and only wants the occurrence of favorable
circumstances to become a duty."[59]

Historical events drove Douglass to his increasingly militant stand
during the 1850s. As southern soil became depleted, slaveholders recognized that slavery would die unless allowed to expand into the territories. The Kansas-Nebraska Act of 1854, engineered by Senator Stephen
A. Douglas, chairman of the Senate's Committee on Territories, dealt
with the issue of slavery in the remaining territories of the Louisiana
Purchase. Designed to organize the territories of Kansas and Nebraska,
the act permitted the people of the new territories to decide for themselves, on the basis of the doctrine of popular sovereignty, whether to
allow slavery within their borders. The bill was approved by the Senate
on March 3 and was sent to the House, where the debate intensified.
Many in the North feared that passage of the bill would open the way
for the southern slaveholders to gain control of the federal government.
On May 10, while the bill was in the House, Frederick Douglass was in
New York City delivering an address at the Broadway Tabernacle.
With the passage of the Kansas-Nebraska Act in May 1854, Douglass
returned to his prevailing theme—the Declaration of Independence as
the nation's defining document. America, he lamented, was in the midst
of a "moral revolution," a "moral darkness," because one half of the nation had replaced freedom with slavery. In doing so, the South and all
those who tolerate slavery were in violation of a transcendent moral
law. "Man can make no compact which is more sacred than the right of
man to Liberty; and he who despises and tramples upon this God-given
right, has qualified himself for any and every possible crime against
God and man." Douglass proceeded to censure those politicians, such
as the Indiana Democrat John Pettit and the late John C. Calhoun,
who had mocked the equality principle of the Declaration of Independence as "a self-evident lie."[60] Douglass's speech received great applause. Later that year, he journeyed to Illinois, Stephen A. Douglas's

home state, to condemn the Kansas-Nebraska Act. "This bill," cried Douglass, "this Nebraska bill, gives to the people of the territories the right to hold slaves. Where did this bill get this right, which it so generously gives away? Did it get it from Hon. Stephen A. Douglas? Then I demand where he got that right?"[61]

Nonetheless, the doctrine of racial inequality won an important victory when the Kansas-Nebraska Act was finally passed on May 22, 1854. The act repealed the Missouri Compromise of 1820, which had prohibited slavery in any part of the Louisiana Purchase north of 36 degrees, 30 minutes north latitude, except for the state of Missouri. Opening all national territory to slavery, the act alarmed many in the North, inducing one newspaper to lament that it was "a triumph of Slavery [and] Aristocracy over Liberty and Republicanism." Many whose opposition to slavery had been lackluster now realized that the institution would not simply fade away. Horace Greeley, editor of the *New York Tribune*, later quipped that the Kansas-Nebraska Act created more abolitionists in two months than William Lloyd Garrison and Wendell Phillips did in twenty years.[62] Characterizing the act as a major victory for "the audacious villainy of the slave power," Douglass called upon all anti-slavery Americans to abandon the establishment parties as patent failures and to organize instead a "great party of freedom" to exterminate slavery. "All compromises with slavery ended. The abolition of slavery is essential to the preservation of liberty."[63]

The Kansas-Nebraska Act had a consequence that would alter American history: it aroused Abraham Lincoln to reenter politics after retiring from Congress in 1849. Perhaps his newly formed Republican Party would fulfill Douglass's expectations. Speaking about the act in Peoria, Illinois on October 16, 1854, Lincoln echoed the American dilemma theme that Douglass had been sounding for years—the contradiction of a nation professing equality yet permitting the extension of slavery. Lincoln declared: "I hate it [the extension of slavery] because of the monstrous injustice of slavery itself. I hate it because it deprives our republican example of its just influence in the world—it enables the enemies of free institutions, with plausibility, to taunt us as hypocrites—causes the real friends of freedom to doubt our sincerity, and especially because it forces so many really good men amongst ourselves into an open war with the very fundamental principles of civil liberty—criticizing the Declaration of Independence, and insisting that there is no right principle of action but *self-interest*."[64] The following month, in a speech in Chicago, Illinois, Frederick Douglass assailed the act's provision that slavery in the territories of Kansas and Nebraska would be determined by popular sovereignty. A principle that allows a majority to trample on the rights of a minority, he argued, makes a mockery of the Declaration of Independence. Neither the people nor Congress, he contended, is justified in robbing any person of the God-given natural right to freedom.[65]

Douglass was confident that slavery's recent victories, including the 1850 Fugitive Slave Act and the 1854 Kansas-Nebraska Act, would rouse the national conscience. Meanwhile, the struggle over slavery reached a fateful climax in the territories. While the free status of Nebraska was never in doubt, thousands of settlers from free and slave states, spurred by the popular sovereignty provision of the Kansas-Nebraska Act, converged upon Kansas, leading to violent conflict in what became known as "Bleeding Kansas." While anti-slavery settlers poured in from New England and New York, slavery supporters, dubbed "border ruffians" by the anti-slavery press, came from Missouri and succeeded in establishing a fraudulent pro-slavery territorial government in 1855. Those opposed to slavery responded by forming a free-state party and establishing a Free Soil government in the winter of 1855–56. After forming a provisional government in the town of Lawrence, they armed themselves for the inevitable violent confrontation. For a time, Kansas had two territorial governments, one slave and one free.

On May 21, 1856, seven hundred "border ruffians" from Missouri attacked Lawrence, Kansas, demolishing the offices of two newspapers, plundering stores, and setting a hotel ablaze. In retaliation, John Brown led a small group, including four of his sons, in a massacre of five pro-slavery settlers at Pottawatomie, in eastern Kansas, cracking their skulls and hacking their bodies with broadswords. As a result of the battle between pro-slavery and anti-slavery forces in Kansas, over two hundred men died in 1856.[66] The violence spilled over into the hallowed halls of the United States Congress. On May 19, 1856, two days prior to the sack of Lawrence, abolitionist Senator Charles Sumner delivered in the Senate his famous harangue, "The Crime Against Kansas," denouncing slavery and disparaging Stephen A. Douglas and South Carolina Senator Andrew Butler. "The harlot slavery," Sumner charged, was the "mistress" of Senator Butler. While Butler had been absent during the offensive speech, on May 22, his nephew, Representative Preston Brooks of South Carolina, entered the Senate chamber and beat Sumner with a wooden cane, leaving him unconscious and unable to return to the Senate for nearly three years. The beating of Sumner precipitated outrage throughout the North, in which nearly every city held a public meeting to protest the assault. The poet William Cullen Bryant was appalled: "Violence reigns in the streets of Washington," he wrote in the *New York Evening Post,* "violence has now found its way into the Senate Chamber. . . . In short, violence is the order of the day."[67] While the North was outraged, the South greeted Brooks as a sectional hero.[68]

When Frederick Douglass learned that Sumner had been attacked, he lamented to a Rochester audience: "I speak but the common judgment of all, when I affirm that this is a profoundly grave and serious, and even critical moment in the history of the Republic, and of the progress of the struggle between Slavery and Freedom, which has so long divided and agitated the public mind." He added ominously: "It seems as if the time for words is passed and the time for blows has come."[69]

The following year, in September 1857, the pro-slavery government in Kansas held a constitutional convention at the town of Lecompton and drew up a state constitution that supported slavery. The Lecompton constitution, supported by President Buchanan, was inspired by Taney's opinion in *Dred Scott,* which concluded that blacks were excluded from the rights guaranteed by the United States Constitution. "The right of property," declared the Lecompton constitution, "is before and higher than any constitutional sanction, and the right of the owner of a slave . . . is as inviolable as the right of the owner of any property whatever."[70] The convention submitted the Lecompton constitution to Congress, asking that Kansas be admitted to the Union as a slave state. The anti-slavery forces countered by sending their own constitution to Congress. After bitter conflict, the Kansas voters rejected the Lecompton constitution, choosing to remain a territory rather than become a slave state. Kansas was eventually admitted to the Union as a free state in 1861. The bloody experience of Kansas offered further evidence of the gathering storm.

The desperate struggle in Kansas aroused by the Kansas-Nebraska Act demonstrated, according to Frederick Douglass, that "the war for and against slavery in Kansas was not to be decided by the peaceful means of words and ballots, but that swords and bullets were to be employed on both sides." Douglass met with John Brown often during this period, "and all I saw of him gave me a more favorable impression of the man, and inspired me with a higher respect for his character." Brown made a number of visits to Rochester, spending several days at the Douglass home and discussing his detailed plans with his gracious host. Brown was determined to wage war on slaveholders in the Kansas territory. Douglass did not condemn Brown for his participation in "Bleeding Kansas," or for his attempt to ignite a slave rebellion at Harpers Ferry. Years later, in his final autobiography, *Life and Times*, Douglass defended Brown's violence against slaveholders: "The horrors wrought by his iron hand cannot be contemplated without a shudder, but it is the shudder which one feels at the execution of a murderer. The amputation of a limb is a severe trial to feeling, but necessity is a full justification of it to reason. To call out a murderer at midnight, and without note or warning, judge or jury, run him through with a sword, was a terrible remedy for a terrible malady."[71] Douglass had envisioned the oppressor crushed by the oppressed. A system of violence, slavery could not be immune from violent reprisal. His hatred of slavery had prepared him to listen to any plan for its destruction that promised success.

Historical events intruded once again in 1857, further radicalizing Douglass, when the U.S. Supreme Court ruled in *Dred Scott v. Sandford* that black Americans, either slave or free, could not be citizens of the United States. According to the Court, the nation's Founders never intended blacks to be included in the equality principle of the Declaration of Independence. Many Americans regarded *Dred Scott* as the death knell for a political solution to the problem of slavery. The Supreme Court had apparently settled the slavery question definitively. The United States Constitution, said the Court, sanctioned slavery. No black person, said the Court, Frederick Douglass included, was a citizen of the United States.

IX

Slavery had to be abolished, by whatever means necessary. Douglass stated his philosophy in a famous speech delivered to a largely black audience of over a thousand in Canandaigua, New York, on August 3,

1857. The occasion was the commemoration of the emancipation of the British West Indian slaves on August 1, 1834—an anniversary American blacks felt more worthy of celebration than the Fourth of July. While it would take the Civil War to end slavery in the United States, the institution had been vanquished in the British Empire as the result of a massive popular movement initiated by Thomas Clarkson in 1787. Douglass's speech, delivered two months after his attack upon the 1857 *Dred Scott* decision, contains what are perhaps his most-quoted words: "Let me give you a word of the philosophy of reform. The whole history of the progress of human liberty shows that all concessions yet made to her august claims, have been born of earnest struggle. . . . If there is no struggle there is no progress. . . . This struggle may be a moral one, or it may be a physical one, and it may be both moral and physical, but it must be a struggle. Power concedes nothing without demand. It never did and it never will. . . . The limits of tyrants are prescribed by the endurance of those whom they oppress." Directing his anger at the southern slaveholders, Douglass concluded: "Find out just what any people will quietly submit to and you have found out the exact measure of injustice and wrong which will be imposed upon them, and these will continue till they are resisted with either words or blows, or with both."[72] For Douglass, the American Revolution, inspired by principles of the Declaration of Independence, had always served as an example of a moral and physical struggle. From his own life, he could have pointed to his violent resistance to Edward Covey, in addition to the moral struggle against slavery that had preoccupied him for so many years. Britain had succeeded in legislating slavery out of existence throughout its empire. Douglass had hoped that America could follow Britain's example. But by 1857, many concluded that slavery had become so entrenched in America that only violence could abolish it.

In the same speech, Douglass saluted Madison Washington and Joseph Cinque, each of whom led successful mutinies aboard slave ships. Thirty-nine Africans rebelled while being transported by Spain to Cuba in 1839 aboard the slave schooner *Amistad*. Led by Cinque, the Africans killed most of the crew, along with the captain. A controversy arose whether the Africans, captured by a U.S. warship, were freemen or slaves who should be returned to Spain. While the Martin Van Buren administration, worried about losing southern support in an election year, held that the Africans were property who should be deported, the abolitionists, led by Lewis Tappan, organized to protect their rights. After the Africans won in the lower federal court, the Van Buren administration appealed to the United States Supreme Court. At this point, John Quincy Adams came to the defense of the Africans. While not an abolitionist, he distinguished himself later in life as a defender of human rights. Standing before the Supreme Court, with a gesture that Frederick Douglass would have appreciated, Adams pointed to a copy of the Declaration of Independence hanging on the wall and proclaimed: "The moment you come to the Declaration of Independence, that every man has a right to life and liberty, as an inalienable right, this case is decided. I ask nothing more on behalf of these unfortunate men, than this Declaration."[73] The court agreed with Adams, issuing a majority decision in 1841 declaring the Africans free. Ironically, the majority included Chief Justice Roger B. Taney.

X

As much as Douglass admired John Brown's motives in attempting to incite a slave rebellion, he knew that the plan had no hope of success. When the two men met secretly at a stone quarry near Chambersburg, Pennsylvania, in the spring of 1859, Brown revealed his boldest scheme. He planned to seize the government arsenal at Harpers Ferry, Virginia (now West Virginia), a small town about seven miles northwest of Washington, D.C., for the purpose of securing arms for slaves in nearby plantations. While he merely hinted at the plan before, Brown was now explicit. "He thought," Douglass later wrote, "that the capture of Harpers Ferry would serve as notice to the slaves that their friends had come, and as a trumpet to rally them to his standard." Brown was confident that his action would ignite a slave rebellion that would bring the South to its knees. He even spent time at Douglass's Rochester home drafting a constitution for a free state to be created in the South after the slave insurrection. But Douglass viewed Brown's scheme as absurd: "I looked at him with some astonishment, that he could rest upon a reed so weak and broken, and told him that Virginia would blow him and his hostages sky-high, rather than that he should hold Harpers Ferry an hour."[74] Nevertheless, Brown persisted in trying to convince Douglass to join him: "Come with me, Douglass. . . . I want you for a special purpose. When I strike, the bees will begin to swarm, and I shall want you to help hive them." Brown's fanaticism had impaired his judgment.

But Douglass refused to join Brown, protesting that his plan was doomed to fail. Douglass had broken with the Garrisonians over the issue of practicality. Simply put, Garrison's plan to defeat slavery by reviling the Constitution and forsaking the political process would not work. It would also bring about more harm than good for the slaves. John Brown's expectation that a raid on Harpers Ferry would arouse a general slave rebellion was equally naive, and he risked creating a backlash that could have irreparably harmed the abolition movement. Douglass opposed Brown with all the arguments he could muster. "It would be an attack upon the federal government," he remonstrated, "and would array the whole country against us." Douglass's skepticism was shared by the leading blacks of his day. As W. E. B. Du Bois explained: "They believed in John Brown, but not in his plan. They knew he was right, but they knew that for any failure in his project they, the black men, would probably pay the cost."[75] While Brown did receive financial assistance from New England and New York abolitionists, the so-called "Secret Six," including Theodore Parker, Thomas Wentworth Higginson, and Gerrit Smith, Douglass distanced himself from the venture. It was one thing to expand the efforts of the Underground Railroad, but quite another to believe that a minority of armed whites and blacks could overturn the institution of slavery. Only the military might of the federal government could destroy slavery in the South.

Nevertheless, convinced that he had been appointed to dispense God's justice, John Brown forged ahead. On the evening of October 16, 1859, Douglass was interrupted while addressing a large audience in National Hall, Philadelphia. He was informed that Brown, with a small band of recruits, sixteen whites (including four of Brown's sons) and five blacks, had seized the government arsenal at Harpers Ferry, killing three men, arming about fifty slaves, and declaring a general emancipation. "The announcement came upon us with the startling effect of an earthquake," Douglass recalled. "It was something to make the boldest hold his breath. I saw at once that my old friend had attempted what he had long ago resolved to do, and I felt certain that the result must be his capture and destruction."[76] Douglass's prediction proved to be correct. After about a day of violence, United States Marines, led by Colonel Robert E. Lee, easily suppressed the insurgents, killing most, including two of Brown's sons, and seriously wounding Brown. No slaves had freely joined the insurrection. Charged with murder, treason, and inciting slaves to rebel, the fifty-nine-year-old Brown was tried, convicted, and hanged in Charleston, Virginia, on December 2, 1859, while church bells pealed in his honor. As he walked to his execution, Brown passed a note to one of his jailers: "I John Brown am now quite *certain* the crimes of this *guilty* land will never be purged *away*, but with Blood."[77]

That Brown had willingly sacrificed his life in an effort, however misguided, to free the slaves greatly endeared him to many Americans in the North, black and white. Had Brown attempted his raid against Harpers Ferry a generation earlier, most northerners would have undoubtedly joined southerners in condemning him. But the mood of the nation had changed drastically by the late 1850s as the conflict over slavery approached the point of no return. Brown's final moving words to the Virginia court, reported widely in the press, induced many northerners to regard him as a martyr: "If it is deemed necessary that I should forfeit my life for the furtherance of the ends of justice, and mingle my blood with the blood of millions in this slave country whose rights are disregarded by wicked, cruel, and unjust enactments, I say let it be done."[78] Some of America's greatest luminaries joined the chorus of national mourning. In New York, black abolitionist Henry Highland Garnet announced from the pulpit of his African Methodist Episcopal Church that December 2, the day of Brown's execution, should henceforth be known as Martyr's Day.[79] In Boston, Unitarian preacher Theodore Parker pronounced Brown "not only a martyr . . . but also a SAINT." Henry Wadsworth Longfellow declared the date of Brown's execution "the date of a new Revolution,—quite as much needed as the old one." Ralph Waldo Emerson predicted that Brown's memory would "make the gallows as glorious as the cross."[80] Brown's execution, as Emerson had predicted, immediately made him a martyr. Like the cross, Brown's gallows became a symbol of selfless sacrifice. He behaved so nobly at his trial, Douglass recalled, that "all over the North men were singing the John Brown song. His body was in the dust, but his soul was marching on. . . . What he had lost by the sword he had more than gained by the truth."[81] Abolitionist Lydia Maria Child proclaimed: "All I know, or care to know, is that his example stirred me up to consecrate myself with renewed earnestness to the righteous cause for which he died so bravely."[82] The death of Brown inspired the poet James Russell Lowell's words: "Truth forever on the scaffold, wrong forever on the throne. But that scaffold sways the future."[83] Composing "A Plea for Captain John Brown" in Concord, Massachusetts, Henry David Thoreau expressed great admiration for Brown's character, a man with "a spark of divinity in him," who responded to the higher law by resisting slavery with physical force. "You who pretend to care for Christ crucified," pleaded Thoreau, "consider what you are about to do to him who offered himself to be the saviour of four millions of men. . . . Some eighteen hundred years ago Christ was crucified; this morning, perchance, Captain Brown was hung. These are the two ends of a chain which is not without its links."[84] Not since George Washington had an American been so mourned.

Although Douglass rejected the plan to raid Harpers Ferry from the beginning as a strategic blunder, he never disavowed Brown. The raid had terrorized the South as never before, arousing a wave of hysteria matched only by the reaction to Nat Turner's rebellion in 1831. Douglass's hatred of slavery induced him to defend Brown's methods: "He has attacked slavery with the weapons precisely adapted to bring it to death. Moral considerations have long since been exhausted upon slaveholders. It is vain to reason with them. . . . Slavery is a system of brute force. It shields itself behind *might,* rather than right. It must be met with its own weapons."[85] Years later, Douglass paid tribute to Brown in the pages of his third autobiography. Although the raid on Harpers Ferry was doomed from the start, Brown did dramatize the evil of slavery and express the anger and frustration of millions of Americans opposed to the institution.

While Douglass sympathized with Brown, he realized that his own calling involved the power of the pen rather than the sword. If Brown considered himself God's instrument, chosen to destroy slavery by violence, Douglass was God's prophet, warning in countless speeches and editorials that the unreformed South would suffer divine vengeance. "The tools to those that can use them," Douglass declared. "Let every man work for the abolition of Slavery in his own way. I would help all and hinder none."[86] Nevertheless, the failed raid on Harpers Ferry drew Douglass closer to concluding that the point of no return had been reached: slavery in the South would be destroyed not by moral argument or party politics, but by war. Douglass proclaimed at a commencement address at Storer College at Harpers Ferry on May 30, 1881: "If John Brown did not end the war that ended slavery, he did at least, begin the war that ended slavery.... When John Brown stretched forth his arm the sky was cleared. The time for compromises was gone—the armed hosts of freedom stood face to face over the chasm of a broken Union—and the clash of arms was at hand."[87]

Many sympathized with Brown's violence because they saw no legal alternative once slavery received the endorsement of the nation's highest judicial authority. In 1857, the United States Supreme Court had handed down its infamous *Dred Scott* decision, affirming the constitutionality of slavery.

CHAPTER 6

THE *DRED SCOTT* DECISION AND THE AMERICAN DILEMMA

They [black people] had for more than a century before [the Decla-ration of Independence] been regarded as beings of an inferior order, and altogether unfit to associate with the white race, either in social or political relations; and so far inferior, that they had no rights which the white man was bound to respect.

—*Roger B. Taney*
Dred Scott v. Sandford

I

Frederick Douglass fought relentlessly for the inclusion of blacks in American society on the basis of political and social equality. At the same time, the supporters of slavery remained steadfast in their belief that from the beginning of the republic, blacks were considered infe-rior beings. As slaves, they were chattel property, devoid of the human rights guaranteed to white Americans under the Constitution. In 1857, the institution of slavery received valuable sanction from the Supreme

Court in the landmark decision of *Dred Scott v. Sandford*.[1] Dred Scott, a slave living in the slave state of Missouri, had been taken in 1834 from St. Louis by his master, army surgeon Dr. John Emerson, to live for two years in the free state of Illinois, where slavery had been forbidden by the 1787 Northwest Ordinance and by the Illinois constitution. Scott was later brought to the new territory of Wisconsin, where slavery had been prohibited under the Missouri Compromise.[2]

In 1846, Dred Scott, with financial assistance from abolitionists, brought suit in the Circuit Court of St. Louis County against Dr. Emerson's widow, claiming that by the terms of the Missouri Compromise, his seven-year residence in a free state and in a territory prohibiting slavery made him free. The principal issue before the Court was whether residence on free soil affected a slave's legal status. Missouri legal precedents supported Scott's claim, particularly *Rachel v. Walker* (1836), in which Rachel, a slave, was granted freedom by the Missouri Supreme Court due to her residence in a free territory. During the early years of the republic, a widely accepted sojourning privilege enabled masters to take slaves temporarily into free soil without jeopardizing their ownership. At the same time, slaves taken to live more or less permanently on free soil were generally recognized as forever free. When Dred Scott, soon to become one of the most famous litigants in American constitutional history, initiated his suit, the established legal principle in Missouri was "once free, always free."[3] In 1850, after many delays, Scott prevailed in the St. Louis Circuit Court. Two years later, Emerson appealed to the Missouri Supreme Court, which reversed the lower Court's decision by a two-to-one vote, explaining that the "times now are not as they were when the previous decisions on this subject were made."[4] According to the Missouri Supreme Court, the relevant law in the case was that of Missouri, where Scott had been a slave, not that of Illinois or Wisconsin territory. In the wake of the Wilmot Proviso—which focused national attention on the question of whether Congress had the authority to forbid slavery in the territories—many Missouri citizens sought greater legal protection for slavery. The Missouri bench having become elective rather than appointed in 1851, the judges were particularly sensitive to public opinion. The same court that had freed the slave Rachel in 1836 now reversed itself, remanding Dred Scott to slavery. Politics and racial bigotry trumped legal precedent.[5] The Missouri Supreme Court's decision that Scott resume his status as a slave when he returned to Missouri was a grim forecast of the decision of the United States Supreme Court five years later.

Failing to win on the state level, Scott appealed in 1853 to a federal court, the United States Circuit Court for Missouri, located in St. Louis. By this time, Mrs. Emerson had remarried and moved to Massachusetts, transferring ownership of Dred Scott to her brother, John Sanford. Scott appealed to the federal court on the grounds that Sanford's New York State residency made possible a case under the diversity-of-citizenship clause in Article III, section 2 of the United States Constitution. A citizen of one state suing a citizen of another state has access to the federal courts. Scott's lawyers claimed that he was a citizen of Missouri. Meanwhile, attorneys for Sanford issued what is known as a plea in abatement to stop or "abate" the case, arguing that Scott was not a citizen of Missouri because he was a "Negro of African descent; his ancestors were of pure African blood, and were brought into this country and sold as Negro slaves."[6] Although United States Circuit Judge Robert W. Wells rejected Sanford's plea, supporting Scott's right to sue in a federal court as a citizen of Missouri, he ultimately upheld the Missouri Supreme Court, ruling that if Scott had acquired freedom by living on free soil, his slave status resumed once he returned to Missouri, where slavery was legal.

But the matter was not settled. In December 1854, Scott's attorneys sought recourse in the nation's highest tribunal, the United States Supreme Court, alleging that Judge Wells had erred in his decision. Although the Kansas-Nebraska Act had repealed the Missouri Compromise that year, Scott's suit was still viable, for he had lived on free soil while the compromise had been in effect. The *St. Louis Herald* registered its sympathy: "Dred is, of course, poor and without any powerful friends. But no doubt he will find at the bar of the Supreme Court some able and generous advocate, who will do all he can to establish his right to go free." Dred Scott's supporters issued a pamphlet summarizing the case, with a preface attributed to Scott, pleading for assistance: "I have no money to pay anybody at Washington to speak for me. My fellow-men, can any of you help me in my day of trial? Will nobody speak for me at Washington, even without hope of other reward than the blessings of a poor black man and his family?"[7] Scott's plea was dated the Fourth of July. After months, Montgomery Blair, a

Washington lawyer and Free Soil Democrat, volunteered to defend him without remuneration. The plaintiff's case, taken to the Supreme Court on a writ of error, was finally argued in February 1856 but held over for re-argument in December because the justices believed that the suit raised important constitutional questions. The Supreme Court, led by Roger B. Taney, successor to the great John Marshall as Chief Justice in 1835, was heavily pro-slavery; five justices were from slaveholding families, and seven had been appointed by pro-slavery presidents. While Dred Scott's case was before the Court, Congress remained divided over the question of the extension of slavery in the territories, and conflict between pro-slavery and anti-slavery advocates led to bloodshed in Kansas. If Congress could not resolve the most serious constitutional crisis in the nation's history, perhaps the Supreme Court could.

In November 1856, Democrat James Buchanan of Pennsylvania was elected the nation's fifteenth president, defeating John C. Frémont, the first Republican candidate for the office. His election did nothing to heal the sectional tensions that gripped the nation. Indeed, the southern states had threatened to secede from the Union if an anti-slavery Republican became President. The month after Buchanan's election, when the significant political implications of the Supreme Court's pending decision became clear, the *Dred Scott* case attracted national attention. By Christmas of that year, the name of Dred Scott had become familiar to most Americans interested in national politics.[8] For the Court had before it not only the fate of Dred Scott, but also the questions of black citizenship and the constitutionality of the Missouri Compromise of 1820, which forbade slavery in the northern territories of the Louisiana Purchase. The issue of slavery in the territories, Buchanan declared in his Inaugural Address on March 4, 1857, "is a judicial question, which legitimately belongs to the Supreme Court of the United States, before whom it is now pending, and will, it is understood, be speedily and finally settled. To their decision, in common with all good citizens, I shall cheerfully submit, whatever this may be."[9] But Buchanan's words were duplicitous, for he had received letters from Justices John Catron and Robert C. Grier, secretly revealing to him in advance the Court's decision to uphold the southern position.

On the morning of March 6, 1857, two days after Buchanan's inauguration, the nine justices filed into the courtroom, crowded with journalists anxiously awaiting the decision of the nation's highest tribunal in the case of *Dred Scott v. Sandford*. Seven of the nine justices—Chief Justice Taney of Maryland, James W. Wayne of Georgia, John Catron of Tennessee, Peter V. Daniel of Virginia, John A. Campbell of Alabama, Robert C. Grier of Pennsylvania, and Samuel Nelson of New York—ruled against Scott. Grier and Nelson were known as "doughfaces"—northerners with southern principles. The two dissenters were John McClean of Ohio and Benjamin R. Curtis of Massachusetts. Chief Justice Taney, almost eighty years old and a supporter of slavery, wrote the majority opinion. With the courtroom crowded with spectators and reporters, Taney, with trembling hands and feeble voice, read his fifty-four-page opinion over the course of the next two hours.[10] The Chief Justice might have been physically frail, but his opinion would strike a mighty blow on behalf of slavery.

Almost half of Taney's lengthy opinion was devoted to excluding black Americans from the nation's fundamental democratic creed. He began by addressing the principal issue before the Court: "The question is simply this: Can a Negro, whose ancestors were imported into this country, and sold as slaves, become a member of the political community formed, and brought into existence by the Constitution of the United States, and as such become entitled to all the rights, and privileges, and immunities, guaranteed by that instrument to the citizen? One of which rights is the privilege of suing in a court of the United States in the cases specified in the Constitution."[11]

Speaking for the Court, Taney answered the question, arguing that black people were not included among the "sovereign people" of the United States. Hence, blacks, either free or slave, could not be citizens of the United States under the Constitution: "We think they are not, and that they are not included, under the word 'citizens' in the Constitution, and can therefore, claim none of the rights and privileges which that instrument provides for and secures to citizens of the United States. On the contrary, they were at that time considered as a subordinate and inferior class of beings, who had been subjugated by the dominant race, and, whether emancipated or not, yet remained subject to their authority, and had no rights or privileges but such as those who held the power and the Government might choose to grant them."[12]

Taking refuge in the doctrine known as judicial restraint, Taney then argued that the function of the Supreme Court is not to make new law, but merely to interpret the Constitution according to the original intention of the framers: "It is not the province of the court to decide upon the justice or injustice, the policy or impolicy, of these laws. The decision of that question belonged to the political or law-making power; to those who formed the sovereignty and framed the Constitution. The duty of the court is, to interpret the instrument they have framed, with the best lights we can obtain on the subject, and to administer it as we find it, according to its true intent and meaning when it was adopted."[13]

While blacks may be granted citizenship by individual states, Taney held that this did not grant them national citizenship. Nevertheless, prior to *Dred Scott,* the popular and judicial consensus held that a state citizen was a national citizen.[14] In fact, "citizenship" would not be defined authoritatively in the Constitution until section 1 of the Fourteenth Amendment in 1868. Nevertheless, Taney ruled that because Dred Scott, like all slaves and their descendants, was not a citizen of the United States, he had no right to bring a suit before the federal courts. Scott's suit, therefore, had been illegitimately brought before the Supreme Court. This ruling would have upheld the Missouri Supreme Court's original decision that Scott remained a slave. As precedent, Taney had the Court's 1850 unanimous decision in *Strader v. Graham,* which declared that the status of slaves was determined not by the law of the state in which they sojourned, but by law of the state to which they returned.[15] Once Dred Scott returned to Missouri, therefore, he resumed his legal status as a slave. On this point, seven of the nine judges had agreed as early as February 1857. Two justices, John McClean and Benjamin Curtis, indicated that they would write dissenting opinions upholding the constitutionality of the Missouri Compromise and supporting Congress' power to prohibit slavery in the territories. In response, the remainder of the Court decided to counter the dissenters by having Taney write an opinion addressing all the substantial issues related to slavery raised by the case. Not satisfied with merely ruling that the Supreme Court lacked jurisdiction in Scott's case, Taney seized the opportunity to make pronouncements on the broader question of slavery that would ignite furious controversy.

Taney sought to demonstrate that slavery had been sanctioned by the nation's Founders. Arguing from a misreading of history that had the support of the South, he proclaimed that the Founders of the republic could not have intended to include blacks under the protection of either the Declaration of Independence or the Constitution:

> It is difficult at this day to realize the state of public opinion in relation to that unfortunate race, which prevailed in the civilized and enlightened portions of the world at the time of the Declaration of Independence, and when the Constitution of the United States was framed and adopted. But the public history of every European nation displays it in a manner too plain to be mistaken. They had for more than a century before [the Declaration of Independence] been regarded as *beings of an inferior order,* and altogether unfit to associate with the white race, either in social or political relations; and so far *inferior,* that they had *no rights which the white man was bound to respect;* and that the Negro might justly and lawfully be reduced to slavery for his benefit. . . . And in no nation was this opinion more firmly fixed or more uniformly acted upon than by the English Government and English people. . . . The opinion thus entertained and acted upon in England was naturally impressed upon the colonies they founded on this side of the Atlantic. And, accordingly, a Negro of the African race was regarded by them as *an article of property,* and held, and bought and sold as such, in every one of the thirteen colonies which united in the Declaration of Independence, and afterwards formed the Constitution of the United States.[16]

The Founders of the republic, Taney alleged, never intended to include blacks within the principle that "all men are created equal," enshrined in the Declaration of Independence. Blacks, both slave and free, could not be citizens of the United States. Applying this reading of the text of the Constitution, the Chief Justice also insisted that, according to the document, blacks were not human beings but property. Yet the historical context he used to support his opinion was not colonial America, where free blacks lived in every state, but the prevailing view in European nations. Taney's argument that blacks were regarded as property under English, and by extension, American law was patently false. English jurist Sir William Blackstone had held that "a slave or Negro, the instant he lands in England, becomes a freeman," entitled to all rights of English citizenship. Furthermore, the English idea of liberty, the same idea that inspired the Declaration of Independence, did not distinguish between whites and blacks.[17]

Taney's opinion did more than deny that Scott's residence on free soil made him a free person once he returned to a slave territory. The Chief Justice excluded blacks from the principles of liberty and equality endorsed by the Declaration of Independence and the rights guaranteed to all citizens by the Constitution. After quoting the famous proclamation from the second paragraph of the Declaration of Independence, "We hold these truths to be self-evident: that all men are created equal; that they are endowed by their Creator with certain unalienable rights; that among them are life, liberty, and the pursuit of happiness," Taney conceded that "the general words above quoted would seem to embrace the whole human family, and if they were used in a similar instrument this day would be so understood." Nevertheless, ignoring the literal text, he confidently proclaimed: "But it is too clear for dispute, that the enslaved African race were not intended to be included, and formed no part of the people who framed and adopted the declaration; for if the language, as understood in that day, would embrace them, the conduct of the distinguished men who framed the Declaration of Independence would have been utterly and flagrantly inconsistent with principles they asserted; and instead of the sympathy of mankind, to which they so confidently appealed, they would have deserved and received universal rebuke and reprobation."[18]

According to Taney, both the Declaration of Independence and the United States Constitution endorse white supremacy. Both documents deny the personhood of black Americans: "[The Preamble] declares that it is formed by the *people* of the United States; that is to say, by those who were members of the different political communities in the several States. . . . It does not define what description of persons are intended to be included under these terms, or who shall be regarded as a citizen and one of the people. . . . But there are two clauses in the Constitution which point directly and specifically to the Negro race as a separate class of persons, and show that they were not regarded as a portion of the people or citizens of the Government they formed."[19]

Even conceding a more liberal American public in 1857, Taney adhered to a rigid understanding of what he regarded as the original intent of the Constitution's framers:

"No one, we presume, supposes that any change in public opinion or feeling, in relation to this unfortunate race, in the civilized nations of Europe or in this country, should induce the court to give to the words of the Constitution a more liberal construction in their favor than they were intended to bear when the instrument was framed and adopted. . . . If any of its provisions are deemed unjust, there is a mode prescribed in the instrument itself by which it may be amended; but while it remains unaltered, it must be construed now, as it was understood at the time of its adoption."[20] In other words, the Taney Court denied that the United States Constitution may be construed as what is called a "living document," subject to new interpretations as society evolves. As far as Taney was concerned, the Constitution is a dead document. On the question of slavery, the Constitution meant in 1857 exactly what it meant in 1787.

On Scott's claim that his residence in the free territory of Wisconsin had made him free, Taney held that Congress had no legal power to prevent the extension of slavery in the territories. The Chief Justice summarily rejected the Missouri Compromise, already repealed by the Kansas-Nebraska Act in 1854. Speaking for the court, he ruled that Congress could not legally deprive southerners of their property in slaves in the territories without, as stipulated by the Fifth Amendment, due process of law[21]:

> [T]he rights of property are united with the rights of person, and placed on the same ground by the fifth amendment to the Constitution, which provides that no person shall be deprived of life, liberty, and property, without due process of law. And an act of Congress which deprives a citizen of the United States of his liberty or property, merely because he came himself or brought his property into a particular Territory of the United States, and who had committed no offense against the laws, could hardly be dignified with the name of due process of law. . . . The right of property in a slave is distinctly and expressly affirmed in the Constitution. . . . The act of Congress which prohibited a citizen from holding and owning property of this kind in the territory . . . is not warranted by the Constitution, and is therefore void; and that neither Dred Scott himself nor any of his family, were made free by being carried into

this territory; even if they had been carried there by the owner, with the intention of becoming a permanent resident.[22]

This section of Taney's opinion converted Dred Scott's private cause into a public issue.[23] Clearly, the Chief Justice's objective was not legal but political. He apparently interpreted the Democratic Party's victory in the presidential election of 1856 as a mandate for the Supreme Court to prevent congressional regulation of slavery in the territories.[24] The Chief Justice made the *Dred Scott* decision a formidable pro-slavery document.

II

The prospects of the anti-slavery movement could not have been bleaker. With a single judicial opinion, *Dred Scott* had driven a battering ram through the argument that the Constitution opposed slavery. The decision had also rendered unconstitutional the most important plank in the Republican Party's platform: preventing the extension of slavery in the territories. Even if Republicans were elected to national office, they could not implement their anti-slavery program. Northern Democrat Stephen A. Douglas's position that, on the basis of popular sovereignty, the people could reject slavery was also rendered null and void.

The *Dred Scott* decision was only the second time that the Supreme Court declared an act of Congress unconstitutional. The first was in *Marbury v. Madison* (1803), in which Chief Justice John Marshall established the right of judicial review. *Dred Scott* in effect nullified Frederick Douglass's contention, the core of his abolitionist message, that black Americans were originally included within the principles and rights professed by the nation's founding documents. The nation's highest court, following Taney's specious reasoning, decided that Dred Scott was still a slave.[25] Affirmed as property, denied rights, even basic humanity, black Americans faced a dim future. For Douglass, accepting the Supreme Court's decision would mean that his long battle against slavery had been misguided and his goal to achieve equality for black Americans was unconstitutional. Many northerners were now convinced that, with the Missouri Compromise invalidated, southern slaveholders would make every effort to extend their tentacles not only throughout the territories, but also in free states, eventually gaining control of Congress. The nationalization of slavery seemed imminent. Indeed, historian David M. Potter observes that *Dred Scott* fundamentally altered the position of slavery in America. The American people always "regarded slavery as having only a local sanction, and freedom as having a national sanction. . . . The argument [of the South] was not without legal plausibility, but it fatally reversed the place of slavery and freedom in the American system. It made freedom local—an attribute of those states which abolished slavery, but not of the United States; it made slavery national, in the sense that slavery would be legal in any part of the United States where a state government had not abolished it."[26]

Despite Taney's confidence that *Dred Scott* would settle definitively the problem of slavery, the decision aroused a storm of protest, pushing the nation inexorably toward civil war. The Supreme Court could have stopped at ruling that it lacked jurisdiction in Scott's case. But it went on to strike down the constitutionality of the Missouri Compromise, prompting northern critics to charge that much of Taney's opinion was not law but extrajudicial *obiter dictum*, dealing with issues not relevant to the case at hand. In fact, only 2 percent of the opinion dealt with the original question before the Court: whether Scott's residence on free soil affected his legal status as a slave. In contrast, 44 percent of the opinion dealt with black citizenship and 38 percent with slavery in the territories.[27] Taney and his defenders maintained that the Court was justified in considering all constitutional issues raised by the case. Indeed, Scott's legal opponents had originally raised the issue of black citizenship and the constitutionality of the Missouri Compromise. Taney anticipated criticism, arguing in his opinion: "The correction of one error in the court below," he alleged, "does not deprive the appellate court of the power of examining further into the record, and correcting any other material errors which may have been committed by the inferior court."[28] At the same time, critics maintained that Taney had engaged in reckless judicial legislation, gratuitously intervening in politics. According to the leading authority on *Dred Scott*, Don E. Fehrenbacher, the decision "remains the most striking instance of the Supreme Court's attempting to play the role of *deus ex machina* in a setting of national crisis." *Dred Scott* is "certainly the prime historical example of judicial power exercised in the interest of racial subordination."[29]

Regardless of the appropriateness of Taney's comprehensive opinion, *Dred Scott* did not resolve but exacerbated the constitutional conflict over slavery. The decision further divided the nation and induced many more northerners to support the anti-slavery movement. Until *Dred Scott,* slavery had been recognized as merely a local institution, supported by state law; now slavery was recognized as a right anywhere in the nation.[30] Characterized by historian William M. Wiecek as the "*summa* of proslavery constitutionalism," the decision made slavery part of the supreme law of the land.[31] Even free blacks, who regarded themselves as citizens even though deprived of full civil rights, were now denied by the Court inclusion in the body politic.

Abraham Lincoln would register his firm opposition to *Dred Scott.* After Democrat Stephen A. Douglas gave a speech in Springfield, Illinois, defending the decision, Lincoln justified Republican opposition. On June 26, 1857, he argued that Judge Taney's opinion misinterpreted the Declaration of Independence. Lincoln noted that the Chief Justice had conceded that the words of the Declaration, asserting that "all men are created equal," seemed broad enough to include "the whole human family." Nevertheless, Taney took the position that the signers of the Declaration never intended to include blacks within its equality principle. This view, Lincoln argued, does "obvious violence to the plain unmistakable language" of the Declaration of Independence, which affirms that "*all*" men are created equal—equal in "certain inalienable rights, among which are life, liberty, and the pursuit of happiness." "I think the authors of that notable instrument," Lincoln affirmed, "intended to include *all* men, but they did not mean to say all were equal *in all respects*. They did not mean to say all were equal in color, size, intellect, moral development, or social capacity." The signers of the Declaration meant to declare that all men are equal in rights. "They did not mean to assert the obvious untruth, that all men were then actually enjoying that equality, nor yet, that they were about to confer it immediately upon them. In fact, they had no power to confer such a boon. They meant simply to declare the *right,* so that the *enforcement* of it might follow as fast as circumstances should permit." Political necessity dictated that the Declaration's equality principle could not immediately be implemented for all. Exercising prudence, the Founders established a goal of equal rights for all humans that would be progressively realized. "They meant to set up a standard maxim for free society, which should be familiar to all, and revered by all; constantly looked to, constantly labored for, and even though never perfectly attained, constantly approximated, and thereby constantly spreading and deepening its influence, and augmenting the happiness and value of life to all people of all colors everywhere."[32]

The *Dred Scott* case and slavery became a subject of controversy in the famous debates between Abraham Lincoln and Stephen A. Douglas during their campaigns for the Senate in Illinois in 1858. On behalf of the northern Democrats, Douglas argued that the people themselves, on the basis of the doctrine of popular sovereignty, should decide the existence of slavery in the territories. Setting forth what is known as the "Freeport Doctrine," he held that a territorial legislature could exclude slavery by refusing to pass laws to protect the institution, thus circumventing of the Supreme Court's ruling in *Dred Scott*. At the same time, in his final debate with Lincoln on October 15, 1858, Douglas attempted to write black Americans, along with a multitude of oppressed people, out of the nation's foundation documents. "I hold that the signers of the Declaration of Independence," he proclaimed, "had no reference to Negroes at all when they declared all men to be created equal. They did not mean Negro, nor the savage Indians, nor the Fejee Islanders, nor any other barbarous race." But Lincoln adhered to his inclusive interpretation of the Declaration. He continued to argue the Republican position that slavery must be excluded from the territories.

A clear victory for slavery, the *Dred Scott* decision aroused Lincoln's apprehension about the future of the Union. In his famous "House Divided" speech in Springfield, Illinois, on June 16, 1858, Lincoln charged that the decision was part of a conspiracy to nationalize slavery. The Supreme Court, he predicted, would soon issue a decision that exceeded *Dred Scott*, "declaring that the Constitution of the United States does not permit a *state* to exclude slavery from its limits. . . . Such a decision is all that slavery now lacks of being alike lawful in all the States. And welcome or unwelcome, such decision *is* probably coming, and will soon be upon us, unless the power of the present political dynasty shall be met and overthrown. We shall *lie down* pleasantly dreaming that the people of *Missouri* are on the verge of making their State *free;* and we shall *awake* to the *reality,* instead, that the *Supreme Court* has made *Illinois* a *slave* state."[33] Lincoln was not about to allow this to happen. Less than two weeks later, while assuring that he would "offer no *resistance*" to the Court, he nevertheless proclaimed: "We think the *Dred Scott* decision is erroneous. We know the court that made it, has often over-ruled its own decisions, and we shall do what we can to have it over-rule this."[34]

Dred Scott sparked a predictably partisan reaction from the press in 1857. The *New York Tribune,* edited by Horace Greeley, assailed *Dred Scott,* the decision being "entitled to just as much moral weight as would be the judgment of a majority of those congregated in any Washington bar-room."[35] Four days later, the paper declared: "Until that remote period when different Judges sitting in this same Court shall reverse this wicked and false judgment, the Constitution of the United States is nothing better than the bulwark of inhumanity and oppression."[36] The *Chicago Tribune* was equally critical: "We must confess we are shocked at the violence and servility of the Judicial Revolution caused by the Decision of the Supreme Court of the United States. . . . To say or suppose, that a Free People can respect or will obey a decision so fraught with disastrous consequences to the People and their Liberties, is to dream of impossibilities."[37]

At the same time, the pro-slavery Democratic press rushed to declare their support. "The decision is right, and the argument unanswerable, we presume," announced the Louisville *Democrat.* The Charleston *Daily Courier* predicted, with unfounded optimism, that the decision "that the Missouri Compromise is unconstitutional . . . and that free Negroes have no rights as citizens, under the Constitution of the United States . . . will, we confidently believe, settle these vexed questions forever, quiet the country, and relieve it of abolition agitation, and tend to perpetuate the Union."[38] According to the Augusta, Georgia *Constitutionalist:* "Southern opinion upon the subject of slavery . . . is now the supreme law of the land and opposition to southern opinion upon this subject is now opposition to the Constitution and morally treason against the Government."[39]

This single Supreme Court decision further polarized the nation, making the Civil War between the North and the South virtually inevitable. By declaring congressional regulation of slavery in the territories unconstitutional, *Dred Scott* provided judicial sanction for the doctrine of state sovereignty propounded by South Carolina's John C. Calhoun. He had argued that when the states formed the Union by ratifying the Constitution in 1787, they retained the exclusive right to regulate their own domestic institutions.[40] A staunch opponent of rights for black Americans, Calhoun, who died in 1850, espoused the view that the states had a right to nullify acts of the federal government they deemed unconstitutional. With *Dred Scott*, the Supreme Court accomplished what the states had wished to do: strike down the constitutionality of the Missouri Compromise. Emboldened by the Court's decision, the South would now be even more insistent about its "rights." At the same time, the decision convinced many northerners that slavery would be imposed upon the entire nation, and that further compromise was futile.[41] With each side rigidly holding its ground, few would be surprised when the nation plunged into civil war.

Dred Scott cast a shadow over the reputation of the Supreme Court. Modern jurists have condemned the decision. Judge A. Leon Higginbotham characterized the decision as "by far the most articulate and authoritative defense of the precept of black inferiority ever mounted by the American legal process." In fact, Taney made twenty-one references in his opinion to black inferiority and white supremacy.[42] Supreme Court Justice Thurgood Marshall included *Dred Scott* among the "unfortunate examples" of "what happens when the courts have permitted themselves to be moved by prevailing political pressures, and have deferred to the mob rather than interpret the Constitution."[43] Historian John Hope Franklin viewed the decision as another step toward civil war: "With the highest court in the land openly preaching the proslavery doctrine, there was little hope that anything short of a most drastic political or social revolution would bring an end to slavery."[44] Taney's opinion was riddled by historical errors and pro-slavery prejudice. He misread history and distorted the Constitution to further his goal of extending slavery into the territories. In the words of Constitution historian Peter Irons: "Taney's opinion was a travesty of the judicial craft, riddled with obvious errors and outright lies."[45] Perhaps the most famous barb was that of Charles Evans Hughes, later Chief Justice of the Supreme Court, who denounced *Dred Scott* in 1927 as the first of a number of "self-inflicted wounds" which damaged the Court's authority and prestige.[46]

The *Dred Scot* decision demolished the legal rationale not only of the abolitionists, but also of those who sought to prevent the spread of slavery in the territories. Against the Garrisonians, Taney declared that the liberty and equality principles of the Declaration of Independence did not include black Americans. At the same time, the Chief Justice corroborated Garrison's view that the Constitution was a pro-slavery document. Against the Free Soilers and the Republicans, such as Abraham Lincoln, *Dred Scott* affirmed that Congress had no constitutional authority to prevent slavery in the territories. Against the political abolitionists, including Frederick Douglass, who claimed that the Declaration of Independence and the Constitution guaranteed freedom and equal rights to blacks, *Dred Scott* held that such an inclusive reading of the nation's founding documents violated the Founders' original intentions. The powerful abolition arguments that Douglass had been making for years, founded on the Declaration of Independence and the Constitution, had been undermined by judicial decree.

Dred Scott also nullified the principal argument of Douglass's 1852 July Fourth oration that America had a serious moral dilemma to resolve. The Supreme Court had ruled that blacks were aliens in America, excluded from the "all men are created equal" principle of the Declaration of Independence, and from the "people" who ordained and established the Constitution of the United States. Even freed slaves like Douglass had been denied United States citizenship. If *Dred Scott* were to prevail, there was no American dilemma, for blacks had been excluded from the nation's ideals from the beginning.[47] Indeed, the nation's founding documents would have to be interpreted as supporting white supremacy. Black slaves would be relegated to an inferior position in America, regardless of whether they were born in the United States or not, or whether they were "free" or slave. As G. Edward White concludes, the infamy attached to the *Dred Scott* decision stems from the fact that it "made the alleged inferiority of blacks a matter of law." The Supreme Court provided "*open justification* of discrimination by the legal system—the announcement that in a constitutional sense blacks were not equal, not deserving of fair treatment, and not entitled to the full panoply of inalienable natural rights."[48] The nation's highest court having sanctioned a system of human bondage, the future of America's slave population seemed hopeless.

III

In the course of a speech in New York City on May 14, 1857, celebrating the anniversary of the American Abolition Society, Frederick Douglass delivered his opening salvo against the *Dred Scott* decision. The

Taney "settlement," he charged, "settled first—that there is no such thing as justice and mercy in the United States for persons of the colored race. The temple of justice is barred against them. No wrong or outrage to be inflicted upon them can ever bring them within the range of the temple of American justice. They are kicked out of the Supreme Court of the United States, and, of course they are kicked out of the courts of all the States."[49] Douglass knew the devastating legal consequences of *Dred Scott*. He amplified his assault on the decision in the June 12, 1857 edition of *Frederick Douglass' Paper.*[50] Douglass spelled out the ominous effects of the decision:

> This infamous decision of the Slave-holding wing of the Supreme Court maintains that slaves are within the contemplation of the Constitution of the United States, property; that slaves are property in the same sense that horses, sheep, and swine are property; that the old doctrine that slavery is a creature of local law is false; that the right of the slaveholder to his slave does not depend upon the local law, but is secured wherever the Constitution of the United States extends; that Congress has no right to prohibit slavery anywhere; that slavery may go in safety anywhere under the star-spangled banner; that colored persons of African descent have no rights that white men are bound to respect; that colored men of African descent are not and cannot be citizens of the United States.

Douglass predicted that *Dred Scott* would arouse great moral indignation: "I have no fear that the National Conscience will be put to sleep by such an open, glaring, and scandalous tissue of lies as that decision is, and has been, over and over, shown to be."[51]

Once again, the battle lines had been drawn between two conflicting interpretations of the Constitution. Douglass argued that Taney and slavery's supporters distorted the document in a number of egregious ways: "First, by discrediting and casting away as worthless the most beneficent rules of legal interpretation; by disregarding the plain and common sense reading of the instrument itself; by showing that the Constitution does not mean what it says, and says what it does not mean, by assuming that the written Constitution is to be interpreted in the light of a secret and unwritten understanding of its framers, which understanding is declared to be in favor of slavery. It is in this mean, contemptible, underhand method that the constitution is pressed into the service of slavery."[52] Refusing to surrender to despair, Douglass struggled to find a silver lining in *Dred Scott*, declaring that "my hopes were never brighter than now."[53] Throughout the 1850s, as the anti-slavery movement met disappointment after disappointment, Douglass—armed with his providential view of history and the Enlightenment idea of human progress—continued to counsel hope and perseverance among his black brethren, promising final victory.[54] While many believed that *Dred Scott* provided the final solution to the question of slavery, Douglass reminded his New York audience that several times in the past, from the 1820 Missouri Compromise to the Compromise of 1850 to the Kansas-Nebraska Act of 1854, the slavery question had been allegedly "settled." Yet each settlement had been merely a postponement, a temporary retreat from the brink of civil war. "The fact is," he observed, "the more the question has been set-tled, the more it has needed settling."[55] As long as slavery remained in the United States, there could be no "final settlement." Yet Douglass's conviction, informed by his reading of the Book of Exodus, that God was on the side of the slaves and the abolitionists, made him confident that the slave owners would soon be subjected to divine punishment.[56]

In confronting *Dred Scott*, Douglass resorted to the natural law ar-guments that sustained him in the past. Like the constitutional theorist Lysander Spooner, Douglass argued that any law or court decision, in-cluding *Dred Scott*, in violation of God's eternal justice was invalid. "The Supreme Court of the United States," he proclaimed, "is not the only power in this world. It is very great, but the Supreme Court of the Almighty is greater. . . . Judge Taney can do many things, but he can-not perform impossibilities. . . . He cannot reverse the decision of the Most High. He cannot change the essential nature of things—making evil good, and good evil. Happily for the whole human family, their rights have been defined, declared, and decided in a court higher than the Supreme Court." Adhering to the eternal principles of the Declara-tion of Independence that he had celebrated in his 1852 July Fourth oration, Douglass reminded his audience that freedom is a God-given natural right. Governments are institutions to secure, not to create, natural rights. As a clear violation of the natural right of black people to be free, *Dred Scott* was invalid. "Your fathers have said that man's right to liberty is self-evident," Douglass declared, "man was born with it. It was his before he comprehended it. . . . To decide against this right in the person of Dred Scott, or the humblest and most whip-scarred bondman in the land, is to decide against God. It is an open rebellion against God's government." Consistent with the jeremiadic tradition, Douglass was confident that slavery would ultimately be abolished through divine providence. Despite the disappointing setbacks, Douglass believed that America would fulfill its promise.[57] God's justice must prevail: "I am superstitious to believe," he confessed, "that the finger of the Almighty may be seen bringing good out of evil." *Dred Scott,* Douglass predicted, will arouse the "national conscience." "All measures devised and executed with a view to allay and diminish the anti-slavery agitation, have only served to increase, intensify, and embolden that agitation. . . . The American people have been called upon . . . to abolish and put away forever the system of slavery." With slavery abolished, America would be able to fulfill its founding egalitarian ideal. "The Constitution," Douglass asserted, "as well as the Declaration of Independence, and the sentiments of the Founders of the Republic, give us a platform broad enough, and strong enough, to support the most comprehensive plans for the freedom and elevation of all the people of this country, without regard to color, class, or clime."[58]

Continuing his offensive against *Dred Scott,* Douglass rejected the view that the Supreme Court should be the sole interpreter of the United States Constitution. In his 1852 July Fourth oration, Douglass had affirmed the right of American citizens to interpret the Constitution and to exercise every legal means to enable their interpretation to prevail. He refused to believe that the Constitution is whatever the Supreme Court declares, what is known as the doctrine of judicial supremacy. Douglass's speech attacking *Dred Scott* reflected his conviction that American constitutionalism could be shaped not only by public officials, but also by ordinary persons.[59] Abraham Lincoln agreed. While conceding that *Dred Scott* had decided the fate of the particular litigants, Lincoln believed that the interpretation of the Constitution was too important to be left in the hands of the Supreme Court alone. The future president refused to submit to the Court's ruling that Congress had no power to prevent slavery in the territories. Questions concerning constitutional meaning, he argued, should be addressed not only by the Court, but also by the American voters and the other branches of government, Congress and the executive. Lincoln struck a blow against judicial supremacy by claiming that Taney's ruling imposed no obligation on the other branches of the federal government. In Lincoln's judgment, the issues treated in *Dred Scott* had remained open, especially since the decision had been rendered by a partisan court and contradicted the sentiments of a large portion of the nation.

Lincoln was adamant that the Supreme Court should not be allowed to usurp its power, and he was not the first to demand the exercise of checks and balances incorporated into the Constitution. In 1832, President Andrew Jackson had contended that "Congress, the Executive, and the Court must each for itself be guided by its own opinion of the Constitution." Moreover, all public officers, federal and state, take an oath to support the Constitution as they understand it. They do not take an oath to support the Supreme Court's interpretation.[60] Whether Congress should be permitted to outlaw slavery in the territories, Lincoln affirmed, will be determined by the votes of the congressmen. Speaking in Chicago, Illinois on July 10, 1858, he proclaimed: "If I were in Congress, and a vote should come up on a question whether slavery should be prohibited in a new territory, in spite of that Dred Scott decision, I would vote that it should."[61] Elected President in 1861, with the nation close to civil war, Lincoln used the occasion of his First Inaugural Address on March 4 to state his unequivocal opposition to Taney's ruling. If the Supreme Court alone is allowed to determine the meaning of the Constitution, Lincoln argued, "the people will have ceased, to be their own rulers, having, to that extent, resigned their government, into the hands of that eminent tribunal."[62] Ironically, the man who had issued President Lincoln the oath of office was Chief Justice Roger B. Taney.

IV

Although both Frederick Douglass and Abraham Lincoln believed that *Dred Scott* violated fundamental natural law principles, neither argued that the decision should be disobeyed. While Douglass had supported disobedience to the 1850 Fugitive Slave Law, he hoped that Taney's ruling would be overturned legally as a result of the moral outrage it aroused. Furthermore, since *Dred Scott* involved an interpretation of the Constitution, his greatest legal weapon against slavery, Douglass decided to confront the decision by returning once again to the question of the constitutionality of slavery. "I have a quarrel with those who fling the Supreme Court of this land between the slave and freedom," he declared. "It is a serious matter to fling the weight of the Constitution against the cause of human freedom."[63]

Determined to expose the faulty reasoning that led to the *Dred Scott* decision, Douglass turned to three rules of legal interpretation. He explained: "These rules are as old as law. They rise out of the very elements of law. It is to protect human rights, and promote human welfare." First, the intention of a legal instrument, such as the Constitution, must be found in the very words of the document, not in any alleged intentions of its framers. Second, any infringement on human rights must be stated explicitly by the words of the document. Third, when interpreting a legal instrument one must look to its declared ends. Based on the first rule, Douglass could argue that nowhere does the Constitution expressly establish a right to own property in human beings. In alleging that slaves were property under the Constitution, Taney had merely imposed his personal prejudice upon the text, substituting partisan politics for the law.

The second rule of legal interpretation derived from Chief Justice Marshall's 1805 opinion in *United States v. Fisher.* According to Marshall: "Where rights are infringed, where fundamental principles are overthrown, where the general system of law is departed from, the legislative intention must be expressed with *irresistible clearness,* to induce a court of justice to suppose a design to effect such objects."[64] Abolitionist theorists Lysander Spooner and William Goodell adhered to Marshall's rule of textual interpretation: the language of any statute or constitution must be construed "strictly" in favor of freedom and natural rights. If the Constitution supported the right to own slaves, its language must be crystal clear.

According to the third rule, a "rule of law as well as of common sense," the ends of the United States Constitution, the aspirations of the Founders, Douglass asserted, are clearly stated in the language of its Preamble: "We the people of the United States, in order to form a more perfect Union, establish justice, insure domestic tranquility, provide for the common defense, promote the general welfare, and secure the blessings of liberty to ourselves and our posterity, do ordain and establish this Constitution for the United States of America." Based on the Constitution's ends alone—justice, liberty, and the general welfare—slavery should be abolished. Douglass held that the federal government had the legal authority and the means to abolish slavery throughout the United States. Congress should outlaw slavery, the Supreme Court should declare slavery unconstitutional, and the President, as the nation's chief executive, should enforce the Constitution, according to Article VI the "supreme law of the land." Taney had erroneously and unjustly subjected the Constitution to a racist reading. The words "slave," "slaveholder," and "slavery"—a point Douglass often made on the lecture circuit—are absent from the language of the Constitution. Moreover, contrary to Taney's opinion, "we the people" does not specify "white people."[65] The Constitution is color-blind.

Douglass also exposed Taney's grievous historical errors. The Chief Justice was wrong in claiming that at the time of the Declaration of Independence and the adoption of the Constitution, "the enlightened and civilized portion of the world" regarded blacks as "beings of an inferior order," justly reduced to slavery. Douglass pointed to the anti-slavery sentiment among the various American religious denominations, the existence of abolition societies in the various states, North as well as South, and the acknowledgment of the Founders of the republic that slavery was immoral. Finally, Douglass argued that in eleven of the thirteen original States, free blacks were eligible to vote during the period when the Constitution was ratified.[66] Within the Taney Court, Justice Benjamin Robbins Curtis, wrote a famous seventy-page dissent from the majority opinion in *Dred Scott*, arguing that free blacks had political rights when the Constitution was adopted. Indeed, when the Articles of Confederation were eventually ratified in 1781, free blacks, even though descended from slaves, were citizens of the states of New Hampshire, Massachusetts, New York, New Jersey, and North Carolina.[67]

V

Three years after *Dred Scott*, during his second lecture tour of the British Isles, Douglass reaffirmed his view of an anti-slavery Constitution by returning to the rules of interpretation that had guided him since his conversion to political abolitionism. If the Garrisonian abolitionists, the pro-slavery South, and the United States Supreme Court were correct in reading the Constitution as establishing slavery, the American dilemma that Douglass stressed in his 1852 July Fourth oration, and in countless other speeches, did not exist. If the *Dred Scott* decision were followed as the law, black Americans would be regarded as mere chattel, perpetually excluded from the freedoms proclaimed by the Declaration of Independence and protected by the Constitution. Speaking in Poughkeepsie, New York, on August 1, 1858 to commemorate the abolition of slavery in the British West Indies in 1833, Douglass declared that the principles that made America's Fourth of July "glorious have been buried out of sight, and Slavery, with the Negro's bleeding bones in his mouth, is now *stamping* on Freedom's grave. . . . The Fourth of July is still celebrated, but not as a festival of Liberty. With many it is the great day for the assassination of Liberty." Beneath the eloquent declarations of praise for the Union "is veiled the hideous and hell-black imp of Slavery."[68]

To confront the devastating consequences of the *Dred Scott* decision, Douglass was impelled to meet his adversaries head on. He began to formulate his most comprehensive refutation of the pro-slavery interpretation of the Constitution. As he had declared in an address delivered in Manchester, New Hampshire, on January 24, 1854: "The great mistake of the anti-slavery men of modern times, is that they have too easily given up the Constitution to slavery."[69] At a time when many Americans—not only slaveholders, but also the Garrisonians and moderate anti-slavery proponents—probably agreed with the Supreme Court's reading of the Constitution in *Dred Scott,* Frederick Douglass faced one of his greatest challenges.

CHAPTER 7

THE UNITED STATES CONSTITUTION IS ANTI-SLAVERY

In all matters where laws are taught to be made the means of oppression, cruelty, and wickedness, I am for strict construction. I will concede nothing.

—Frederick Douglass,
"The Constitution of the United States:
Is It Pro-Slavery or Anti-Slavery?"

I

Frederick Douglass was determined to reclaim the United States Constitution for the abolitionist cause. On March 26, 1860, he delivered a major speech in Glasgow, Scotland's largest and finest Victorian City, entitled, "The Constitution of the United States: Is it Pro-Slavery or Anti-Slavery?" The speech, among the most significant in his life, was delivered in the Queen's Rooms, located in Glasgow's West End, a neighborhood dominated by the University of Glasgow, founded in 1451. Frederick Douglass, a self-educated former slave, not a professional judge, lawyer, or constitutional scholar, argued his view of the correct reading of the Constitution. He would not leave the interpretation of America's founding document solely to members of the legal establishment or the Supreme Court. As Justice Joseph Story wrote in his *Commentaries on the Constitution of the United States* (1833), "Constitutions . . . are instruments of a practical nature, founded on the common business of human life, adapted to common wants, designed for common use, and fitted for common understanding. The people make them . . . ; the people adopt them; the people must be supposed to read them; and cannot be presumed to admit in them any recondite meaning."[1] Douglass understood that significant reform is often spearheaded by those who succeed in convincing the democratic majority of a more just way of construing the Constitution.[2]

When Douglass delivered his Glasgow speech, he had been away from his homeland for about four months. His implication in John Brown's raid on Harpers Ferry in 1859 had placed him in danger in the United States. The Virginia authorities had discovered Douglass's name among Brown's papers, and a warrant had been issued for his arrest. Learning that he was being pursued, Douglass fled to New York. He then took a ferry across the Hudson River to Hoboken, New Jersey, where he took temporary refuge at a boarding house with a white woman named Ottilie Assing. A journalist and staunch abolitionist from Germany, Assing had met Douglass in 1856, when she sought him out in Rochester. Arriving at the office of the *North Star* on 25 Buffalo Street one morning and not finding Douglass there, she proceeded to walk a half hour to his home to interview him. Douglass turned out to be even more impressive than she had imagined. The two quickly became friends and worked closely during the ensuing years to combat slavery in America. Ottilie Assing would spend many summers in Rochester with Douglass and his family, leading to speculation that she and Douglass had a sexual relationship. While in Rochester, Assing prepared a German translation of Douglass's *My Bondage and My Freedom*, the book that had inspired her to meet him.[3] From Hoboken, Douglass returned to Rochester before fleeing to Canada and finally to Britain where he had a prior commitment to deliver a series of lectures.

On November 12, 1859, Douglass sailed to Liverpool, England aboard the *Nova Scotian*. His tour of Britain inspired him to expound further on his abolitionist thinking, just as he had done during his first lecture tour there in the mid-1840s, leading him to launch a frontal assault upon the view that slavery was constitutional. His trip would energize the British anti-slavery movement. Crowds flocked to hear him speak on John Brown and to argue his aspirational reading of the Constitution, rooted in the ethical principles of the Declaration of Independence. Leeds abolitionist James Walker testified that Douglass's *"powerful* and eloquent appeals deepen our detestation of slavery, and have imparted to us a stronger impulse for, and led us more actively and devotedly into anti-slavery work than ever before."[4]

Douglass explained in the November 1859 issue of *Douglass' Monthly,* a journal launched the previous year, that his prearranged trip made necessary a temporary suspension of his editorial duties. Regarding the efforts to charge him for connection to John Brown, Douglass, still fuming over *Dred Scott,* issued a revolutionary statement: "A government which refuses to acknowledge—nay, denies that I can be a citizen, or bring a suit into its courts of justice—in a word brands me as an outlaw in virtue of my blood, now professes a wish to try me for being a traitor and an outlaw! To be a traitor, two conditions are necessary: First—one must have a government; secondly—he must be found in armed rebellion against that government. I am guilty of neither element of treason. The American government refuses to shelter the Negro under its protecting wing, and makes him an outlaw. The government is therefore quite unreasonable and inconsistent. Allegiance and protection are said to go together, and depend upon each other. When one is withdrawn, the other ceases."[5] Arriving in England, Douglass visited Julia Griffiths, who had assisted him in the publication of his abolitionist newspapers, and her husband in Halifax, Yorkshire. During this time, Douglass received news that on December 2, 1859, John Brown was hanged in Virginia.

In Glasgow, Scotland, with his home country on the brink of civil war, Douglass had an opportunity to continue the battle he had waged for years over the proper reading of the United States Constitution. His Glasgow speech displays a mastery of the principles of constitutional interpretation, derived from considerable study of the writings of the radical abolitionists. The impetus for Douglass's Glasgow address was provided by George Thompson, a prominent British abolitionist, who had recently attacked the United States Constitution as a pro-slavery document in a speech at the Glasgow City Hall. Seeking to embarrass Douglass, Thompson had cited some of Douglass's attacks upon the Constitution, made while he was a Garrisonian, prior to his conversion to political abolitionism.[6] Douglass's rebuttal of Thompson, delivered shortly before Abraham Lincoln's nomination for the presidency of the United States, is the most comprehensive statement of his mature position on the Constitution.[7]

Douglass's interpretation of the Constitution was not original, but his rhetorical brilliance did more to publicize an abolitionist reading of the nation's charter than did the tortuous reasoning of his legal mentors, Lysander Spooner and William Goodell. Throughout the 1850s, Douglass's eloquence reached thousands of people who were not inclined to study constitutional history, and many had heard him profess that the Constitution nowhere explicitly endorses or establishes slavery.[8] Lawrence H. Tribe argues in his standard text, *American Constitutional Law*, that Douglass's "extraordinary address" warrants inclusion with Chief Justice Taney's opinion in *Dred Scott* as part of the canon of constitutional texts to be studied.[9] Not only does Douglass explicate the political abolitionist view of the Constitution, but his arguments also aim to refute both the Garrisonians and supporters of *Dred Scott*.

II

Stepping up to the speaker's platform in Glasgow, with a copy of the Constitution in hand, Douglass faced a daunting challenge. As the debate over slavery raged in the United States, and the political parties prepared for the presidential election of 1860, Douglass brought his argument for an abolitionist United States Constitution before an international forum. He sought to demonstrate that the United States Constitution, the supreme law of the land, is anti-slavery. Douglass would argue that all three branches of the federal government have the legal power and the moral responsibility not only to prevent the spread of slavery, but also to abolish the institution immediately and unconditionally in the South. He applied the standard rules of interpretation that had guided him in his conversion to the Constitution, deriving its meaning from the language of the text alone.

Douglass expounded his literal rules of constitutional interpretation for his 1860 Glasgow audience. He presented the first rule: "In all matters where laws are taught to be made the means of oppression, cruelty, and wickedness, I am for strict construction. I will concede nothing."[10] Douglass quoted from Chief Justice John Marshall's opinion in the 1805 *Fisher* case, which said that the language of the law must always be interpreted in favor of liberty and justice. We cannot conclude that the Constitution establishes slavery unless its language explicitly does so. Douglass then introduced a second rule, which can be referred to as the innocent interpretation rule: "Where a law is susceptible of two meanings, the one making it accomplish an innocent purpose, and the other making it accomplish a wicked purpose, we must in all cases adopt that which makes it accomplish an innocent purpose." When construing a law, unless the language expressly forbids, one must give it an interpretation consistent with justice and virtue. Driving his point home, Douglass asserted: "When it is proposed to transform person into 'property' and men into beasts of burden, I demand that the law that contemplates such a purpose shall be expressed with irresistible clearness. The thing must not be left to inference, but must be done in plain English."[11] The third and final rule, which may be called the consistency rule, states: "The details of a law are to be interpreted in the light of the declared objects sought by the law."[12] Douglass called the attention of his Glasgow listeners to the objects for which the Constitution was framed and adopted. Slavery, he contended, was not among them. He quoted the Constitution's Preamble: "We the people of the United States, in order to form a more perfect union, establish justice, insure domestic tranquility, provide for the common defense, promote the general welfare, and secure the blessings of liberty to ourselves and our posterity, do ordain and establish this Constitution for the United States of America."

Douglass insisted that the Preamble, proclaiming the ethical purpose of the Constitution, carries the same force of law as the rest of the document. In fact, as he argued in several speeches, the Preamble should govern the interpretation of the Constitution. According to the express language of the Preamble, the government must fulfill the six ends: "Union, defense, welfare, tranquility, justice, and liberty. These are all good objects, and slavery, so far from being one of them, is a foe to them all." Seeking to demolish *Dred Scott*, Douglass returns to Chief Justice Taney's claim that blacks are "not included within the benefits sought" under the Preamble. But this exclusion is not expressly stated in the Constitution. As Douglass pointed out, the phrase "we the people" does not specify white people, or citizens, or the privileged class. It simply reads "we the people." Nowhere does the Preamble exclude black Americans. "The constitutionality of slavery can be made out," Douglass warned, "only by disregarding the plain and common-sense reading of the Constitution itself. . . . By assuming that the Constitution does not mean what it says, and that it says what it does not mean; by disregarding the written Constitution, and interpreting it in the light of a secret understanding."[13] Douglass's argument that a literal reading of the Constitution did not support slavery had been a staple argument of the abolitionists. The abolitionist historian and jurist Richard Hildreth wrote in 1854 that the clauses of the Constitution alleged to establish slavery do no such thing: "They contain no endorsement of the slave laws of the states; no recognition of slavery as a state institution; no express recognition even of the bare fact of the existence of slavery, and much less of its existence as an institution entitled to the favorable regard and protecting care of the Federal government."[14] The abolitionists would take the framers of the Constitution at their literal word.

Having clarified his rules of interpreting the United States Constitution for his audience at Glasgow, Douglass got down to business. He argued that, based on a strictly literal view, the following extratextual elements must be dismissed as irrelevant: that slavery existed in the United States when the Constitution was adopted; that some framers were slaveholders; that these slaveholders intended to secure by the Constitution certain advantages for slavery; that the American government has acted to support slavery for seventy-two years; and that the American courts have applied a pro-slavery interpretation to the Constitution. The real questions, Douglass insisted, are: "[First], Does the United States Constitution guarantee to any class or description of people in that country the right to enslave, or hold as property, any other class or description of people in that country? [Second], is the dissolution of the Union between the slave and free States required by fidelity to the slaves, or by the just demands of conscience? In other words, is refusing to exercise the ballot, and to hold political office, the surest, wisest, and best way to abolish slavery in America?"[15]

Douglass reminded his audience that the Garrisonians answered these two questions affirmatively. Led by the fiery rhetoric of William Lloyd Garrison, they condemned the Constitution as a diabolical pact, called for the North to secede from the Union, and scorned politics. Douglass's goal was to prove that the Garrisonian beliefs and practice were fundamentally flawed. Much was at stake; if Garrison's pro-slavery reading of the Constitution were correct, slavery could never be abolished within the context of the American political system. If slavery was constitutional, *Dred Scott* had legally settled the slavery question. If the United States Constitution supported slavery, the document must be either destroyed or at least amended before slavery could be abolished. Moreover, if slavery was constitutional, opponents of slavery would be justified in abstaining from party politics and seceding from the Union. But to destroy the Union would abandon the slaves to perpetual bondage. To reject politics would play into the hands of southern politicians.

The Constitution, Douglass insisted, is "no vague, indefinite, floating, unsubstantial, ideal something, coloured according to any man's fancy," but instead a "plainly written document, . . . a written instrument full and complete in itself." The explicit text of the Constitution must rule: "No Court in America, no Congress, no President, can add a single word thereto, or take a single word therefrom." The American government had been instituted to implement the Constitution, "a great national enactment done by the people," which "can only be altered, amended, or added to by the people."[16] Douglass told his Glasgow audience that the Constitution's clauses allegedly protecting slavery are ambiguous. Slaveholders relied upon flimsy evidence of the framers' original intentions while disregarding the fact that the literal text of the Constitution did not explicitly support slavery. The Garrisonians, Douglass argued, erred by confusing the government's failure to implement the Constitution's ethical goals with the document itself.[17] Douglass's friend Gerrit Smith emphasized this point by asking: "Is the Constitution pro-slavery, because the government of the United States has, from its beginning, been administered for the advantage of slavery? As well might you hold the Constitution responsible for any other trampling on its principles. . . . The fact, that the nation, in its national capacity, favors and upholds slavery, proves nothing against the Constitution."[18] Throughout the antebellum years, the federal government, including the Supreme Court, deviated from the ideals of the Founders each time it compromised with slavery. The abolitionist quarrel was not with the Constitution. Douglass defended the Constitution from those, including the presidency, Congress, and the Supreme Court, whose tolerance of slavery undermined the document's republican values. The Constitution must not be wrested from the sovereign people.

Let the people read the document themselves to determine whether it establishes or prohibits slavery. If they did so, Douglass was confident that they would see that nowhere does the Constitution explicitly recognize slavery as a legitimate part of American society.

Prudence dictated that the many framers of the Constitution who opposed slavery had to accept, at least temporarily, concessions to the institution in the interest of creating "a more perfect union." Even in those provisions that by implication referred to slavery, the framers refrained from language that might give the institution moral sanction. Instead of "slaves," the Constitution refers to "three-fifths of all other persons," the "migration or importation of such persons," and "persons held to service or labor." Abolished in the North after the American Revolution, slavery was confined to the southern states, where it was regarded as a product of state law, not natural law or right. The framers' intent to limit slavery to the South was reflected by the Northwest Ordinance of 1787, which prohibited slavery in the vast territory of the Ohio Valley—what became the states of Ohio, Indiana, Illinois, Michigan, Wisconsin, and Iowa. As historian Don E. Fehrenbacher observes: "It is as though the framers were half-consciously trying to frame two constitutions, one for their own time and the other for the ages, with slavery viewed bifocally, that is, plainly visible at their feet, but disappearing when they lifted their eyes."[19]

III

Based upon his rules for properly interpreting the Constitution, Douglass declared to his Glasgow audience that the "text, and only the text, and not any commentaries or creeds written by those who wished to give the text a meaning apart from its plain reading," is the Constitution of the United States.[20] Perhaps the closest analogue to Douglass in modern times is the Supreme Court Justice Hugo Black, known for always carrying a copy of the Constitution in his pocket and consulting its literal common-language meanings. Black's veneration of the nation's charter, set forth in *A Constitutional Faith* (1969), induced him to discount any interpretation that strayed from a precise wording of the text.[21] Douglass rejected what is known today as originalism, interpreting the Constitution based on the alleged personal extratextual intentions of the framers derived from examining the document's historical and political context. In accord with the common law understanding endorsed by most of the Constitution's framers, adopters, and early interpreters, Douglass insisted that the "intentions" must be evidenced in the language of the document itself.[22] We will recall that prior to converting fully to the Constitution, Douglass admitted that strictly construed according to its letter, the document opposed slavery. Nevertheless, he could not at that early time relinquish his view that the original intent of the framers, as well as subsequent interpretations by the federal courts, made the Constitution a pro-slavery instrument. Douglass later realized that many questionable interpretations of the Constitution had been propounded under the umbrella of so-called original intent.

To read the Constitution accurately, Douglass elucidated, one must reject any intent beyond that found explicitly in the words of the text itself.[23] Searching for intentions, good or evil, beyond the text is futile. He argued: "It would be the wildest of absurdities, and lead to endless confusions and mischiefs, if, instead of looking to the written paper itself, for its meaning, it were attempted to make us search it out, in the secret motives, and dishonest intentions, of some of the men who took part in writing it. It was what they said that was adopted by the people, not what they were ashamed or afraid to say, and really omitted to say."[24] If the framers intended to provide a constitutional sanction for slavery, binding not only on the present but also on future generations, they would have done so in language that was crystal clear.

Douglass told his Glasgow audience that the delegates to the 1787 Constitutional Convention in Philadelphia had acted under a secrecy rule that prohibited making their deliberations public. This enabled the people to judge solely the written text, uninfluenced by whatever unexpressed motives and intentions that might have moved the framers. "The fact is an important one, that the framers of the Constitution sat with closed doors, and that this was done purposely, that nothing but the result of their labors should be seen, and that that result should be judged of by the people free from any of the bias shown in the debates." Douglass stressed: "These debates were purposely kept out of view, in order that the people should adopt, not the secret motives or unexpressed intentions of any body, but the simple text of the paper itself."[25]

The publication in 1840 of Madison's detailed *Notes* on the Philadelphia Convention's debates raised the question of the intentions of the framers. While the text of the Constitution refrained from using the words "slave" and "slavery," Madison's work revealed that the words had dominated many of their debates. To what extent should the framers' intentions, insofar as they can be ascertained from the debates, determine the interpretation of the Constitution with regard to slavery? An acrimonious controversy ensued, with each side finding evidence corroborating its position. The ambiguity surrounding the framers' intentions sparked disagreements even among the abolitionists. Garrisonians found justification in Madison's revelations for their attack upon the Constitution. Free Soilers argued that while the framers struck compromises with slavery, they also provided a means in the Constitution to prohibit its extension that would lead to its early demise. Douglass insisted that the framers' intentions could not be derived from anywhere except the plain, unmistakable language of the Constitution itself: "I repeat, the paper itself, and only the paper itself, with its own plainly-written purposes, is the Constitution. It must stand or fall, flourish or fade, on its own individual and self-declared character and objects." He asks rhetorically: "Where would be the advantage of a written Constitution, if, instead of seeking its meaning in its words, we had to seek them in the secret intentions of individuals who may have had something to do with writing the paper?" He then dismissed those who continued to speak of the "original intent" of the framers. "What will the people of America a hundred years hence care about the intentions of the scriveners who wrote the Constitution? . . . They were for a generation, but the Constitution is for ages." Using an argument of reversal, Douglass indicated that those who go outside the Constitution to prove that it is pro-slavery unwittingly support his anti-slavery view. "It is an admission that the thing for which they are looking is not to be found where only it ought to be found, and that is in the Constitution itself."[26]

IV

Having established his strict textual basis for reading the Constitution, Douglass turned to the document, examining each of the clauses alleged to support slavery. To refute the Garrisonians, as well as the Taney Court and the southern ideologues who interpreted the Constitution as pro-slavery, Douglass began by referring to the relevant clauses of the text. According to the British abolitionist George Thompson, as well as the Garrisonians, Article I, section 9 provided for the continuation of the African slave trade for twenty years, until 1808; Article I, section 2, granted the slave states a representation of three-fifths of their entire slave population; Article I, section 8, authorized the federal government to suppress slave insurrections; and Article IV, section 2, provided for the recovery of fugitive slaves from other states. These sections of the Constitution had been the basis for Wendell Phillips's assault upon the document years before.[27] Douglass's response to Thompson therefore may also be read as a response to Phillips and the Garrisonians. Regarding the clauses in the Constitution allegedly supporting slavery, Douglass inquired: "Why did he [Thompson] not read the Constitution? . . . The words of the Constitution were before him. Why then did he not give you the plain words of the Constitution?" Douglass explained the reason for Thompson's evasion: "It so happens that no such words as 'African slave trade,' no such words as 'slave representation,' no such words as 'fugitive slaves,' no such words as 'slave insurrections,' appear anywhere in that instrument. These are the words of that orator, and not the words of the Constitution of the United States."[28]

Turning to the text of the Constitution itself, Douglass raised the document in his hands and read, "word for word," each of the provisions purported by Thompson to bolster slavery. Douglass allowed the audience to hear for themselves a literal reading of the Constitution's provisions, which, in fact, are subject to interpretations disadvantageous to slavery. He began with Article I, section 2: "Representatives and direct taxes shall be apportioned among the several States which may be included within this Union, according to their respective numbers, which shall be determined by adding to the whole number of free persons, including those bound to service for a term of years, excluding Indians not taxed, three-fifths of all other persons."

The three-fifths compromise issued from the debate in the 1787 Constitutional Convention over political representation. The delegates had agreed upon a bicameral Congress, with proportional representation in the House of Representatives. But the southern delegates made it clear that they would reject a Union that did not include slavery. They desired a Constitution that supported the right to own slaves. On the question of representation in the Senate, the

Convention agreed that each state, regardless of size, would have two Senators. Since representation in the House would be determined by population, the Convention had to consider the question of who should be counted. The South, wishing to increase its electoral power in the House of Representatives, wanted to count slaves as whole people. Holding greater numbers, the South would be able to protect the system of slavery. If all slaves were included in the population count, the South would have had 50 percent of the seats in the House. Regarding human bondage as a blatant contradiction to the equality principle of the Declaration of Independence, most northern delegates believed that the Constitution should not endorse slavery. They wanted no slaves to be counted, thus granting them greater voting power to control Congress. If no slaves were included in the population count, the South would have had only 41 percent of the seats in the House. Northern delegates also believed that allowing the South to count slaves for purposes of representation would provide an incentive to increase the slave population.

After more than a month of vigorous debate, the impasse in the Constitutional Convention was resolved by a compromise stipulating that for representation and direct taxation a slave would count neither as a whole person nor as a non-person, but as three-fifths of a person. This was known as the "federal number," in which three-fifths of the slave population would be added to the entire white population for the purpose of determining the number of seats in the House of Representatives. The greater the number of seats in the House, the greater the direct taxation. This compromise gave the South 47 percent of the seats in the House, making it easier for the North to prevail on slavery issues.[29] Because free blacks constituted 8 percent of the total population in 1790, as "free persons," they were, according to the clause, counted as full persons, like free whites, for purposes of representation.[30] Both sides looked to the compromise's brighter side. According to Charles Pinckney, delegate of South Carolina, the southern delegates "made the best terms for the security of [slavery] it was in our power to make. We would have made better if we could, but on the whole, I do not think them bad." At the same time, delegate James Wilson of Pennsylvania concluded that the northern delegates had succeeded in "laying the foundation for banishing slavery out of this country," albeit "the period is more distant than I could wish."[31] For the sake of establishing "a more perfect union," both the North and the South had compromised.

Addressing the three-fifths compromise, Douglass conceded, only for the purpose of argument, that "all other persons" refers to slaves. Indeed, the clause does acknowledge the existence of non-free persons in the United States. Nevertheless, he argued, granting the "worst construction" to the provision amounts to a "downright disability laid upon the slaveholding States," depriving them of two-fifths of their basis for representation. "A black man in a free State is worth just two-fifths more than a black man in a slave State, as a basis of political power under the Constitution."[32] Over the years, critics have alleged that the three-fifths clause reflects that the framers regarded slaves as less than complete humans.[33] Modern neo-Garrisonian interpreters of the Constitution have condemned the framers, alleging that after proclaiming that "all men are created equal" in the Declaration of Independence, they produced a Constitution that denied that blacks were men at all.[34] But the charge of relegating blacks to mere chattel status is more applicable to Justice Taney than to someone who understood the three-fifths clause as an unavoidable compromise. Regardless of whether some framers believed that black persons were not entitled to full civic rights, the three-fifths clause had nothing to do with this prejudice. Northern delegates wanted to exclude blacks from being counted, not because they believed them to be less than human, but because they sought to weaken the power of the slaveholding South in Congress. At the same time, southern delegates wanted every slave counted, not because they acknowledged that blacks were human beings equal to whites, but because they wanted to increase the voting power of the South in Congress. The three-fifths clause related not to the humanity or moral worth of slaves, but to their legal status. In fact, under the clause, free blacks would be counted as free persons for purposes of representation. The compromise was not about race, but about political and economic power.

In any case, Douglass claimed that the three-fifths clause favored freedom by giving an increase of "two-fifths" of political power to free over slave states. He thus reinterpreted a clause usually condemned as favoring slavery into an outright disadvantage to the South. "Instead of encouraging slavery," he concluded, "the Constitution encourages freedom by *holding out to every slaveholding State the inducement of an increase of two-fifths of political power by becoming a free State.*"[35] But as long as the southern economy depended heavily upon slavery, the slave states would see no political advantage in freeing their slaves. Moreover, the three-fifths compromise increased the number of votes the southern states had in the electoral college, thus giving them more power in choosing the nation's president. Indeed, five of the first seven American presidents—Washington, Jefferson, Madison, Monroe, and Jackson—were slaveholders from slave states. Nevertheless, Douglass was adamant in maintaining that the three-fifths clause, as well as the other allegedly pro-slavery provisions of the Constitution, was open to mitigating interpretations. The literal phrasing of the clause did not sanction slavery. Examining each of the document's allegedly pro-slavery clauses, Douglass would capitalize on the framers' circumlocutions, language that clearly reflected their conflict over the issue of slavery. A correct reading of the Constitution, he believed, would justify it as an abolition document.

V

Building his argument, Douglass next considered Article I, section 9: "The migration or importation of such persons as any of the States now existing shall think proper to admit, shall not be prohibited by the Congress prior to the year one thousand eight hundred and eight, but a tax or duty may be imposed on such importation, not exceeding ten dollars for each person."

For those who believed that the clause refers to slavery, Douglass clarified that its specific language "does not warrant any such conclusion." Even if one grants, for the sake of argument, that the clause is about slavery, one cannot deny that it permits Congress to abolish the African slave trade in twenty years, by 1808.[36] The clause entered the Constitution in 1787 as a result of a compromise between the North, which demanded complete prohibition of the slave trade, and the South, which held that the federal government should have power to interfere. Northern delegates who found slavery morally reprehensible sought to end the traffic in human beings. Southern delegates, in contrast, sought to continue the supply of slave labor as an economic necessity. The plantation, which brought the South millions of dollars in profit, depended on an enslaved labor force. Thus the Constitutional

Convention arrived at the best possible compromise, with many northern delegates expecting the eventual demise of slavery.

The compromise on the slave trade prevented the South from having its complete way. While the Founders may not have desired to attack slavery where it already existed in the South, their decision to terminate the slave trade in 1808 indicates that many believed that slavery was a dying institution.[37] Congress having abolished the trade at the earliest possible date, Douglass reminded his audience that the provision "became a dead letter more than fifty years ago, and binds no man's conscience for the continuance of any slave trade whatever." Applying a liberal construction to the clause, Douglass argued: "This very provision, if made to refer to the African slave trade at all, makes the Constitution anti-slavery rather than for slavery, for it says to the slave States, the price you will have to pay for coming into the American Union is, that the slave trade, which you would carry on indefinitely out of the Union, shall be put an end to in twenty years if you come into the Union." The provision was deliberately phrased not to guarantee the right, but to postpone the power to prohibit, looking to "the abolition of slavery rather than its perpetuity."[38] The clause may have been a reluctant and temporary concession, applicable only to "States now existing," that is, in 1787, and made in the interest of creating "a more perfect Union."[39] As such, the majority of the slave states in the nineteenth century were not included in the clause's provision. As the historian Herbert J. Storing concludes: "The clause, fairly interpreted, gives a temporary respite to an illicit trade; the presumption was that Congress would, after twenty years, forbid this trade . . . and in fact Congress did so."[40] Moreover, since the language of the clause refers to "States now existing," it would appear that Congress could legitimately restrict the slave trade in new states and in the territories of the nation.

Douglass insisted that the slave trade provision demonstrated the reverse of what his Garrisonian opponents contended. It reveals that the framers did not favor slavery and intended to hasten its extinction. At the time of the American Revolution, slavery existed in each of the thirteen colonies and the slave trade flourished. In the revolution's aftermath, the states of the North proceeded to abolish slavery, and the Constitution expressed an intention to cut off the stream of slaves to the South in the near future. "Men at the time, both in England and in

America, looked upon the slave trade as the life of slavery. The abolition of the slave trade was supposed to be the certain death of slavery. Cut off the stream, and the pond will dry up, was the common notion at the time." The provision demonstrates, Douglass declared, that the "intentions of the framers of the Constitution were good, not bad."[41] Contrary to the Garrisonian interpretation, therefore, the slave trade provision was designed not to perpetuate, but ultimately to abolish slavery.[42] In a debate with the black Garrisonian abolitionist Charles Lenox Remond in New York City in May 1857, Douglass—citing James Kent's classic *Commentaries on American Law* (1826–30)—argued that when the Constitution was adopted, the expectation was that the abolition of the slave trade would mark the abolition of slavery.[43] But the nation would pay a price for the slave trade compromise. Many northern delegates underestimated the resolve of the South to bolster slavery. The slave trade clause provided a twenty-year opportunity for the slave owners to augment the slave population by hundreds of thousands, thus further entrenching slavery as the basis for the economy of the South.

Although the framers may have intended to set slavery on a course to extinction with the Constitution's slave trade clause, they were wrong in expecting its imminent demise. The invention of the cotton gin in 1793 made slavery even more profitable. But Douglass provided a credible argument that the slave trade clause struck a significant blow against slavery. Having granted Congress the power to end the trade in twenty years, both sides at the Constitutional Convention believed that they surrendered substantial ground. While opponents of slavery resented that the federal government would be tied by the Constitution for two decades, slavery's proponents became resigned to the fact that Congress would end the slave trade as it was authorized to do. Rather than perpetuating slavery, Douglass believed that the slave trade clause provided a constitutional means to accomplish its ultimate extinction. Don E. Fehrenbacher points out that the clause was "probably a necessary concession to the lower South—one that proved, however, to be antislavery in its ultimate effect." The expectation was that the South would eventually be deprived of its major source of forced labor. While the clause did allow the importation of some slaves, "at the same time it *expressly confirmed* the power of Congress to prohibit the trade eventually, and more than that, it fostered a general ex-

pectation of federal legislation and federal enforcement at the desig-
nated time."[44] Those framers who opposed slavery had discovered a
way to preserve the Union and to strike a blow at slavery by eventually
depriving the South of its supply of slave labor.

VI

Douglass next examined Article I, section 8, referred to as the "slave
insurrection" clause: "Congress shall have the power . . . to provide for
calling forth the militia to execute the laws of the Union, suppress insurrections and repel invasions."

This clause, according to Douglass, "has nothing whatever to do
with slaves or slaveholders." Construing the text literally, "it is only a
law for the suppression of riots or insurrections."[45] Based on a literal
reading, the clause does not refer specifically to insurrections by slaves.
Instead, it authorizes Congress to suppress any insurrection. During
the period of the Constitutional Convention there was no obvious
threat of significant slave violence. In fact, the framers were probably
more alarmed by recent outbreaks of white violence, specifically
Shays's 1787 uprising in Massachusetts, which inspired resistance to
debt recovery and tax collection throughout much of the nation. If this
clause had been omitted from the Constitution, the federal government
would have lacked the authority to suppress insurrections such as the
Whiskey Rebellion in 1794. President Abraham Lincoln would have
been deprived of the constitutional authority to quell a rebellion not of
slaves, but of southern slaveholders in 1861.[46]

Douglass seized the ambiguity in the insurrection clause, reading it
as a potential legal instrument for the abolition of slavery. Considering
hypothetically that the clause was intended to refer to slave insurrections, he explains, it would not protect slavery. In fact, many political
abolitionists argued that the Constitution empowered Congress to prohibit or abolish slavery, not only in the western territories, but also in
the States. But Douglass was more radical than most. To make a point,
he offered a hypothetical scenario: If an opponent to slavery became
President of the United States, "and the day that shall see this case is
not distant," the power to suppress a slave insurrection could actually
end slavery. "If it should turn out that slavery is a source of insurrection, that there is no security from insurrection while slavery lasts,

why, the Constitution would be best obeyed by putting an end to slavery, and an anti-slavery Congress would do that very thing."[47] Douglass used the insurrection clause to indicate the potential of an anti-slavery Congress that would abolish slavery in order to prevent disastrous slave rebellions. Considering the escalating conflict between pro-slavery and anti-slavery proponents, the political climate could be swayed to favor the abolitionist position. Hence, slavery could be abolished in order to prevent violent revolution. Moreover, the clause works both ways. If the southern states were ever to rebel against a law of Congress forbidding slavery, the federal government would be authorized to crush such an insurrection. Douglass ingeniously showed, therefore, that the insurrection clause does not necessarily favor slavery but may be read literally to provide a constitutional weapon against slavery.

VII

Finally, Douglass dealt with the "fugitive slave" clause. He quoted the relevant phrases from Article IV, section 2, letting his audience hear the very words of the Constitution so that he could make the case that the clause does not expressly recognize slaves as property: "No person held to service or labor in one State, under the laws thereof, escaping into another, shall, in consequence of any law or regulation therein, be discharged from such service of labor, but shall be delivered up on claim of the party to whom such service or labor may be due."

Conceding that the provision may have been introduced originally for the purpose of capturing fugitive slaves, Douglass insisted that the literal wording lends no credence to the view that the clause establishes slavery. Above all, the Constitution nowhere refers specifically to "fugitive slaves." The word "servitude," Douglass clarified, had been omitted from the written provision, "for the very reason that it applied to slaves." He reminded his Glasgow audience that James Madison reported that the word "servitude" had been struck from the Constitution "because the convention would not consent that the idea of property in men" should be found in the document.[48] The clause, Douglass alleged, does not use the word "slave," nor does it expressly recognize slaves as property. Attributing allusions to slavery in the words "service" and "labor" are yet another instance of misreading the Constitution. Advocates of slavery, therefore, impose a construction upon the Constitution unsupported by the words of the document. Many framers were opposed to slavery, but because the institution was protected by local law in the South, they were reluctant to encourage defiance of the law, even in the interest of justice.[49] The Union, they knew, could not survive without respect for the rule of law. While acknowledging that, given the Constitution's ambiguous language, Madison's testimony might be offered to support either side of the slavery issue, Douglass contended that "this is another evidence of the folly and absurdity of making the secret intentions of the framers the criterion by which the Constitution is to be construed."[50] The meaning of the Constitution must be determined not by ascribing alleged intentions to its framers, but by the exact language of the text.

If not to "slaves," then to whom does the language of the fugitive clause apply? Once directing his Glasgow listeners to consider the framers' language, Douglass argued that the clause applies only to apprentices and indentured servants. "Its object plainly is, to secure the fulfillment of contracts for 'service and labor.'"[51] The abolitionist Richard Hildreth had made this point in 1854.[52] Such a construction, Douglass alleged, referred only to those servants who are obligated by contracts. Since slaves could not make contracts, the clause did not refer to them. "The legal condition of the slave puts him beyond the operation of this provision. He is not described in it. He is a simple article of property. He does not owe and cannot owe service. He cannot even make a contract. It is impossible for him to do so. He can no more make such a contract than a horse or an ox can make one."[53] Thus, the language of the clause does not include slaves. Applying Chief Justice John Marshall's rule in *United States v. Fisher*, Douglass showed his audience that the Constitution's clause dealing with fugitives from labor does not support slavery. Unless a statute or constitution expressly deprives a person of a fundamental liberty, the framers' intent must be interpreted as not denying the rights of any person. The oblique language of the Constitution indicated to Douglass that many framers intended to leave open a legal avenue for the eventual extinction of slavery in America. Confronted by a Constitution that neither sanctioned nor condemned slavery explicitly, Douglass felt justified, following the *Fisher* rule, in construing the document strictly in favor of liberty and equality. Read in light of its Preamble and its intimate relationship to the Declaration of Independence, the Constitution condemned slavery.

The records of the 1787 Constitutional Convention show that most framers were careful to avoid granting legal sanction to slavery through what became known as the fugitive slave clause. Reading the evolving drafts of the clause, we note that "the person justly claiming their service or labor" was revised to "the party to whom such service or labor may be due." Hence, "justly claiming" was altered to "may be due." Moreover, "person bound to service or labor" was revised to "person legally held to service." This wording was ultimately revised: "legally" was removed, while "under the labor of one State, under the Laws thereof" remained. According to Madison, this revision was made "in compliance with the wish of some who thought the term [legal] equivocal, and favoring the idea that slavery was legal in a moral view."[54]

At Glasgow, Douglass also adverted briefly to other sections of the Constitution that are inconsistent with slavery. Proponents of slavery conveniently ignored the Fifth Amendment, which declares that "no person shall be deprived of life, liberty, or property without due process of law." The rights of millions of slaves had been violated. Not only does the Constitution guarantee to "every State in the Union a republican form of government" (Article IV, section 4), it also guarantees all persons the privilege of the writ of habeas corpus (Article I, section 9), and the right to trial by jury (Article III, section 2). Moreover, the Constitution "forbids the passing of a bill of attainder: that is, a law entailing upon the child the disabilities and hardships imposed upon the parent." On the basis of this provision alone, Douglass insisted, "every slave law in America might be repealed." He concluded: "In the hands of abolitionist statesmen, and backed up by a right moral sentiment" these sections of the Constitution would abolish slavery in the United States. And yet, Douglass conceded, the practice of the American people would lead one to an opposite conclusion. "I admit it. They have given the Constitution a slaveholding interpretation. I admit it. They have committed innumerable wrongs against the Negro in the name of the Constitution. Yes, I admit it all; and I go with him who goes farthest in denouncing these wrongs. But it does not follow that the Constitution is in favor of these wrongs because the slaveholders have given it that interpretation."[55]

Douglass's Glasgow speech was a brilliant legal brief on behalf of a Constitution that forbade slavery everywhere in the United States. He was tenacious in his effort to save the Constitution from an erroneous pro-slavery reading. Clause by clause, word by word, he insisted, the text must stand on its substance. The misconstrued, extratextual interpretations have led many on the unrighteous path, to the detriment of America and its Constitution, a "glorious liberty document." In the words of Don E. Fehrenbacher: "On the eve of Lincoln's nomination for the presidency, Frederick Douglass held up for public view the constitutional surgical tools that could be used at the proper moment."[56] But Douglass's abolitionist reading of the Constitution was too radical to be accepted by most Americans of his day, in the North as well as in the South. Even if the federal government had been persuaded to uphold the Constitution and abolish slavery in the states, either by Congressional legislation or by presidential executive order, such action would have been overturned by the pro-slavery Taney Court.

VIII

Having argued that the United States Constitution is a liberty document, that fulfilling the ethical goals of its Preamble mandated the abolition of slavery, Douglass went on to the question of the Union. Many abolitionists, frustrated by the failure of the federal government to abolish slavery, continued to favor abolishing the Union. If the South would not reform, the only recourse, other than civil war, would be for the North to secede from the Union. Better no Union than a Union with slavery. But dissolving the Union, Douglass maintained, would fail to bring the North a "single advantage over slavery, but would take from it many. Within the Union, we have a firm basis of opposition to slavery. It is opposed to all the great objects of the Constitution." Rejecting the South's conception of states' rights, used to defend slavery as a local institution under the protection of the individual states, Douglass advocated "drawing the bond of the Union more closely, and bringing the slave States more completely under the power of the free States." While Douglass agreed with division between the federal and the state governments established by the framers, he insisted that no state should be permitted to use the doctrine of states' rights as a shield to protect slavery, an institution that deprived blacks of rights guaranteed by the Constitution. As for the Garrisonian argument that remaining in the Union morally implicated northerners in supporting slavery, Douglass refused to believe that seceding from the Union would fulfill any moral obligation. "There now clearly is no freedom from responsibility for slavery to any American citizen short of the abolition of slavery," he declared.[57] Morality demands abolishing slavery, not the federal Union.

From the podium at Glasgow, Douglass sent a message to Americans at home to use the political process to defeat slavery. Aiming to overturn *Dred Scott*, Douglass urged all those opposed to slavery to use the ballot box to influence the composition of the Supreme Court. "What do we want? We want this:—whereas slavery has ruled the land, now must liberty; whereas pro-slavery men have sat in the Supreme Court of the United States, and given the constitution a pro-slavery interpretation against its plain reading, let us by our votes put men into that Supreme court who will decide, and who will concede, that that constitution is not [pro-] slavery."[58] Opponents of slavery must also "reform the government" by electing to Congress persons committed to the abolition of slavery.

Before closing his Glasgow speech, Douglass interjected a personal note of great importance. The wrong perception of him, he realized, could hurt his credibility in the fight against slavery. His British abolitionist adversary George Thompson had emphasized in various speeches that Douglass once held the opposite view of the Constitution. We recall that, early in his abolitionist career, while a staunch Garrisonian, Douglass had stood on many platforms to condemn the Constitution as a pro-slavery document. He told his Glasgow listeners that when he escaped slavery in his youth, he adopted many views of the Garrisonians. "When I was a child, I thought and spoke as a child." Having studied little, especially in constitutional law, he was persuaded by their pro-slavery reading of the Constitution. After years of experience and reflective reading, Douglass had revised his views on the Constitution and politics. His Glasgow address was a palinode, enabling him to retract the misguided pro-slavery interpretation of the Constitution that he had proclaimed throughout his first lecture tour of the British Isles from 1845 to 1847. The mature Douglass concluded that attacking the Constitution and shunning politics, as the Garrisonians counseled, deprived the abolition movement of the most effective weapons against slavery. Slavery would be defeated not by a secession of the North from the Union, and not by ignoring the power of the ballot, but by political reform under the Constitution. "My position now is one of reform, not of revolution. I would act for the abolition of slavery through the Government—not over its ruins."[59]

Douglass's speaking tour of Britain would be brought to a sad end by the news that his daughter, Annie, the youngest of his children, had died in Rochester on March 13, 1860, just prior to her eleventh birthday. Douglass characterized her as "the light and life of my house." The grieving Douglass, still at risk of arrest for his association with John Brown, journeyed home to Rochester to be with his "sorrow-stricken family," his wife Anna and their remaining four children.[60] He soon learned that Congress had agreed to put the matter of his criminal prosecution to rest. Although Douglass promised to resume his tour of Britain, he did not return until long after the Civil War.

When Douglass returned to Rochester, the United States was in the midst of the 1860 presidential campaign. The slavery controversy had split the Democrats—who had controlled the White House for most of the past forty years—into two factions, one led by Stephen A. Douglas, the other by John C. Breckinridge of Kentucky. That May, the Republicans met for their convention in Chicago and nominated Abraham Lincoln as their candidate for the presidency. Douglass praised Lincoln's character in the pages of *Douglass' Monthly*, but affirmed that the candidate still had to prove himself. "His political life is thus far to his credit, but it is a political life of fair promise rather than one of rich heritage."[61]

IX

Over the ensuing months, Douglass came to see civil war as inevitable. As the nation passed the point of no return, he reluctantly concluded that slavery would have to be defeated not by reform but by violence. He wrote to journalist and abolitionist James Redpath of Massachusetts in June 1860:

I have little hope of the freedom of the slave by peaceful means. A long course of peaceful slaveholding has placed the slaveholders beyond the reach of moral and humane considerations. They have neither ears nor hearts for the appeals of justice and humanity. While the slave will tamely submit his neck to the yoke, his back to the lash, and his ankle to the fetter and chain, the Bible will be quoted, and learning invoked to justify slavery. The only penetrable point of a tyrant is the *fear of death*. The outcry that they make, as to the danger of having their *throats cut* is because they deserve to have them *cut*. The efforts of John Brown and his brave associates, though apparently unavailing, have done more to upset the logic and shake the security of slavery, than all other efforts in that direction for twenty years.[62]

By the end of 1860, the national crisis over slavery reached its boiling point. In November, Lincoln was elected the sixteenth president of the United States on a platform dedicated to preventing the extension of slavery. According to Douglass, the election "demonstrated the possibility of electing, if not an Abolitionist, at least an *anti-slavery reputation* to the Presidency of the United States."[63] But the South did not trust the new president. Convinced that Lincoln would endeavor not only to stop the spread of slavery into the territories but also to destroy the institution where it already existed, South Carolina seceded from the Union on December 20, 1860. On December 3, an angry Douglass reluctantly declared to an audience at Tremont Temple, Boston, that dissolving the Union would unite the North behind a war to abolish slavery in the South. "I am for a dissolution of the Union," he proclaimed, "decidedly for a dissolution of the Union!"[64]

Douglass's hope in the new president would soon be disappointed. Striving to prevent a civil war, Lincoln sought to placate the South with his First Inaugural Address on March 4, 1861. On a cold, windy day in the nation's capital, the president, while denying the right of any state to secede from the Union, also pledged that he had neither the "lawful right" nor the "inclination" to interfere with the institution of slavery in the states. Lincoln concluded his address with a conciliatory note: "We are not enemies, but friends. Though passion may have strained, it must not break our bonds of affection." His eloquence soared: "The mystic chords of memory, stretching from every battlefield, and patriot grave, to every living heart and hearthstone, all over this broad land, will yet swell the chorus of the Union, when again touched, as surely they will be, by the better angels of our nature."[65] But Frederick Douglass could not share the president's optimism. An angry Douglass accused Lincoln of "prostrating himself before the foul and withering curse of slavery." He "stands upon the same moral level with [the slaveholders], and is in no respect better than they." Readers of *Douglass' Monthly* were reminded that Lincoln took an oath to defend the Constitution of the United States which, read correctly, Douglass insisted, is an abolition document. "The American people have placed the Government in the hands of Abraham Lincoln for the next four years, and his instructions are in the Constitution."[66]

By this time, Douglass had become resigned to war: "Let the conflict come, and God speed the Right, must be the wish of every true-hearted American, as well as of that of an onlooking world."[67] By April 1861, South Carolina had been joined by ten other seceding states, which ultimately became the Confederate States of America, under a Constitution that specifically recognized slavery in the states as well as in the territories. Early that month, in a rare moment of desperation, Douglass planned a visit to the black republic of Haiti to explore the possibility of encouraging black Americans to emigrate to a land more conducive to freedom. Scheduled to sail by steamer on April 25, his trip was suddenly canceled. On April 12, 1861, six weeks after Abraham Lincoln took office, Confederate batteries opened fire upon Fort Sumter, a Union stronghold in Charleston harbor, South Carolina. The Civil War had begun.

EPILOGUE

There are principles in the Declaration of Independence which would release every slave in the world and prepare the earth for a millennium of righteousness and peace.
— *Frederick Douglass, "The Slaveholders' Rebellion"*

I

Throughout the Civil War, the Fourth of July continued to symbolize for Frederick Douglass America's failure to fulfill the ideals of the Declaration of Independence. On July 4, 1862, he delivered another speech celebrating the nation's founding, this time in the small town of Himrods Corners, in Yates County, New York. That morning, as a marching band played, a crowd of two thousand people, many having arrived by train from the nearby towns of Canandaigua and Penn Yan, assembled at a pine grove to hear Douglass speak.[1] Once again, he had an opportunity to assess the nation on the occasion of the anniversary of its independence. For him, the Fourth of July remained a solemn occasion, one demanding that the nation reflect upon the tragic contradiction of slavery in a republic. While he had criticized the Lincoln administration for not making the Civil War a war against slavery, for supporting the constitutionality of the 1850 Fugitive Slave Law, and for failing originally to enlist blacks in the Union army, the tone of Douglass's oration contrasts markedly with that of his Rochester July Fourth speech a decade before.

Delivered a year after the outbreak of the Civil War, Douglass's Himrods Corners address, entitled "The Slaveholders' Rebellion," does not reflect the profound sense of black alienation that marked his 1852

Rochester address. The tone of the Himrods Corners address is less strident, more conciliatory. Douglass's anti-slavery cause was no longer that of a minority. Having been vilified by the Garrisonians as an "apostate" ten years earlier, Douglass confessed in June 1861 a "personal, if not a little malicious pleasure" in seeing William Lloyd Garrison and his followers now embrace the Union. Douglass now saw vindicated his conviction that "the battle of freedom should be fought within the Union, and not out of it; that instead of leaving the Union on account of slavery, we should stand by the Union, and drive out slavery."[2] From the beginning, Douglass had insisted that the Civil War was a war to end slavery as well as to save the Union. He remained hopeful that America would fulfill for all persons, regardless of race, the liberty and equal rights promised by the Declaration of Independence and the protections guaranteed by the Constitution.

At Himrods Corners, Douglass sternly rebuked former President James Buchanan, whose Democratic Party had been a major bulwark of slavery. Douglass called Buchanan a "traitorous Democratic President" for doing nothing to end slavery, thus helping to make the Civil War inevitable.[3] Nevertheless, instead of the relentless "your," a censuring refrain in his 1852 July Fourth oration, Douglass now employed the inclusive "our." Presenting a united front against the slaveholders now took precedence over highlighting the nation's failings. When Douglass distinguished between "your fathers" and "our fathers," it was to emphasize the common cause that united white and black Americans seeking to defeat the rebellious slave states. In defending freedom against slavery, "we are only continuing the tremendous struggle, which your fathers and my fathers began eighty-six years ago." Douglass here paid tribute to the black heroes of the past who had fought for the nation's independence in 1776. The North, he argued, like Abraham Lincoln, was engaged in defending the Constitution against "the slaveholder's mutiny." The rebellion of the South, he insisted, was a rebellion by those who reject the Declaration of Independence and "pervert the free principles of the Constitution to slavery."[4] The Civil War was being fought to defend the freedom proclaimed in the Declaration and guaranteed by the Constitution.

Delivering his July Fourth 1862 address at Himrods Corners, Douglass continued to speak truth to America. The Civil War, he affirmed, is "the logical and inevitable result of a long and persistent course of national transgression." Reflecting on American history since the Revolution, he recalled the missed opportunities to resolve the slavery question. In 1776, the United States was young and anti-slavery sentiment high, yet slavery was not exterminated; in 1787, when the Constitution established the nation's government, the document's framers mistakenly believed that ending the slave trade after twenty years would sound the death knell for slavery. The Missouri Compromise of 1820, permitting Missouri to enter the Union as a slave state, "forms the beginning of that political current," Douglass lamented, "which has swept us on to this rebellion, and made the conflict unavoidable. . . . We became a nation of Compromisers."[5] This was followed by a series of victories for the slaveholders: the annexation of Texas, the war with Mexico, and the Kansas-Nebraska Act. Such is the sorry record of the United States.

At Himrods Corners, Douglass returned to the themes of his 1852 July Fourth Corinthian Hall oration. He praised the Declaration of Independence, the document that had inspired his struggle against slavery. "No people," he proclaimed, "ever entered upon the pathway of nations, with higher and grander ideas of justice, liberty and humanity than ourselves. There are principles in the Declaration of Independence which would release every slave in the world and prepare the earth for a millennium of righteousness and peace." Echoing his 1852 oration, Douglass again emphasized the American dilemma, the contradiction between promise and fulfillment. The "glorious truths" of the Declaration of Independence have been "craftily perverted into seeming falsehoods. Instead of treating it, as it was intended to be treated, as a full and comprehensive declaration of the equal and sacred rights of mankind, our contemptible Negro-hating and slaveholding critics have endeavored to turn it into absurdity by treating it as a declaration of the equality of man in his physical proportions and mental endowments." This perversion of the Declaration, Douglass held, was sanctioned by the Supreme Court's 1857 decision in *Dred Scott*, which declared that "'all men' means some men, and those white men." The Founders failed to abolish slavery in 1787, compromising with the evil institution. Successive generations of politicians dashed the Founders' expectation that slavery would soon be eradicated in compliance with "the principles of the Constitution and the spirit of the age." Having ignored the noble principles of the Declaration of Independence, denying human rights to black Americans, and "yielding to the extravagant pretensions set up by the slaveholder under the plausible color of State rights," America betrayed the ideals of the Founders, making the Civil War inevitable.[6] Douglass then appealed to President Lincoln, still reluctant to make the abolition of slavery the major war aim of the North, to issue an Emancipation Proclamation to end slavery once and for all. It would take Lincoln another year before acceding to Douglass's request. While actually freeing few slaves, the Emancipation Proclamation of January 1, 1863 did sound the death knell for slavery in the South, easing Douglass's criticism of Lincoln. But the Civil War did not resolve the American dilemma. While slavery was abolished, racism and inequality continue to plague the nation.

II

Douglass's prophetic view of the Civil War would be echoed by Abraham Lincoln. On March 4, 1865, five weeks before his assassination, Lincoln delivered his Second Inaugural Address. The North was on the verge of final victory. A large crowd of over thirty thousand gathered in Washington to hear the president's reflections on the carnage that had devastated the nation for the past four years. The morning had been cold and rainy. People cheered and bands played as the president rode up Pennsylvania Avenue to a wooden platform on the east front of the Capitol Building, with its recently completed iron dome, crowned with a statue of Armed Liberty. Douglass stood in the crowd facing the president. Among the crowd, standing on the balustrade above the president, was his future assassin, the actor John Wilkes Booth, a fervent supporter of slavery.

As the Civil War was now drawing to a close, Frederick Douglass remembered the mood that day in the nation's capital: "The whole proceeding was wonderfully quiet, earnest, and solemn."[7] When Abraham Lincoln was introduced, "a roar of applause shook the air, and again, and again repeated."[8] The president stepped to the platform. As he did so, the sun burst through the clouds that had covered the nation's capital since that morning. Douglass might have perceived it as an auspicious omen. He stared intently at Lincoln.

Lincoln recalled that four years ago, when he delivered his First Inaugural Address, the nation had been on the verge of a civil war between the North and the South. "Both parties," Lincoln declared, "deprecated war; but one of them would *make* war rather than let the nation survive; the other would *accept* war rather than let it perish." Then those painful four words: "And the war came."

The president then admitted what Douglass had known from the beginning: Slavery had been the cause of the war. As Douglass looked over the crowd, Lincoln declared: "These slaves constituted a peculiar and powerful interest. All knew that this interest was, somehow, the cause of the war. To strengthen, perpetuate, and extend this interest was the object for which the insurgents would rend the Union, even by war; while the government claimed no right to do more than to restrict the territorial enlargement." Striving to find some ultimate meaning in the war, Lincoln resorted to divine providence. "The Almighty has His own purposes." Quoting the Gospel of Matthew, the president drew near the end of his speech: "Woe unto the world because of offences! For it must needs be that offences come; but woe to that man by whom the offence cometh!" For years, Frederick Douglass had warned that the nation would suffer God's wrath for the evil of slavery. Now he heard Lincoln proclaim that "this terrible war" was God's punishment upon a sinful nation. Echoing Douglass's 1852 July Fourth oration, the president referred to "American Slavery," not southern slavery. The South was punished for perpetuating slavery. The North was punished for compromising with slavery. Some 620,000 Union and Confederate soldiers had lost their lives.

Lincoln expressed resignation: "Fondly do we hope—fervently do we pray—that this mighty scourge of war may speedily pass away. Yet, if God wills that it continue, until all the wealth piled by the bond-man's two hundred and fifty years of unrequited toil shall be sunk, and until every drop of blood drawn with the lash, shall be paid by another drawn with the sword, as was said three thousand years ago, so still it must be said 'the judgments of the Lord, are true and righteous altogether.'"

Lincoln ended with an eloquent peroration calling for compassion rather than vengeance towards the vanquished, a compassion stemming from the realization that the North had been as guilty as the South. "With malice towards none; with charity for all; with firmness in the right, as God gives us to see in the right, let us strive on to finish the work we are in; to bind up the nation's wounds; to care for him who shall have borne the battle, and for his widow, and his orphan—to do all which may achieve and cherish a just, and a lasting peace, among ourselves, and with all nations."[9]

After thunderous applause, Lincoln turned to Chief Justice Salmon Chase, placed his left hand on the Bible, raised his right hand, and took the oath of office. The Constitution he swore to defend would soon incorporate the Thirteenth Amendment, which went into effect on December 18, 1865. It made explicit what Frederick Douglass had argued for years could be found in the plain words of the Preamble, that slavery violated the Constitution's ethical objectives to establish justice, secure the blessings of liberty, and promote the general welfare of all Americans.

Lincoln's Second Inaugural Address stirred Frederick Douglass, who recalled that it "sounded more like a sermon than like a state paper." The occasion demanded religious eloquence. On that day, only Abraham Lincoln, the nation's representative, was capable of healing the deep wounds brought about by slavery. "I know not how many times and before how many people," said Douglass, "I have quoted these solemn words of our martyred President." When Douglass was barred from a reception held at the Executive Mansion that evening, Lincoln ordered that he be admitted, welcoming him warmly: "Here comes my friend Douglass." Lincoln asked Douglass what he thought of his inaugural. "There is no man in the country," the president declared, "whose opinion I value more than yours." Douglass responded: "Mr. Lincoln, that was a sacred effort."[10]

On April 9, 1865, the Civil War ended. General Robert E. Lee surrendered to General Ulysses S. Grant at Appomattox Court House in Virginia. On April 14, Good Friday evening, Abraham Lincoln was shot by John Wilkes Booth while attending a performance at Ford's Theater in Washington, D.C. Lincoln died the following morning.

III

Years later, Frederick Douglass had an opportunity to assess Abraham Lincoln from the perspective of black Americans. On April 14, 1876, Douglass was invited to speak on Lincoln in the nation's capital. The challenge he faced would be similar to that he met at Corinthian Hall on July 5, 1852: to deliver a speech that both praised what should be praised and criticized what had to be criticized. The occasion was the unveiling of the Freedman's Memorial Monument to the former president in Lincoln Park, Washington, D.C.[11] A twelve-foot-high bronze and granite statue by Thomas Ball, mounted on a ten-foot pedestal, shows a standing Lincoln holding the Emancipation Proclamation in his right hand with his left hand held over a slave, rising from his knees, with his wrist shackles broken. While many approved of the statue, seeing the slave looking upward to accept the gift of freedom, Douglass later expressed misgivings, saying that rather than depicting a black slave on his knees, "a more manly attitude would have been indicative of freedom."[12] The monument had been initiated by black Americans, former slaves, and was largely financed through their contributions.

Douglass, now almost sixty years old and with white hair, was the featured speaker on this day to honor the martyred president. By this time, Lincoln had assumed the stature of an iconic figure, elevated into the pantheon of American heroes. Ever since the Civil War, many blacks viewed Lincoln as their Moses. Indeed, Lincoln was hailed as the Great Emancipator. On the eve of the war, there existed approximately one-half million free blacks in the North, and four million slaves in the South. To many freed slaves, Lincoln was "Father Abe," who delivered them from bondage. On three occasions Douglass and Lincoln met at the White House, and they had grown to respect each other. When Lincoln was assassinated, Douglass delivered a stirring eulogy for the martyred president in Rochester's City Hall on April 15, 1865. Seated on the platform with Douglass in Washington, D.C. in 1876 were President Grant and his cabinet, justices of the Supreme Court, diplomats, and many members of the Senate and the House. A joint resolution of Congress made April 14 a national holiday. A parade had proceeded down Washington, D.C.'s Pennsylvania Avenue to the Capitol, and continued to Lincoln Park. A large crowd, black and white, had gathered in the park. Black Americans waited in anticipation for a speech that reflected their admiration for the assassinated president. With rapt attention, the audience listened to a reading of the Emancipation Proclamation. Douglass later recalled that the occasion, bringing him into "mental communication with a greater number of the influential and distinguished men of the country than any I had before known," ranked "among the most interesting incidents of my life."[13]

In honor of Lincoln, Douglass chose to begin his address by praising the president. "We stand today at the national center to perform
something like a national act—an act which is to go into history." A
great celebration attended by blacks and whites, he notes, would not
have been possible twenty years earlier when the storm over slavery
ravaged the nation. "That we are here in peace today is a compliment
and a credit to American civilization, and a prophecy of still greater national enlightenment and progress in the future." With a rhetorical
tribute to Lincoln's Second Inaugural Address—"with malice toward
none, with charity for all"—Douglass indicated that he would not
dwell on old injuries: "I refer to the past not in malice, for this day is
not a day for malice."[14] Like Lincoln, Douglass had sought to heal the
nation's wounds after the terrible years of civil war. Instead of recrimi-
nations, he would focus on "the glorious change which has come to
both our white fellow-citizens and ourselves, and to congratulate all
upon the contrast between now and then." He affirmed: "We are here
to express . . . our grateful sense of the vast, high and preeminent services rendered to ourselves, to our race, to our country, and to the whole
world by Abraham Lincoln." Black Americans, Douglass explained,
have chosen this day to dedicate a monument to "the exalted character
and great works of Abraham Lincoln, the first martyr President of the
United States."[15]

While honoring the memory of Lincoln, Douglass expressed his
honest reservations in a manner that would not insult the occasion. He
would not dishonor the memory of the president. But he had to express how black people should view Lincoln. Given that the day was
one of consecration, it would have been easier for Douglass to give a
speech of unmitigated adulation. But as a representative of black
America, he felt compelled to offer his people an honest assessment of
Lincoln's legacy. His speech would reflect the same profound ambivalence about the president seen in his speeches and writings prior to
and during the Civil War. Douglass shared the frustration of other
abolitionists who campaigned to have the president make the Civil
War a war to end slavery. Yet Lincoln had hesitated. To some, it
seemed that he would not take action on his own to end slavery. He
had to be compelled. Indeed, during the Civil War, a disheartened
Douglass wrote that as a statesman, Lincoln had virtually set this rule:
"*Do evil by choice, right from necessity.*"[16]

While Lincoln believed that slavery was constitutionally protected, he agreed with Free Soilers and the Republican Party that the federal government had the legal authority to prevent the extension of slavery in the territories. Like the framers of the Constitution, he hoped that if contained, slavery would eventually die a natural death. When the *Dred Scott* decision in effect legalized slavery throughout the nation in 1857, Lincoln joined the chorus of protest, pledging to support efforts to overturn the decision. Nevertheless, when the conflict between the North and the South led to Civil War, Lincoln declared that his primary objective was not the abolition of slavery, but the preservation of the Union. His sentiment was made public in a famous letter to Horace Greeley, editor of the *New York Tribune,* on August 22, 1862: "My paramount object in this struggle is to save the Union, and is *not* either to save or to destroy slavery. . . . What I do about slavery, and the colored race, I do because I believe it helps to preserve the Union."[17] In contrast, Douglass would not have emphasized one over the other, but rather aimed to accomplish both, that is, to abolish slavery within the context of the Constitution and to preserve the Union. In the antebellum years, Douglass's progressive goals made him, in the words of Eric Sundquist, "the truer 'son,' a truer inheritor than Lincoln of the flawed yet redeemable ideals of the Revolution."[18]

Continuing his Lincoln Park oration, Douglass turned to the question of how black Americans ought to regard the president: "We fully comprehend the relation of Abraham Lincoln both to ourselves and to the white people of the United States. . . . It must be admitted, truth compels me to admit, even here in the presence of the monument we have erected to his memory, Abraham Lincoln was not, in the fullest sense of the word, either our man or our model." Douglass knew that Lincoln believed slavery to be immoral. "As I would not be a slave," declared Lincoln in 1858, "so I would not be a master."[19] In his well-known letter to Albert G. Hodges on April 4, 1864, the president proclaimed: "If slavery is not wrong, nothing is wrong. I cannot remember when I did not think so, and feel." Then came the proviso: "And yet I have never understood that the Presidency conferred upon me an unrestricted right to act officially upon this judgment and feeling. It was in the oath I took that I would, to the best of my ability, preserve, protect, and defend the Constitution of the United States."[20] Lincoln believed that his personal morality was restrained by his constitutional duty. He never grasped the cogency of Douglass's argument that slavery violated the ethical objectives of the Constitution's Preamble.

Douglass could not ignore Lincoln's failings in his 1876 oration. Speaking to the white people in the audience, he declared: "You are the children of Abraham Lincoln." Speaking to the black people in the audience, he confessed: "We are at best only his stepchildren; children by adoption, children by forces of circumstances and necessity." While Lincoln saved the country for white people, "he delivered us from a bondage." Great as Lincoln was, he never believed in racial equality. Douglass explained: "In his interest, in his associations, in his habits of thought, and in his prejudices, he was a white man. He was preeminently the white man's President, entirely devoted to the welfare of the white man. He was ready and willing at any time during the first years of his administration to deny, postpone, and sacrifice the rights of humanity in the colored people to promote the welfare of the white people of this country."[21]

As the nation paused to give honor to a revered president, Douglass was saddened by the limitations of Lincoln's legacy. Whereas Douglass had taken the lead on the problem of slavery, Lincoln had merely followed. The president had not envisioned the America, with equal rights for all, blacks and whites, that Douglass had sought to make a reality. Black people could never forget that they had been enslaved by a nation that had been founded upon freedom. Douglass could not forget that Lincoln believed that preserving the Union was more important than abolishing slavery. But the Union could not have continued to survive with slavery. Douglass could not forget that Lincoln began his administration by proclaiming that he had neither the authority under the Constitution, nor the personal desire, to abolish slavery in the states. Douglass could not forget that Lincoln, despite his moral condemnation of slavery, was never an abolitionist. Douglass could not forget that to a large extent, the emancipation of the slaves was forced upon Lincoln as a means to save the Union. Douglass could not forget that throughout most of his political life, Lincoln supported efforts to colonize freed slaves in Africa or Latin America, thus removing them from the land of their birth. Douglass could not forget that Lincoln supported the constitutionality of the Fugitive Slave Law. Douglass could not forget that the Emancipation Proclamation of January 1, 1863, while an inspiration to blacks, actually freed only a portion of the slaves, for it officially freed only the slaves in the rebelling states. It did not apply to the border states or to areas under Union control. As Douglass later wrote, the Emancipation Proclamation "only abolished slavery where it did not exist, and left it intact where it did exist."[22] He could not forget that Lincoln rescinded anti-slavery General John C. Frémont's August 1861 order emancipating the slaves of Missouri. Douglass could not forget that Lincoln was dilatory in allowing blacks to enter the Union army to fight for freedom; yet, by the end of the war, more than 250,000 blacks had fought in the Union army, contributing significantly to the defeat of the Confederacy. Douglass could not forget that while Lincoln believed slavery to be immoral, he catered to popular prejudice during his campaign for the Senate in white supremacist Illinois in 1858. Lincoln assured an audience that he opposed not only political and social equality between the white and black races, but also blacks voting, holding political office, and intermarrying with whites.[23]

But Douglass recognized that, under Lincoln's administration, blacks made progress. The Emancipation Proclamation, although it did not go far enough, turned the tide against slavery. Douglass would never "forget the outburst of joy and thanksgiving that rent the air when the lightening brought us the emancipation proclamation. In that happy hour we forgot all delay. . . . And we were thenceforward willing to allow the President all the latitude of time, phraseology, and every honorable device that statesmanship might require for the achievement of a great and beneficent measure of liberty and progress."[24] Douglass's experience of Lincoln's leadership during the Civil War led him to reexamine the political difficulties faced by the president in striving to save the Union. Political necessity had compelled Lincoln to make the preservation of the Union a more important goal of the Civil War than the abolition of slavery. Douglass declared: "Had he put the abolition of slavery before the salvation of the Union, he would have inevitably driven from him a powerful class of the American people and rendered resistance to rebellion impossible." Douglass realized that if Lincoln had taken a more aggressive stand against slavery at the beginning of the Civil War, he would have risked losing the support of many whites in the North, Democrats who refused to view the conflict as a war against slavery, in addition to the loyal border slave states—Missouri, Kentucky, Maryland, and Delaware—who were willing to fight for the preservation of the

Union, but not for the abolition of slavery.[25] Lincoln's "great mission," Douglass argued, was both to save the Union and to abolish "the sin of slavery." Yet to accomplish one or both of these ends, he conceded, the president had to "have the earnest sympathy and the powerful cooperation of his loyal fellow-countrymen. Without this primary and essential condition of success his efforts must have been vain and utterly fruitless." In words that could have been addressed to William Lloyd Garrison, a moral absolutist who would rather sink a ship than reform it, Douglass argued: "Viewed from the genuine abolition ground, Mr. Lincoln seemed tardy, cold, dull, and indifferent; but measuring him by the sentiment of his country, a sentiment he was bound as a statesman to consult, he was swift, zealous, radical, and determined."[26]

Let history judge Lincoln, Douglass intoned. "Whatever else in this world may be partial, unjust, and uncertain, time, time is impartial, just, and certain in its action. . . . The honest and comprehensive statesman, clearly discerning the needs of his country, and earnestly endeavoring to do his whole duty, though covered and blistered with reproaches, may safely leave his course to the silent judgment of time." Douglass acknowledged that the president had to consider the needs of the entire nation, "his whole duty," in determining his policy. Steering the ship of state through the most perilous waters, Lincoln was attacked from all sides. "Few great public men have ever been the victims of fiercer denunciation than Abraham Lincoln was during his administration. . . . He was assailed by the Abolitionists; he was assailed by the slaveholders; he was assailed by the men who were for peace at any price; he was assailed by those who were for a more vigorous prosecution of the war; and he was bitterly assailed for making the war an abolition cause."[27] Douglass had come to see Lincoln in a better light, cognizant of the important distinction in politics between the "is" and the "ought." Political limitations had constrained the president. Douglass thus placed Lincoln in the context of his times, the political circumstances that were the reality of antebellum America. Douglass affirmed: "The judgment of the present hour is, that taking him for all in all, measuring the tremendous magnitude of the work before him, considering the necessary means to ends, and surveying the end from the beginning, infinite wisdom has seldom sent any man into the world better fitted for his mission than Abraham Lincoln."[28]

Douglass's view of Lincoln as a political realist would be endorsed by the modern black historians Benjamin Quarles and John Hope Franklin, who saw the president as a practical politician. Reviewing Lincoln's record on the question of slavery, Quarles concludes: "In running the country, as Lincoln knew, the give-and-take of compromise was essential. . . . Daily the Lincoln of the White House had to make choices between unpleasant alternatives. Perfectionism could be practiced only by men not burdened."[29] Franklin wrote that "Lincoln was a practical man, a realist in the best sense of the term. . . . He subscribed to the view that the central idea behind the national political philosophy was the equality of men. But practical man that he was, he doubted that the monstrous evil of slavery could be dealt with summarily."[30] Douglass admitted that as president, Lincoln did as much as he could. "Though he loved Caesar less than Rome, though the Union was more to him than our freedom or our future, under his wise and beneficent rule we saw ourselves gradually lifted from the depths of slavery to the heights of liberty and manhood."[31] Douglass understood that politics, especially in a democracy with a multitude of interests, is the art of achieving the possible.

IV

Frederick Douglass has earned a place among the great intellectual luminaries of the United States. He demonstrated extraordinary fortitude, maintaining his integrity in the face of great opposition during one of the nation's most trying periods. American history knows no better representative of the power of the word wielded on behalf of human rights. Douglass was the foremost advocate of the Declaration of Independence and the Constitution when many sought to betray the fundamental values of the nation's Founders. Applying a moral lens to the nation's founding documents, he did more than any person of his age to call attention to the American dilemma. On the Fourth of July 1852, when most Americans gave mere lip service to liberal ideals, Douglass held the nation accountable, challenging it to fulfill its democratic promise. When many abolitionists were prepared to forsake the Constitution as a slave document, he perceived its powerful antislavery potential, offering a radical interpretation of the document in light of the ethical principles of the Declaration of Independence. If the original, unamended Constitution did endorse slavery, it contradicted not only the Declaration of Independence but also its own Preamble. Douglass refused to view the United States Constitution as a Janus-faced document, supporting both liberty and slavery. The Constitution, as he proclaimed in his momentous 1852 July Fourth oration, was a "glorious liberty document." The Constitution did not have to be amended to abolish slavery; it merely had to be implemented. The Constitution and the Declaration of Independence, Douglass believed, embody the aspirations to liberty, equal rights, and human dignity that inspired the nation's Founders. While these aspirations have not been fully realized in fact, they continue to serve as the standard by which each generation should be judged.

In 1894, a year before Douglass's death, a young black man sought his counsel on how he could make the best of his life. Douglass responded: "Agitate, Agitate, Agitate."[32] He had composed his own fitting epitaph. When slavery deprived him of human dignity, he seized his freedom, creating an identity for himself by his autonomous actions and by sharing the inspirational story of his life with his fellow Americans. Condemned to silence by slavery, he found his voice, one that would express the sentiments and aspirations of millions of black Americans. He inspired the downtrodden, provoked the complacent, and shamed the wicked. He understood the potential of oratory to change the world. If he could inspire people to think differently by changing their perceptions, and get them to look at themselves honestly, he could get them to act differently. When the majority of the nation tolerated slavery, Douglass became a crusader for human rights, demanding the immediate abolition of slavery, not only in the federal territories but also in the South. When Congress passed the Fugitive Slave Law of 1850, effectively nationalizing slavery, Douglass raised his voice in protest. When Congress passed the Kansas-Nebraska Act in 1854, conceding more territory to slavery, Douglass raised his voice in protest. When the Supreme Court ruled in 1857 in *Dred Scott* that blacks were not citizens but mere property, Douglass raised his voice in protest. When many, not only in the South but also in the North, argued that the Constitution protected slavery, Douglass raised his voice in protest. In 1860, on the eve of the Civil War, he had presented the case for an anti-slavery Constitution in a major address in Glasgow, Scotland.

Frederick Douglass devoted his life to the struggle to make the liberty and equality principles of the Declaration of Independence a reality for all Americans, regardless of race or gender. The Fourth of July, he insisted, should not be a day of complacent self-congratulation, but a day in which all Americans reflect on how far they have come in realizing the noble ideals of the nation's Founders. An apostle of freedom and a tireless agitator, Douglass stood like a titan among his contemporaries. He was the conscience of America. When many remained silent, he spoke against oppression, proclaiming his abolitionist and integrationist message at home and abroad. With a single-minded drive, he confronted power—the slaveholders, the slave states, even the federal government. His spirit remained indomitable. When many vacillated, he was committed. When many despaired, he never lost hope. He was determined to redeem the soul of America.

Frederick Douglass was quintessentially the voice of black America. In writing his three autobiographies, he did more than create his own identity, more than gain recognition as the foremost black American orator, and more than articulate for blacks their demand that the American dilemma be resolved. He achieved much more. He succeeded against the odds by inscribing himself in the history of the nation. Frederick Douglass, the former slave, changed the course of American history. Throughout the years prior to the Civil War, he employed the full power of his oratory to speak the truth to America, unleashing a storm of angry reproach against the institution of slavery. He was the nation's gadfly. He directed his wrath against the southern slaveholders who perpetuated the institution. He directed his wrath against southerners who, while not owning slaves, nevertheless defended slavery. He directed his wrath against northerners who compromised with slavery. He directed his wrath against the federal government for failing to abolish slavery. He directed his wrath against a hypocritical white church for justifying slavery and preaching submission. Until slavery was eradicated, America had no right to celebrate freedom on the Fourth of July. And in his wrath, Frederick Douglass was majestic.

NOTES

PROLOGUE

1. Corinthian Hall, constructed by William Reynolds on Corinthian Street in Rochester, New York, opened in 1849. It was the setting for many lectures, orations, banquets, exhibitions, fairs, women's rights meetings, and music events. Speakers included Daniel Webster, Susan B. Anthony, and Ralph Waldo Emerson. Jenny Lind sang there in 1852. William H. Seward, the future Secretary of State under Abraham Lincoln, delivered his famous "Irrepressible Conflict" speech in Corinthian Hall on October 25, 1858.

2. Douglass's speech, originally published as a pamphlet, entitled *Oration, Delivered in Corinthian Hall, Rochester, July 5th, 1852* became better known by its central question: "What to the Slave is the Fourth of July?" Douglass's important speeches were published in his newspapers, giving them a wide circulation. Most of Douglass's speeches cited in this book are from Philip Foner, *The Life and Writings of Frederick Douglass*, 5 volumes (New York: International Publishers, 1950–1975). Hereafter cited as *Life and Writings*.

3. Gunnar Myrdal, *An American Dilemma: The Negro Problem and Modern Democracy*, revised edition (New York: Harper and Row, Publishers, 1962). First edition, 1944.

4. *Life and Times*, 938. In Frederick Douglass, *Autobiographies: Narrative of the Life of Frederick Douglass, an American Slave* (1845); *My Bondage and My Freedom* (1855); and *Life and Times of Frederick Douglass* (Boston, 1893; first published in 1881). Ed. Henry Louis Gates, Jr. New York: The Library of America, 1994. Page citations to Douglass's three autobiographies will be to this edition.

5. Gregory Stephens, "Frederick Douglass' Multiracial Abolitionism: 'Antagonistic Cooperation' and 'Redeemable Ideals' in the July 5 Speech," *Communication Studies* 48 (1997), 176.

6. *Herald of Freedom* (Concord, New Hampshire), December 10, 1841. Quoted in George Asher Hinshaw, "A Rhetorical Analysis of the Speeches of Frederick Douglass During and After the Civil War." Doctoral dissertation, University of Nebraska, 1972, 36.

7. John W. Blassingame, ed., *The Frederick Douglass Papers*, 5 volumes (New Haven: Yale University Press, 1979–92), 1: xxxv, lxix. Hereafter cited as *Frederick Douglass Papers*.

8. Lerone Bennett, Jr., *Before the Mayflower* (New York: Penguin Books, sixth revised edition, 1993), 156.

9. Philip S. Foner and Robert James Branham, eds., *Lift Every Voice: African American Oratory 1787–1900* (Tuscaloosa: University of Alabama Press, 1998), 243.

10. James Monroe Gregory, *Frederick Douglass, the Orator* (New York: Thomas Y. Cromwell, 1893), 89–92.

11. Quoted in William L. Andrews and William S. McFeely, eds., *Narrative of the Life of Frederick Douglass, An American Slave, Written By Himself.* Norton Critical Edition (W.W. Norton and Company, 1997), 130.

CHAPTER 1: FREDERICK DOUGLASS AND THE FOURTH OF JULY

1. The Rochester Ladies' Society was founded on August 20, 1851. Susan Farley Porter was president, Julia Griffiths was secretary, and Maria G. Porter was treasurer. By March 1852, the Society had nineteen members. Devoted to the immediate abolition of slavery, the Society was instrumental in raising funds for the abolition movement, sponsoring lectures and bazaars and providing financial support for fugitive slaves escaping to Canada.

2. See Howard H. Martin, "The Fourth of July Oration," *The Quarterly Journal of Speech* 44 (1958), 393–401.

3. Benjamin Quarles, *Black Mosaic: Essays in Afro-American History and Historiography* (Amherst: University of Massachusetts Press, 1988), 98.

4. Leonard I. Sweet, "The Fourth of July and Black Americans in the Nineteenth Century: Northern Leadership Opinion within the Context of the Black Experience," *Journal of Negro History* 61 (1976), 259.

5. Philip Foner, ed., *We, the Other People: Alternative Declarations of Independence by Labor Groups, Farmers, Women's Rights Advocates, Socialists, and Blacks, 1829–1975* (Urbana: University of Illinois Press, 1976), 14–15.

6. James Oliver Horton and Lois E. Horton, "A Federal Assault: African Americans and the Impact of the Fugitive Slave Law of 1850." In Paul Finkelman, *Slavery and the Law* (Lanham, MD: Rowman and Littlefield Publishers, Inc., 2002), 146.

7. Patrick Rael, *Black Identity and Black Protest in the Antebellum North* (Chapel Hill: University of North Carolina Press, 2002), 78.

8. *Narrative*, 16.

9. *My Bondage and My Freedom*, 217–18.

10. *Narrative*, 38.

11. *My Bondage and My Freedom*, 235.

12. Henry Louis Gates, Jr., Introduction to *Narrative of the Life of Frederick Douglass, An American Slave: Written By Himself* (New York: Laurel-Bantam Doubleday Dell, 1997), xiii.

13. *Narrative*, 42; *My Bondage and My Freedom*, 226.

14. *My Bondage and My Freedom*, 233. Emphases in original.

15. Ibid., 362–63.

16. *Frederick Douglass Papers*, 1:3.

17. *Narrative*, 96.

18. *My Bondage and My Freedom*, 364.
19. *Narrative*, 3–4.
20. *My Bondage and My Freedom*, 337. The passage is repeated verbatim in *Life and Times*, 634. A briefer version is in the *Narrative*, 83–84.
21. *Life and Writings*, I, 155. This speech was appended to Douglass's second autobiography, *My Bondage and My Freedom*.
22. Houston A. Baker, Jr., *The Journey Back: Issues in Black Literature and Criticism* (Chicago: University of Chicago Press, 1980), 32.
23. Waldo E. Martin, Jr., *The Mind of Frederick Douglass* (Chapel Hill: University of North Carolina Press, 1984), 25.
24. James Olney, "Founding Fathers, Frederick Douglass and Booker T. Washington." In *Slavery and the Literary Imagination*, ed. Deborah E. McDowell and Arnold Rampersad (Baltimore: Johns Hopkins University Press, 1989), 7.
25. *Narrative*, 102. Emphasis in original.
26. Foner, *The Story of American Freedom*, 89.
27. Benjamin Quarles, *Black Mosaic*, 92. The Liberty Bell's inscription is taken from the Book of Leviticus 25:10.
28. Benjamin Quarles, *Black Abolitionists* (New York: Oxford University Press, 1969), 25.
29. Ibid., 23.
30. William S. McFeely, *Frederick Douglass* (New York: W. W. Norton, 1991), 110.
31. Frederic May Holland, *Frederick Douglass: The Colored Orator* (New York: Funk and Wagnalls, 1891), 115.
32. *Life and Writings*, I, 138.
33. *Frederick Douglass Papers*, 1:128.
34. *Life and Writings*, I, 127.
35. Ibid., 133.
36. Ibid., 127–28.
37. *The North Star*, consisting of four pages of seven columns each, included texts of anti-slavery abolition speeches, delivered either in Congress or at abolition meetings; reports of anti-slavery meetings, national, state, local, and foreign; Douglass's editorials; news; correspondence; and a page devoted to book reviews, poetry, and fiction.
38. Benjamin Quarles, *Frederick Douglass*, 70–71.
39. Eugene E. Du Bois, *The City of Frederick Douglass: Rochester's African-American People and Places*, third edition (Landmark Society of Western New York, 1998), 13.
40. *My Bondage and My Freedom*, 389.
41. *Life and Writings*, V, 69. Italics in original.
42. Ibid., I, 281.
43. Ibid., 282.
44. *Life and Times*, 709.
45. Robert T. Oliver, *History of Public Speaking in America* (Boston: Allyn and Bacon, 1965), 249.
46. *Frederick Douglass Papers*, 1: xxv.
47. *Life and Writings*, V, 82.

48. George Whitfield, "Frederick Douglass: Negro Abolitionist," *Today's Speech* 11 (1963), 7.
49. See, for example, Garrison's July Fourth Address, 1838, in *Forerunners of Black Power: The Rhetoric of Abolition*, ed. Ernest G. Borman. (Englewood Cliffs, N.J.: Prentice-Hall, 1971), 96–103.
50. *Life and Writings*, II, 132–33. Italics in original.
51. Ibid., 139.
52. *Frederick Douglass Papers*, 1: xxii.
53. Gregory Clark and S. Michael Halloran, *Oratorical Culture in Nineteenth-Century America: Transformations in the Theory and Practice of Rhetoric* (Carbondale and Edwardsville: Southern Illinois University Press, 1993), 15.
54. Hugh Blair, *Lectures on Rhetoric and Belles Lettres*, seventh American edition (New York: George Long, 1817), 235–36.
55. *Frederick Douglass Papers*, 1: xxviii.
56. Ibid., xlii.
57. Ibid., lxiv–lxiv.
58. Ibid., 181–82.
59. Ibid., 182.
60. John W. Blassingame notes that Douglass often began his speeches by declaring that he was unfit for the occasion, a common nineteenth-century rhetorical technique designed to create a rapport with the audience. *Frederick Douglass Papers*, 1:xxx.
61. The degree to which slavery inculcated subservient behavior has been a source of contention among scholars. In *Slavery: A Problem in American Institutional and Intellectual Life*, third edition (Chicago: University of Chicago Press, 1976), Stanley Elkins argued that slavery created the childlike, dependent, deferential, content "Sambo." This thesis provoked many challenges. See, for example, John W. Blassingame, *The Slave Community: Plantation Life in the Antebellum South* (New York: Oxford University Press, 1972); Eugene D. Genovese, *Roll, Jordan, Roll: The World the Slaves Made* (New York: Random House, 1974); Herbert G. Gutman, *The Black Family in Slavery and Freedom, 1750–1925* (New York: Pantheon, 1976); Ann J. Lane, ed., *The Debate Over Slavery: Stanley Elkins and His Critics* (Urbana: University of Illinois Press, 1971). While many slaves were psychologically harmed by slavery, Frederick Douglass exemplifies those who refused to allow the brutal system to destroy their spirit and dignity.

Chapter 2. Narrating America's Revolutionary Past

1. *Life and Writings*, II, 182.
2. In a speech occupying thirty printed pages, Douglass employs the accusatory pronoun "your," "your fathers," "your nation," "your independence," "your freedom," "your Christianity," etc., seventy-eight times, and "you" thirty-four times. Throughout our text, "your" will be emphasized whenever it appears in Douglass's July Fourth speech.

3. W. E. B. Du Bois, *The Souls of Black Folk*. Norton Critical Edition. Ed. Henry Louis Gates, Jr., and Terri Hume Oliver (New York: W.W. Norton, 1999), 11.

4. Jacqueline Bacon, "'Do you Understand Your Own Language?' Revolutionary Topoi in the Rhetoric of African-American Abolitionists," *Rhetoric Society Quarterly* 28 (1998), 55–75, at 57.

5. William Lee Miller, *Arguing About Slavery: John Quincy Adams and the Great Battle in the United States Congress* (New York: Vintage Books, 1995), 16–21.

6. Thomas Jefferson, *Notes on the State of Virginia*, Query XVIII, in *Jefferson: Writings*, ed. Merrill D. Peterson (New York: Library of America, 1984), 289.

7. Bernard Bailyn, *The Ideological Origins of the American Revolution* (Cambridge: Harvard University Press, 1967), 232–246. On the contradiction between the Declaration of Independence and slavery, see also William M. Wiecek, *The Guarantee Clause of the U.S. Constitution* (Ithaca: Cornell University Press, 1972), 137–40.

8. David Walker, *Appeal to the Coloured Citizens of the World*, ed. Peter P. Hinks (University Park: Pennsylvania State University Press, 2000), 78.

9. *Life and Writings*, II, 182.

10. See Albert J. Raboteau, "African-Americans, Exodus, and the American Israel," in *African-American Christianity: Essays in History*, ed. Paul E. Johnson (Berkeley: University of California Press, 1994), 1–17; and Eddie S. Glaude, Jr., *Exodus!: Religion, Race, and Nation in Early Nineteenth-Century Black America* (Chicago: University of Chicago Press, 2000).

11. Gordon Wood, *The Radicalism of the American Revolution* (New York: Alfred A. Knopf, 1988), 336.

12. Robert N. Bellah, "Civil Religion in America," *Daedalus* 96 (1967), 1–21.

13. James Jasinski, "Rearticulating History in Epideictic Discourse: Frederick Douglass's "The Meaning of the Fourth of July to the Negro,'" in *Rhetoric and Political Culture in Nineteenth-Century America*, ed. Thomas W. Benson (East Lansing: Michigan State University Press, 1997), 71–89.

14. Manning Marable, *Black Leadership* (New York: Columbia University Press, 1998), 4.

15. Jasinski, "Rearticulating History," 84.

16. Winthrop D. Jordan, *White Over Black: American Attitudes Toward the Negro, 1550–1812* (Chapel Hill: University of North Carolina Press, 1968), 342. Italics in original.

17. *Life and Writings*, II, 182–83.

18. Ibid., 183–84.

19. Ibid., 184–85. Emphases added.

20. Pauline Maier, Introduction, *The Declaration of Independence and the Constitution of the United States* (New York: Bantam Books, 1998), 1.

21. *Life and Writings*, V, 36.

22. Ibid., 401. Douglass and the abolitionists were not alone in regarding the Declaration of Independence instead of the Constitution as America's primary founding document. Daniel Webster, Abraham Lincoln, and Chief Justice Joseph Story, among others, shared this view. As Lincoln declared in his First Inaugural Address, "The Union is much older than the Constitution." See Garry Wills, *Lincoln at Gettysburg: The Words That Remade America* (New York: Simon and Schuster, 1992), 130–33. For Lincoln's assumption that the nation was founded in 1776, not 1787, see Harry Jaffa, "Abraham Lincoln," in *Encyclopedia of the Constitution,* ed. Leonard W. Levy, Kenneth L. Karst, and Dennis J. Mahoney (New York: Macmillan, 1986), Vol. 3, 1162–63; see also George P. Fletcher, *Our Secret Constitution: How Lincoln Redefined American Democracy* (Oxford: Oxford University Press, 2001), 36.

23. Dennis J. Mahoney, "The Declaration of Independence as a Constitutional Document," in *The Framing and Ratification of the Constitution,* ed. Leonard W. Levy and Dennis J. Mahoney (New York: Macmillan, 1987), 54–55.

24. Jacobus tenBroeck, *Equal Under Law* (originally published as *The Antislavery Origins of the Fourteenth Amendment* (1955) new enlarged edition (New York: Collier Books, 1965), 85, n.20.

25. Charles L. Black, Jr., *A New Birth of Freedom: Human Rights, Named and Unnamed* (New Haven: Yale University Press, 1997), 8–9.

26. Mahoney, "The Declaration of Independence," 54.

27. Ibid., 65, 67–68.

28. *Life and Writings,* II, 185.

29. Lincoln, "Speech at Galesburg, Illinois, October 7, 1858," in Don E. Fehrenbacher, ed., *Lincoln: Speeches and Writings: 1832–1858* (New York: Library of America, 1989), 702.

30. Lincoln, "Speech on the Kansas-Nebraska Act at Peoria, Illinois, October 16, 1854," in Fehrenbacher, *Lincoln: Speeches and Writings: 1832–1858,* 328, 340.

31. Lincoln, "Speech at Independence Hall, Philadelphia, Pennsylvania, February 22, 1861," in Fehrenbacher, ed. *Abraham Lincoln: Speeches and Writings: 1859–1865* (New York: Library of America, 1989), 213.

32. Roy P. Basler, ed., *The Collected Works of Abraham Lincoln* (New Brunswick, N.J.: Rutgers University Press, 1953), IV; 168–69 (ca. January 1861). Italics in original; see Allen C. Guelzo, "Apple of Gold in a Picture of Silver: The Constitution and Liberty," in *The Lincoln Enigma,* ed. Gabor Boritt (Oxford: Oxford University Press, 2001), 86–107.

33. Robert Lowell, "On the Gettysburg Address," in *Lincoln and the Gettysburg Address: Commemorative Papers,* ed. Allan Nevins (Urbana: University of Illinois Press, 1964), 89.

34. *Life and Writings,* II, 307–308. Italics in original.

35. Ibid., V, 306.

36. Ibid., III, 45.

37. Ibid., I, 321.

38. Philip S. Foner, ed., *Frederick Douglass on Women's Rights* (New York: Da Capo Press, 1992), Introduction, 14, 41.

39. Wilson Jeremiah Moses, *Black Messiahs and Uncle Toms: Social and Literary Manipulations of a Religious Myth* (University Park: Pennsylvania State University Press, 1982), 31.

40. David Howard-Pitney, *The Afro-American Jeremiad: Appeals for Justice in America* (Philadelphia: Temple University Press, 1990), 8.

41. Moses, *Black Messiahs and Uncle Toms*, 30–48; and Howard-Pitney, *The Afro-American Jeremiad*.

42. *Life and Writings*, II, 214.

43. Ibid., 185.

44. Ibid., 186.

45. Ibid., 186–87.

46. William E. Cain, ed., *William Lloyd Garrison and the Fight Against Slavery: Selections from the Liberator* (Boston: Bedford Books, St. Martin's Press, 1995), 24.

47. Ibid., 49.

48. Nathan Irvin Huggins, *Slave and Citizen: The Life of Frederick Douglass* (New York: Longman, 1980), 50.

49. James Brewer Stewart, *Holy Warriors: The Abolitionists and American Slavery* (New York: Hill and Wang, 1976), 125; and Howard-Pitney, *The Afro-American Jeremiad*, 33. See also Leon F. Litwack, *North of Slavery: The Negro in the Free States: 1790–1860* (Chicago: University of Chicago Press, 1961).

50. *Life and Writings*, II, 187.

CHAPTER 3: DENOUNCING AMERICA'S PRESENT

1. *Life and Writings*, II, 188.

2. Ibid. The italics for "yours" and "mine" are in original. Other italics added.

3. Ibid., 189–90.

4. Ibid., 190.

5. Ibid., 190–91.

6. David A. J. Richards, *Conscience and the Constitution: History, Theory, and Law of the Reconstruction Amendments* (Princeton: Princeton University Press, 1993), 61.

7. *Life and Writings*, II, 191.

8. Ibid., 191–92. Italics in original.

9. Ibid., 289.

10. Ibid., 295.

11. Ibid., 192.

12. Ibid.

13. *Frederick Douglass Papers*, 2: 6, 61. Italics in original.

14. Ibid., 103.

15. *Life and Writings*, II, 193–95.

16. On the effect of the Fugitive Slave Law of 1850, see Merton L. Dillon, *The Abolitionists: The Growth of a Dissenting Minority* (DeKalb: Northern Illinois University Press, 1974), 175–98.

17. The eleven free states were Massachusetts, Vermont, New Hampshire, Rhode Island, Connecticut, New York, New Jersey, Pennsylvania,

Ohio, Indiana, and Illinois; the eleven slave states were Virginia, Delaware, Maryland, North Carolina, South Carolina, Georgia, Kentucky, Tennessee, Alabama, Mississippi, and Louisiana.

18. *Life and Writings*, II, 277, 279.
19. Bernard Schwartz, *A History of the Supreme Court* (New York: Oxford University Press, 1993), 107.
20. Thoreau, "Civil Disobedience," in Henry David Thoreau, *Civil Disobedience and Other Essays* (New York: Dover Publications, Inc., 1993), 3. Italics in original.
21. *Life and Writings*, II, 70.
22. Calhoun, "Speech on the Introduction of His Resolution on the Slave Question [February 19, 1847]," in *Union and Liberty: The Political Philosophy of John C. Calhoun*, ed. Ross M. Lence (Indianapolis: Liberty Fund, 1992), 516.
23. McPherson, *Ordeal by Fire*, Vol. I, *The Coming of War*, second edition (New York: McGraw-Hill, 1993), 50.
24. Ibid., 110.
25. Calhoun, "Speech on the Oregon Bill [June 27, 1848]," in Lence, *Union and Liberty*, 565–70.
26. Quoted in Paul Finkelman, "The Centrality of Slavery in American Legal Development," in Paul Finkelman, *Slavery and the Law*, 11.
27. *Life and Writings*, I, 291–96, 300; *Frederick Douglass Papers*, Vol. 1: 308, 419.
28. Quoted in Eric Foner and Olivia Mahoney, *A House Divided: America in the Age of Lincoln* (New York: W.W. Norton, 1990), 49.
29. McPherson, *Ordeal by Fire*, Vol. 1, 70.
30. Harold M. Hyman and William M. Wiecek, *Equal Justice Under Law: Constitutional Development: 1835–1875* (New York: Harper and Row, 1982), 144.
31. Horton and Horton, "A Federal Assault: African Americans and the Impact of the Fugitive Slave Law of 1850," 145.
32. Forrest McDonald, *States' Rights and the Union: Imperium in Imperio, 1776–1876* (Lawrence: University Press of Kansas, 2000), 160.
33. *Life and Writings*, II, 106–107. Italics in original.
34. McPherson, *Ordeal by Fire*, Vol. I, 70, 72.
35. Stewart, *Holy Warriors*, 153.
36. Quarles, *Black Mosaic*, 107.
37. *Life and Writings*, II, 226. Italics in original.
38. Carleton Mabee, *Black Freedom: The Nonviolent Abolitionists from 1830 through the Civil War* (London: Collier-Macmillan, 1970), 291.
39. Russell B. Nye, *William Lloyd Garrison and the Humanitarian Reformers* (Boston: Little, Brown and Company, 1955), 157.
40. Thoreau, "Slavery in Massachusetts," An Address at the Anti-Slavery Celebration at Framingham, July 4th, 1854, in Thoreau, *Civil Disobedience and Other Essays*, 23.
41. Horton and Horton, "A Federal Assault: African Americans and the Impact of the Fugitive Slave Law of 1850," 151.
42. *Life and Writings*, II, 43.
43. Stanley W. Campbell, *The Slave Catchers: Enforcement of the Fugitive Slave Law, 1850–1860* (Chapel Hill: University of North Carolina Press, 1970).

44. Bennett, *Before the Mayflower,* 151, 464.
45. Nye, *William Lloyd Garrison,* 158.
46. Mabee, *Black Freedom,* 292.
47. Larry Gara, *The Liberty Line: The Legend of the Underground Railroad* (Lexington: University of Kentucky Press, 1961), 102.
48. McFeely, *Frederick Douglass,* 263. Douglass's letter was dated August 29, 1868.
49. *Life and Writings,* II, 195–96. Italics in original.
50. *Frederick Douglass Papers,* 2: 417–18.
51. *Life and Writings,* II, 196–98.
52. Ibid., 200. Italics in original.
53. Ibid., 201. Italics in original.
54. Ernest Lee Tuveson, *Redeemer Nation: The Idea of America's Millennial Role* (Chicago: University of Chicago Press, 1968), 188–91.
55. Charles M. Wiltse, *John C. Calhoun: Sectionalist, 1840–1850* (Indianapolis: The Bobbs-Merrill Company, Inc., 1951), 334–35.
56. Stewart, *Holy Warriors,* 152.

CHAPTER 4: CONVERTING TO
THE UNITED STATES CONSTITUTION

1. *Life and Writings,* I, 207.
2. The *Liberator,* September 13, 1844. Quoted in Cain, *William Lloyd Garrison,* 31–32.
3. *Life and Writings,* I, 329.
4. Ibid., 275.
5. Ibid., 353; see also *Life and Writings,* V, 183.
6. *Frederick Douglass Papers,* 2: 193–7.
7. Eric Foner, *Free Soil, Free Labor, Free Men: The Ideology of the Republican Party before the Civil War* (New York: Oxford University Press, 1970), 73.
8. Robert C. Dick, *Black Protest: Issues and Tactics* (Westport, CT: Greenwood Press, 1974), 61.
9. Harry H. Wellington, *Interpreting the Constitution: The Supreme Court and the Process of Adjudication* (New Haven: Yale University Press, 1990), 48.
10. Madison, *Federalist,* number 37. Quoted in Walter F. Murphy, "The Art of Constitutional Interpretation: A Preliminary Showing," in *Essays on the Constitution of the United States,* ed. M. Judd Harmon (Port Washington, N.Y.: Kennikat Press, 1978), 130.
11. *Life and Writings,* I., 352.
12. Donald G. Nieman, *Promises to Keep: African-Americans and the Constitutional Order, 1776 to the Present* (New York: Oxford University Press, 1991), viii.
13. *Life and Writings,* II, 201.
14. Ibid., V, 368.
15. McPherson, *Ordeal By Fire,* Vol. I, 47.
16. Fehrenbacher, *The Dred Scott Case: Its Significance in American Law and Politics* (Oxford: Oxford University Press, 1978), 191.
17. Ibid., 617–18.

18. *Life and Writings*, II, 351–52.
19. Ibid., 352.
20. *Life and Times*, 708.
21. *My Bondage and My Freedom*, 364–67. Italics in original.
22. Ibid., 392.
23. George Anastaplo, *The Constitution of 1787: A Commentary* (Baltimore: Johns Hopkins University Press, 1989), 22.
24. Don E. Fehrenbacher, *The Slaveholding Republic: An Account of the United States Governments' Relations to Slavery.* Completed and edited by Ward M. McAfee (Oxford: Oxford University Press, 2001), 39. The controversy over the original Constitution and slavery rages on. For recent anti-slavery interpretations, see Fehrenbacher, *The Dred Scott Case*,11–47; Fehrenbacher, *The Slaveholding Republic*, 15–47, 298–300; Herbert J. Storing, "Slavery and the Moral Foundations of the American Republic," in Horwitz, *The Moral Foundations of the American Republic*, 313–32. For examples of the neo-Garrisonian pro-slavery interpretation of the Constitution, see Thurgood Marshall, "Reflections on the Bicentennial of the United States Constitution," *Harvard Law Review* 101 (1987), 1–5; John Hope Franklin, "The Moral Legacy of the Founding Fathers," in John Hope Franklin, *Race and History: Selected Essays: 1938–1988* (Baton Rouge: Louisiana State University Press, 1989), 153–62; William M. Wiecek, *Sources of Antislavery Constitutionalism* (Ithaca: Cornell University Press, 1977), 62–83; Paul Finkelman, "Slavery and the Constitutional Convention: Making a Covenant with Death," in *Beyond Confederation: Origins of the Constitution and American National Identity*, ed. Richard Beeman, Stephen Botein, and Edward C. Carter II (Chapel Hill: University of North Carolina Press, 1987), 188–225.
25. Thomas G. West, *Vindicating the Founders: Race, Sex, Class, and Justice in the Origins of America* (Lanham, MD: Rowman and Littlefield, 1997), 15.
26. Don E. Fehrenbacher, "Slavery, the Framers, and the Living Constitution," in *Slavery and Its Consequences: The Constitution, Equality, and Race*, ed. Robert A. Goldwin and Art Kaufman (Washington, D.C., American Enterprise Institute, 1988), 6.
27. Joseph Ellis, *Founding Brothers: The Revolutionary Generation* (New York: Alfred A. Knopf, 2001), 93.
28. *The Liberator*, September 13, 1844, in Cain, *William Lloyd Garrison*, 31–32.
29. Lincoln, "Speech on the Kansas-Nebraska Act at Peoria, Illinois, October 16, 1854," in Fehrenbacher, *Lincoln: Speeches and Writings 1832–1858*, 338.
30. Lincoln, "Speech at New Haven, Connecticut, March 6, 1860," in Fehrenbacher, *Lincoln: Speeches and Writings 1859–1865*, 142.
31. West, *Vindicating the Founders*, 15–16.
32. F. Michael Higginbotham, *Race Law: Cases, Commentary, and Questions* (Durham, North Carolina: Carolina Academic Press, 2001), 74.
33. McKivigan, "The Frederick Douglass-Gerrit Smith Friendship," in *Frederick Douglass: New Literary and Historical Essays*, ed. Eric J. Sundquist (Cambridge: Cambridge University Press, 1990), 212.

34. David W. Blight, *Frederick Douglass' Civil War: Keeping Faith in Jubilee* (Baton Rouge: Louisiana State University Press, 1989), 30.

35. *Life and Writings*, II, 118–19.

36. Ibid., 149. Italics in original.

37. Ibid., 149–50. Italics in original.

38. Ibid., 150.

39. T. Gregory Garvey, "Frederick Douglass' Change of Opinion on the U.S. Constitution: Abolitionism and the 'Elements of Moral Power,'" *American Transcendental Quarterly* 9 (1999), 229–43.

40. Quoted in Rossiter, *Seedtime of the Republic: The Origin of the American Tradition of Political Liberty* (New York: Harcourt, Brace and Company, 1953), 368.

41. Garrison, "Declaration of Sentiments of the National Anti-Slavery Convention . . . assembled in the City of Philadelphia, December 4, 1833," in *The Antislavery Argument*, ed. William H. Pease and Jane H. Pease (Indianapolis: The Bobbs-Merrill Company, 1965), 65–71, at 68.

42. Robert M. Cover, *Justice Accused: Antislavery and the Judicial Process* (New Haven: Yale University Press, 1975), 1–41.

43. Ibid., 21.

44. Alfred H. Kelly, Winfred A. Harbison, and Herman Belz, *The American Constitution: Its Origins and Development*, seventh edition, Vol. I (New York: W.W. Norton and Company, 1991), 244.

45. On the moral reading of the Constitution, see Ronald Dworkin, *Freedom's Law: The Moral Reading of the American Constitution* (Cambridge: Harvard University Press, 1996), 2–12.

46. Richards, *Conscience and the Constitution*, 99–102.

47. *Life and Writings*, II, 152–53.

48. For the Constitution as part of America's political religion, see Michael Kammen, *A Machine That Would Go of Itself: The Constitution in American Culture* (New York: Alfred A. Knopf, 1987); and Sanford Levinson, *Constitutional Faith* (Princeton: Princeton University Press, 1988).

49. On the aspirational theory of the Constitution, see Sotirios A. Barber, *On What the Constitution Means* (Baltimore: Johns Hopkins University Press, 1984), 55–62;.Herman Belz, *Abraham Lincoln, Constitutionalism, and Equal Rights in the Civil War Era* (New York: Fordham University Press, 1998), 88; Philip Bobbitt, *Constitutional Fate: Theory of the Constitution* (New York: Oxford University Press, 1982),93–177; Gary J. Jacobsohn, *The Supreme Court and the Decline of Constitutional Aspiration* (Totowa, N.J.: Rowman and Littlefield, 1986), 1–11, 95–112; and Walter F. Murphy, James E. Fleming, and William F. Harris, II, *American Constitutional Interpretation* (Mineola, N.Y.: The Foundation Press, Inc., 1986), 1–3; 290–91.

50. Wiecek, *Sources of Antislavery Constitutionalism*, 63.

51. Herbert J. Storing, "Slavery and the Moral Foundations of the American Republic," in Horwitz, The Moral Foundations of the American Republic, 324.

52. See James A. Colaiaco, *Martin Luther King, Jr.: Apostle of Militant Nonviolence* (New York: St. Martin's Press, 1988, paperback edition, with preface, 1993).

53. Jacobus tenBrock, *Equal Under Law*, 66–93; see also Dwight Lowell Dumond, *Anti-Slavery: The Crusade for Freedom in America* (Ann Arbor: University of Michigan Press, 1961), 293–95.
54. *Life and Writings*, II, 381.
55. Ibid., 337.
56. Ibid., III, 365.
57. Lincoln, "Speech at Alton, Illinois, October 15, 1858," in Fehrenbacher, *Lincoln: Speeches and Writings: 1832–1858*, 802.
58. Lincoln, "House Divided Speech at Springfield, Illinois, June 16, 1858," in Fehrenbacher, *Lincoln: Speeches and Writings, 1832–1858*, 426. Italics in original.
59. Douglass, "Freedom in the West Indies: An Address Delivered in Poughkeepsie, New York, on 2 August 1858." *Frederick Douglass Papers*, 3: 237.
60. Fehrenbacher, *The Dred Scott Case*, 21, 27.
61. Lincoln, "Address at Cooper Institute, New York City," in Fehrenbacher, *Lincoln: Speeches and Writings: 1859–1865*, 126–27,130. Emphasis in original. Cooper Institute, located on Astor Place in Manhattan, later became known as Cooper Union.
62. Lincoln, "First Inaugural, March 4, 1861," in Fehrenbacher, *Lincoln: Speeches and Writings: 1859–1865*, 215.
63. Charles L. Black, Jr., *Structure and Relationship in Constitutional Law* (Baton Rouge: Louisiana State University Press, 1969), 7; see also Phillip Shaw Paludan, "Hercules Unbound: Lincoln, Slavery, and the Intentions of the Framers," in *The Constitution, Law, and American Life: Critical Aspects of the Nineteenth-Century Experience*, ed. Donald G. Nieman (Athens: University of Georgia Press, 1992), 7–9.
64. Murphy, Fleming, and Harris, *American Constitutional Interpretation*, 292–94.
65. *Life and Writings*, V, 196.
66. Kammen, *A Machine That Would Go of Itself*, 99.
67. Ralph Waldo Emerson, "The Fugitive Slave Law," 7 March 1854, in Len Gougeon and Joel Myerson, eds., *Emerson's Antislavery Writings* (New Haven: Yale University Press, 1995), 73–89, at 82. Italics in original.
68. Eric Foner, *The Story of American Freedom* (New York: W. W. Norton & Co., 1998), 36. Italics in original.
69. Fehrenbacher, *The Dred Scott Case*, 21.
70. A. Leon Higginbotham, Jr., *Shades of Freedom: Racial Politics and Presumptions of the American Judicial Process* (New York: Oxford University Press, 1996), 68–69.
71. *My Bondage and My Freedom*, 392.
72. Ibid., 391–92.
73. Quarles, *Frederick Douglass*, 74.
74. *Frederick Douglass Papers*, 4: 507.
75. *Life and Writings*, II, 213–14.
76. Ibid., 350.
77. Ibid., 177.

78. *Frederick Douglass Papers*, 2: 395–96.
79. Blight, *Frederick Douglass' Civil War*, 35.
80. *Life and Writings*, II, 214.
81. For Douglass and party politics during the antebellum period, see Blight, *Frederick Douglass' Civil War*, 26–58.
82. *Life and Writings*, II. 514.
83. Ibid., 397. See Herbert J. Storing, "The Case against Civil Disobedience," in *Toward a More Perfect Union: Writings of Herbert J. Storing*, ed. Joseph M. Bessette (Washington, D.C.: The American Enterprise Institute, 1995), 250.
84. *Life and Writings*, II, 155–56. Italics in original.
85. Ibid., 53–54.
86. Ibid., 210.
87. Quarles, *Frederick Douglass*, 74.
88. *Life and Writings*, II, 55.
89. Ibid., 425.
90. Ibid., V, 183.
91. McKivigan, "The Frederick Douglass-Gerrit Smith Friendship," in Sundquist, *Frederick Douglass: New Literary and Historical Essays*, 205–32; see also Leon F. Litwack, "The Emancipation of the Negro Abolitionist," in *The Antislavery Vanguard: New Essays on the Abolitionists*, ed. Martin Duberman (Princeton: Princeton University Press, 1965), 137–55.
92. Mrs. Anna Murray Douglass responded to the charge against her husband by sending a note to Garrison: "It is not true, that the presence of a certain person in the office of Frederick Douglass causes unhappiness in his family. . . ." *Life and Writings*, II, 58.
93. Wilson J. Moses, "Frederick Douglass and the Constraints of Racialized Writing," in Sundquist, *Frederick Douglass: New Literary and Historical Essays*, 77.
94. *Life and Writings*, II, 55.
95. Quarles, *Frederick Douglass*, 74.
96. *Life and Writings*, II, 63.
97. William Goodell, *Views of American Constitutional Law and Its Bearing upon American Slavery* (Utica, N.Y.: Lawson and Chapin, 1845, second edition), 134–42; Lysander Spooner, *The Unconstitutionality of Slavery* (Boston: Bela Marsh, 1846), 36–9.
98. *Life and Writings*, II, 202. Italics and emphasis in original.
99. Ibid., 353. Italics in original.
100. H. Jefferson Powell, "The Original Understanding of Original Intent," in *Interpreting the Constitution: The Debate Over Original Intent*, ed. Jack N. Rakove (Boston: Northeastern University Press, 1990), 82.
101. Leonard W. Levy, *Original Intent and the Framers' Constitution* (Chicago: Ivan R. Dee, 1988), 2.
102. Fletcher, *Our Secret Constitution*, 30; see also Bobbitt, *Constitutional Fate*, 9–13.
103. Lawrence H. Tribe, *American Constitutional Law*, Vol. One, third edition (New York: Foundation Press, 2000), 57.

104. William J. Brennan, Jr., "The Constitution of the United States: Con-
     temporary Ratification," in Rakove, *Interpreting the Constitution*, 25.
105. *Life and Writings*, I, 355.
106. Ibid., I, 356, 363.
107. Ibid., II, 157. Italics in original.
108. Tribe, *American Constitutional Law*, 32.
109. Spooner, *The Unconstitutionality of Slavery*, 57–60.
110. Powell, "The Original Understanding of Original Intent," in Rakove,
     ed. *Interpreting the Constitution: The Debate over Original Intent* (Boston:
     Northeastern University Press, 1990), 58–59, 62.
111. Spooner, *The Unconstitutionality of Slavery*, 82, 115. Italics in original.
     Ogden v. Saunders (12 Wheaton, 332).
112. *Gibbons v. Ogden* (9 Wheaton, 1) 1824, in *Documents of American History*,
     ninth edition, Vol. I, ed. Henry Steele Commager (Englewood Cliffs,
     N.J.: Prentice-Hall, 1973), 239.
113. For Marshall's method of interpreting the Constitution, see Charles F.
     Hobson, *The Great Chief Justice: John Marshall and the Rule of Law*
     (Lawrence, K.S.: University Press of Kansas, 1996), 75, 93–94,
     101–102, 199–208.
114. Goodell, *Views of American Constitutional Law*, 21.
115. *Life and Writings*, V, 198. Douglass's point about the difficulty of ascer-
     taining "original intent" outside the literal words of the document itself
     had been made by Justice Joseph Story, *Commentaries on the Constitution
     of the United States*, I, 3rd edition (Boston: Little, Brown and Company,
     1858) [First published 1833], 300–301. Cited by Schrader, "Natural
     Law in the Constitutional Thought of Frederick Douglass," in Bill E.
     Lawson and Frank M. Kirkland, *Frederick Douglass: A Critical Reader*
     (Walden, M.A.: Blackwell, 1999), 88–89.
116. *Life and Writings*, II, 367.
117. Stephens, "Frederick Douglass' Multiracial Abolitionism," 177; see also
     Gregory Stephens, *On Racial Frontiers: The New Culture of Frederick Dou-
     glass, Ralph Ellison, and Bob Marley* (Cambridge: Cambridge University
     Press, 1999), 54–113.
118. *Life and Writings*, III, 348–49. Italics in original.
119. Lawrence H. Tribe believes that the Preamble should play a greater
     role in interpreting the Constitution. See Tribe, *American Constitutional
     Law*, 72 n. 10.
120. On the Preamble of the Constitution as inconsistent with slavery, see
     also Goodell, *Views of American Constitutional Law*, 39–41; and Spooner,
     The Unconstitutionality of Slavery, 89–94.
121. Dennis J. Mahoney, "Preamble," in *Encyclopedia of the Constitution*, Vol.
     3, ed. Levy, Karst, and Mahoney, 1435–36, at 1436.
122. Joseph Story, *A Familiar Exposition of the Constitution of the United States*.
     Originally published in 1840 (Lake Bluff, Illinois: Regnery/Gateway
     Bicentennial Edition, 1986), 58–59.
123. Louis Henkin, *The Age of Rights* (New York: Columbia University Press,
     1990), 95, 202 n.13.

124. *Life and Writings*, II, 54.

125. Aristotle, *Rhetoric*, I. xv. 3–12.

126. Ronald G. Walters, *The Antislavery Appeal: American Abolitionism After 1830* (New York: W.W. Norton and Co., 1978), 42. For Spooner's anti-slavery construction of the Constitution, see Aileen S. Kraditor, *Means and Ends in American Abolitionism: Garrison and His Critics on Strategy and Tactics, 1834–1850* (New York: Pantheon Books, 1969), 187–88; 190–96.

127. *Frederick Douglass Papers*, 3, 159.

128. Bernard Bailyn, *Faces of Revolution: Personalities and Themes in the Struggle for* American Independence (New York: Vintage Books, 1992), 222; see also Jaffa, *Original Intent and the Framers of the Constitution: A Disputed Question* (Washington, D.C: Regnery Gateway, 1994), 95.

129. Sacvan Bercovitch, *The American Jeremiad* (Madison: University of Wisconsin Press, 1978), 6–7, 11; and Howard-Pitney, *The Afro-American Jeremiad*, 7–8.

130. *Life and Writings*, II, 203.

131. Blight, *Frederick Douglass' Civil War*, 1–25.

132. *Life and Writings*, II, 203. See also the conclusion of *My Bondage and My Freedom*, 398.

133. *Life and Writings* II, 203–204.

134. *Frederick Douglass Papers*, 3: 359, headnote.

CHAPTER 5: THE OMINOUS FUTURE:
A NATION ON THE BRINK

1. McFeely, *Frederick Douglass*, 181.

2. William L. Andrews, *"My Bondage and My Freedom* and the American Literary Renaissance of the 1850s," in *Critical Essays on Frederick Douglass*, ed. William L. Andrews (Boston: G. K. Hall and Co., 1991), 138–39.

3. *Narrative*, 102; *My Bondage and My Freedom*, 398. Italics added.

4. *Frederick Douglass Papers*, Vol. 3: 7; Douglass used similar words in a speech in Chicago, Illinois, on October 30, 1854, attacking the Kansas-Nebraska Act. *Frederick Douglass Papers*, Vol. 2: 558.

5. *My Bondage and My Freedom*, 226–227.

6. Eric J. Sundquist, *To Wake the Nations: Race in the Making of American Literature* (Cambridge: Harvard University Press, 1993), 124.

7. *My Bondage and My Freedom*, 106.

8. Sundquist, *To Wake the Nations*, 89–90.

9. Ibid., 125, 132, 137.

10. *Life and Writings*, II, 235.

11. Ibid., 360.

12. Ibid., 122.

13. *My Bondage and My Freedom*, 301–302.

14. *Life and Writings*, II, 244.

15. Ibid., II, 254–55.

16. Ibid., 255, 259.

17. Ronald T. Takaki, *Violence in the Black Imagination: Essays and Documents* (New York: G.P. Putnam's Sons, 1972), 80.
18. *Life and Writings*, I, 97–98.
19. Ibid., II, 443.
20. See Bernard R. Boxill, "Douglass Against the Emigrationists," in Lawson and Kirkland, *Frederick Douglass: A Critical Reader*, 21–49.
21. *Frederick Douglass Papers*, 2: 11.
22. *My Bondage and My Freedom*, 412, 414.
23. Ibid., 418.
24. Sundquist, Introduction, *Frederick Douglass: New Literary and Historical Essays*, 6, 14.
25. *My Bondage and My Freedom*, 398.
26. *Frederick Douglass Papers*, 1: 262.
27. Henry Highland Garnet, "An Address to the Slaves of the United States of America," in *Forerunners of Black Power*, ed. Ernest G. Borman (Englewood Cliffs, N.J.: Prentice-Hall, Inc., 1971), 153–54.
28. Dick, *Black Protest*, 138; and *Life and Writings*, II, 22. On the issue of violence in the abolition movement, see Dick, *Black Protest*, 127–60.
29. *Life and Times*, 719.
30. *Life and Writings*, I, 359–60.
31. Ibid., 398–99.
32. James Oliver Horton and Lois E. Horton, *Hard Road to Freedom: The Story of African America* (New Brunswick, N.J.: Rutgers University Press, 2001), 110.
33. *My Bondage and My Freedom*, 254.
34. *Narrative*, 60.
35. *My Bondage and My Freedom*, 268–69.
36. Ibid., 283–84. Italics in original.
37. Ibid., 286. Emphasis in original.
38. Ibid., 286. Italics in original.
39. Frantz Fanon, *The Wretched of the Earth*, trans. Constance Farrington (New York: Grove Press, Inc., 1968), 94.
40. *Narrative*, 65.
41. Ibid., 304–305. Italics in original.
42. William L. Andrews, Introduction, *Three Classic African-American Novels* (New York: Penguin Books, 1990), 11.
43. Frederick Douglass, "The Heroic Slave," in *Violence in the Black Imagination: Essays and Documents*, ed. Ronald T. Takaki (New York: G. P. Putnam's Sons, 1972), 37–38.
44. *Frederick Douglass Papers*, 1: 67–69, 211, 244–45; 2: 46–47, 131, 153–58.
45. Takaki, *Violence in the Black Imagination*, 37–38. Italics in original.
46. Ibid., 75. Italics in original.
47. *Frederick Douglass Papers*, 2: 151, 153. Italics in original.
48. For Douglass and John Brown, see McFeely, *Frederick Douglass*, 186–200.
49. Hebrews, 9:72.
50. *Life and Times*, 715–19.
51. *Frederick Douglass Papers*, 2: 275.

52. *Life and Writings*, II, 287.
53. Ibid., 206–209.
54. Ibid., 287–88. Italics in original.
55. Ibid., V, 334.
56. *Frederick Douglass Papers*, 3: 88.
57. *My Bondage and My Freedom*, 248.
58. Herbert Aptheker, *To Be Free: Studies in American Negro History* (New York: International Publishers, 1948), 61.
59. November 28, 1856. Date provided by Aptheker, *To Be Free*, 62. For complete text, see *Life and Writings*, II, 406.
60. *Frederick Douglass Papers*, 2: 481, 483, 487–88.
61. *Life and Writings*, II, 331.
62. McPherson, *Ordeal by Fire*, Vol. I, 93.
63. *Life and Writings*, II, 283–84.
64. Lincoln, "Speech on the Kansas-Nebraska Act at Peoria, Illinois, October 16, 1854," in Fehrenbacher, *Lincoln: Speeches and Writings: 1832–1858*, 315, 339. Italics in original.
65. *Life and Writings*, II, 331–32.
66. McPherson, *Ordeal by Fire*, Vol. I, 98.
67. Michael Fellman, Lesley J. Gordon, and Daniel E. Sutherland, *This Terrible War: The Civil War and Its Aftermath* (New York: Longman, 2003), 62.
68. David Donald, *Charles Sumner and the Coming of the Civil War* (New York: Alfred A. Knopf, 1961), 301, 304.
69. *Frederick Douglass Papers*, 3: 115.
70. Peter Irons, *A People's History of the Supreme Court* (New York: Penguin Books, 1999), 177.
71. *Life and Times*, 743–44.
72. *Life and Writings*, II, 437. Misdated August 4th. *Frederick Douglass Papers*, Vol. 3: 182, headnote.
73. Robert V. Remini, *John Quincy Adams* (New York: Henry Holt and Company, 2002), 148.
74. *Life and Times*, 759.
75. W. E. B. Du Bois, *John Brown*, ed. David Roediger (New York: The Modern Library, 2001), 61.
76. *Life and Times*, 748.
77. Stephen B. Oates, *To Purge This Land With Blood: A Biography of John Brown* (New York: Harper and Row, Publishers, 1970), 351.
78. Ibid., 327.
79. Fellman, Gordon, and Sutherland, *This Terrible War,* 6.
80. James M. McPherson, *Battle Cry of Freedom: The Civil War Era* (New York: Oxford University Press, 1988), 209–210.
81. *Life and Times*, 759–64.
82. Richard O. Curry, "Righteous Violence," in *The Abolitionists: Means, Ends, and Motivations*, third edition, ed. Lawrence B. Goodheart and Hugh Hawkins (Lexington, MA: D. C. Heath and Co., 1995), 140.
83. Herbert Aptheker, *Abolitionism: A Revolutionary Movement* (Boston: Twayne Publishers, 1989), 138.

84. Thoreau, "A Plea for Captain John Brown" (1860). In Thoreau, *Civil Disobedience and Other Essays*, 46–48.
85. *Life and Writings*, II, 460. Italics in original.
86. *Life and Times*, 753, 755.
87. Douglass, "Did John Brown Fail?: An Address Delivered in Harpers Ferry, West Virginia, on 30 May 1881," in *Frederick Douglass Papers*, 5, 35.

Chapter 6: The *Dred Scott* Decision
and the American Dilemma

1. The suit was against Scott's owner, John F. A. Sanford of New York. The name was misspelled as "Sandford" in the official court reports, hence *Dred Scott v. Sandford*. The citation is *Dred Scott v. Sandford*, 19 Howard 394 (1857). Benjamin C. Howard was the official reporter of the case. Based upon a later renumbering of U.S. Supreme Court decisions, the case may also be cited: 60 U.S. 393 (1857). The inclusive pages are 393–633.
2. The Wisconsin territory is now part of the state of Minnesota.
3. Irons, *A People's History of the Supreme Court*, 159.
4. Fehrenbacher, *The Dred Scott Case*, 264.
5. Hyman and Wiecek, *Equal Justice Under Law*, 173.
6. Paul Finkelman, *Dred Scott v. Sandford: A Brief History with Documents* (Boston: Bedford Books, St. Martin's Press, 1997), 25.
7. Fehrenbacher, *The Dred Scott Case*, 280.
8. Ibid., 305.
9. Ibid., 313.
10. While all nine justices wrote opinions, Don E. Fehrenbacher observes: "In all branches of government and in popular thought, the 'Dred Scott decision' came to mean the opinion of the Chief Justice. . . . As a matter of historical reality, the Court decided what Taney declared that it decided." Fehrenbacher, *The Dred Scott Case*, 334. Fehrenbacher reiterates this point in another work: "Taney's opinion was accepted as the opinion of the Court by its critics as well as its defenders. As a matter of historical reality, the *Dred Scott* decision is what he declared it to be." See Fehrenbacher, "Dred Scott v. Sandford," in *Encyclopedia of the American Constitution*, Vol. 2, ed. Levy, Karst, and Mahoney, 586.
11. *Dred Scott v. Sandford*, 19 Howard 403.
12. Ibid., 404–405.
13. Ibid., 405.
14. Finkelman, *Dred Scott v. Sandford*, 35.
15. Strader v. Graham, 10 Howard 82 (1850).
16. 19 Howard 407–9. Italics added.
17. Irons, *A People's History of the Supreme Court*, 173–74.
18. 19 Howard 410.
19. Ibid., 410–11. Italics in original.
20. Ibid., 426.
21. *Dred Scott* included the first instance of "substantive due process" in American constitutional law. The "due process" clause of the Fifth

Amendment originally related solely to "process," or fair procedure. That is, the clause was traditionally interpreted as merely stipulating how laws must be applied rather than restricting which laws the government may enact. In ruling that Congress could not legally deprive slave owners of their "property" in the territories, the Taney Court, instead of limiting itself to the process by which law is applied, took upon itself to stipulate the proper substance of the law.

22. 19 Howard 450–52. Italics added.
23. Fehrenbacher, *The Dred Scott Case*, 300.
24. Finkelman, *Dred Scott v. Sandford*, 44.
25. Soon after the Supreme Court's decision, Dred Scott was set free by his owner. He subsequently worked as a porter in St. Louis until his death on September 17, 1858.
26. David M. Potter, *The Impending Crisis: 1848–1861*, Completed and edited by Don E. Fehrenbacher (New York: Harper and Row, Publishers, 1976), 293.
27. Fehrenbacher, "The Dred Scott Case," in *Quarrels that Have Shaped the Constitution*, ed. John A. Garraty (New York: Harper and Row, Publishers, 1987), 96.
28. 19 Howard 428.
29. Fehrenbacher, *The Dred Scott Case*, 5; and "Dred Scott v. Sandford," in *Encyclopedia of the American Constitution*, ed. Levy, Karst, and Mahoney, Vol. 2, 584.
30. Kelly, Harbison, and Belz, *The American Constitution*, I, 274.
31. Wiecek, *The Sources of Antislavery Constitutionalism*, 18.
32. Lincoln, "Speech on the Dred Scott Decision at Springfield, Illinois, June 26, 1857," in Fehrenbacher, *Lincoln: Speeches and Writings: 1832–1858*, 398. Italics in original.
33. Lincoln, "House Divided Speech at Springfield, Illinois, June 16, 1858," in Fehrenbacher, *Lincoln: Speeches and Writings: 1832–1858*, 432. Italics in original.
34. Lincoln, "Speech on the Dred Scott Decision at Springfield, Illinois, June 26, 1857," in Fehrenbacher, *Lincoln: Speeches and Writings: 1832–1858*, 393. Italics in original.
35. *New York Tribune*, March 7, 1857. Quoted in Stanley I. Kutler, ed., *The Dred Scott Decision: Law or Politics?* (Boston: Houghton Mifflin Company, 1967), 47; and Charles Warren, *The Supreme Court in United States History*, Vol. Two: 1836–1918, revised edition (Boston: Little, Brown, and Company 1926), 305.
36. Warren, *The Supreme Court in United States History*, Vol. Two, 305–306.
37. *Chicago Tribune*, March 12, 1857. Quoted in Kutler, *The Dred Scott Decision*, 47–48.
38. *Charleston* [South Carolina] *Daily Courier*, March 9, 1857. Quoted in Kutler, *The Dred Scott Decision*, 54.
39. Fehrenbacher, *The Dred Scott Case*, 418.
40. Kutler, *The Dred Scott Decision*, xv.
41. Potter, *The Impending Crisis*, 291.
42. Higginbotham, *Shades of Freedom*, 61, 65.

43. Thurgood Marshall, "Remarks at the Second Circuit Judicial Confer-
ence [The Importance of Judicial Neutrality], May 8, 1981," in *Thurgood
Marshall: His Speeches, Writings, Arguments, Opinions, and Reminiscences*, ed.
Mark V. Tushnet, The Library of Black America (Chicago: Lawrence
Hill Books, 2001), 188.

44. John Hope Franklin and Alfred A. Moss, Jr., *From Slavery to Freedom: A
History of African Americans*, eighth edition (Boston: McGraw-Hill,
2000), 216.

45. Irons, *A People's History of the Supreme Court*, 176.

46. Fehrenbacher, *The Dred Scott Case*, 573.

47. This position was recently argued by Charles W. Mills, "Whose Fourth
of July? Frederick Douglass and 'Original Intent,'" in *Frederick Douglass: A Critical Reader*, ed. Lawson and Kirkland, 100–42. Mills's interpretation suffers from the same historical flaws as Taney's decision.

48. G. Edward White, *The American Judicial Tradition: Profiles of Leading
American Judges*, expanded edition (New York: Oxford University
Press, 1988), 82. Italics in original.

49. *Frederick Douglass Papers*, 3: 145–46.

50. Douglass's assault on *Dred Scott* received greater circulation when his
speech was published as a pamphlet.

51. *Life and Writings*, II, 410–11.

52. Ibid., 420.

53. Ibid., 411.

54. Blight, *Frederick Douglass' Civil War*, 3–12.

55. *Life and Writings*, II, 410.

56. See Blight, *Frederick Douglass' Civil War*, 101–21.

57. Howard-Pitney, The Afro-American Jeremiad, 20.

58. *Life and Writings*, II, 411–12, 415.

59. Wayne D. Moore, "Constitutional Citizenship," in *Constitutional Politics:
Essays on Constitution Making, Maintenance, and Change*, ed. Sotirios A.
Barber and Robert P. George (Princeton: Princeton University Press,
2001), 248–49.

60. "Andrew Jackson's Veto of the Bank Bill," in Murphy, Fleming, and
Harris, *American Constitutional Interpretation*, 225–26.

61. Lincoln, "Speech at Chicago, Illinois, July 10, 1858," in Fehrenbacher,
Lincoln: Speeches and Writings: 1832–1858, 450–51.

62. Lincoln, "First Inaugural Address March 4, 1861," in Fehrenbacher,
Lincoln: Speeches and Writings: 1859–1865, 221.

63. Life and Writings, II, 418.

64. *United States v. Fisher*, 6 United States Reports (2 Cranch), 358 (1806).
Spooner, *The Unconstitutionality of Slavery*, 18–19. Italics in original; see
also William Goodell, *Slavery and Anti-Slavery*, 574.

65. *Life and Writings*, II, 418–19.

66. Ibid., 420–24.

67. For Curtis's dissenting opinion, see Finkelman, *Dred Scott v. Sandford*,
108–26.

68. *Life and Writings*, V, 403, 406. Italics in original.

69. *Frederick Douglass Papers*, 2: 459.

CHAPTER 7: THE UNITED STATES CONSTITUTION
IS ANTI-SLAVERY

1. Bobbitt, *Constitutional Fate*, 25–26.
2. J. M. Balkin and Sanford Levinson, "The Canons of Constitutional Law," *Harvard Law Review* 111 (1998), 1021–22.
3. On the relationship between Douglass and Ottilie Assing, see McFeely, *Frederick Douglass*, 183–86; 199; and Maria Diedrich, *Love Across Color Lines: Ottilie Assing and Frederick Douglass* (New York: Hill and Wang, 1999).
4. *Life and Writings*, II, 95.
5. Ibid., II, 466.
6. *Frederick Douglass Papers*, 3: 340, headnote.
7. The speech was later published as a pamphlet: Frederick Douglass, *The Constitution of the United States: Is It Pro-Slavery or Anti-Slavery? By Frederick Douglass. A Speech Delivered in Glasgow, March 26, 1860, in Reply to an Attack Made Upon His View by Mr. George Thompson* (Halifax, England: T. and W. Birtwhistle, printers, 1860). In the United States, the speech was printed in *Frederick Douglass' Paper*, April 27, 1860.
8. Cass Sunstein, "Dred Scott v. Sandford and Its Legacy," in *Great Cases in Constitutional Law*, ed. Robert P. George ((Princeton: Princeton University Press, 2000), 65, 75, 88 n.1, 89 n.6.
9. Tribe, *American Constitutional Law*, 2, 2 n. 3. See also Balkin and Levinson, "The Canons of Constitutional Law," 964–67; 1021–24. Balkin and Levinson "suggest, if only symbolically, that Frederick Douglass is on at least the same level of interpretive authority as Roger B. Taney." At 965 n. 8.
10. *Life and Writings*, II, 475–76.
11. Ibid., 476. Ronald Dworkin offers a similar interpretative rule, advocating that legal interpretation should attempt to make the law "the best it can be." Ronald Dworkin, *Law's Empire* (Cambridge: Harvard University Press,1986), 313–14.
12. *Life and Writings*, II, 476.
13. Ibid., 477.
14. Richard Hildreth, *Despotism in America: An Inquiry into the Nature, Results and Legal Basis of the Slaveholding System in the United States* (1854; reprint, New York: Kelley, 1970), 239–40. Quoted in Cain, *William Lloyd Garrison*, 33.
15. Life and Writings, II, 468.
16. Ibid.
17. Fehrenbacher, "Slavery, the Framers, and the Living Constitution," 4; Fehrenbacher, *The Slaveholding Republic*, 13. See also the argument of black abolitionist William Howard Day, "The Constitution as Seen by Negroes, 1851," in Aptheker, *A Documentary History of the Negro People*, 318.
18. Gerrit Smith to John Greenleaf Whittier, July 18, 1844. Fehrenbacher, "Slavery, the Framers, and the Living Constitution," in Goldwin and Kaufman, *Slavery and Its Consequences*, 4.

19. Fehrenbacher, *The Dred Scott Case*, 27.
20. *Life and Writings*, II, 469.
21. Hugo LaFayette Black, *A Constitutional Faith* (New York: Alfred A. Knopf, 1969).
22. Powell, "The Original Understanding of Original Intent," in Rakove, *Interpreting the Constitution*, 88.
23. Keith E. Whittington argues that the strict textualist position was "perhaps most ably stated by Frederick Douglass." See Whittington, *Constitutional Interpretation: Textual Meaning, Original Intent, and Judicial Review* (Lawrence, KS: University Press of Kansas, 1999), 176.
24. *Life and Writings*, II, 469.
25. Ibid.
26. Ibid., 469–70.
27. Wendell Phillips, *The Constitution a Pro-Slavery Document, or Selections from the Madison Papers, etc.* (New York: American Anti-Slavery Society, 1844), 4, 6.
28. *Life and Writings*, II, 471.
29. Robert A. Goldwin, *Why Blacks, Women, and Jews Are Not Mentioned in the Constitution and Other Unorthodox Views* (Washington, D.C.: The American Enterprise Institute, 1990), 12.
30. West, *Vindicating the Founders*, 16.
31. Goldwin, *Why Blacks*, 12–13.
32. *Life and Writings*, II, 472.
33. For examples, see Harding, *There Is a River: The Black Struggle for Freedom in America* (New York: Harcourt Brace Jovanovich, 1981), 46; and Wiecek, *The Sources of Antislavery Constitutionalism in America*, 58.
34. Franklin, "The Moral Legacy of the Founding Fathers," 159.
35. *Frederick Douglass Papers*, 2: 352. Italics in original. The sentence quoted varies slightly from the text of the speech reprinted in *Life and Writings*, II, 472.
36. *Life and Writings*, II, 472.
37. Nathan Irvin Huggins, "Slavery and Its Defense," in Nathan Irvin Huggins, *Revelations: American History, American Myths*, ed. Brenda Smith Huggins (New York: Oxford University Press, 1995), 237.
38. *Life and Writings*, II, 472–73.
39. Wiecek, *The Sources of Antislavery Constitutionalism*, 74.
40. Storing, "Slavery and the Moral Foundations of the American Republic," in Horwitz, *The Moral Foundations of the American Republic*, 322.
41. *Life and Writings*, II, 473.
42. Two years later, in a speech delivered at Himrods Corners, New York on July 4, 1862, Douglass admitted that the framers were mistaken in assuming that stopping the African slave trade would put an end to slavery. "They did not comprehend the radical character of the evil." *Life and Writings*, III, 247.
43. *Frederick Douglass Papers*, 3: 158–59, and n.13.
44. Fehrenbacher, *The Slaveholding Republic*, 41–44. Italics in original.
45. *Life and Writings*, II, 473.
46. Fehrenbacher, *The Slaveholding Republic*, 44–45, 355, n.123.

47. *Life and Writings*, II, 473. In the version of the speech reprinted in *Frederick Douglass Papers*, 2: 354, Douglass uses himself as the example of the person elected president.

48. *Life and Writings*, II, 475. The Madison quotation is from Max Farrand, ed., *The Records of the Federal Convention of 1787*, revised edition (New Haven: Yale University Press, 1937), II, 417 (August 25).

49. Harry Jaffa, *Crisis of the House Divided: An Interpretation of the Issues in the Lincoln-Douglas Debates* (Chicago: University of Chicago Press, 1982), 434.

50. *Life and Writings*, II, 475.

51. Ibid.

52. Staughton Lynd, "The Abolitionist Critique of the United States Constitution," in Duberman, *The Antislavery Vanguard*, 210.

53. *Life and Writings*, II, 475.

54. George Anastaplo, *Abraham Lincoln: A Constitutional Biography* (Lanham, MA: Rowman and Littlefield Publishers, Inc., 1999), 56, 65–66.

55. Life and Writings, II, 477–78.

56. Fehrenbacher, *The Slaveholding Republic*, 300.

57. *Life and Writings*, II, 479.

58. *Frederick Douglass Papers*, 3: 366. These words do not appear in the version of Douglass's speech printed in Foner.

59. *Life and Writings*, II, 480.

60. Ibid., 95.

61. Ibid., 484.

62. Ibid., 487. Italics in original.

63. Ibid., 528. Italics in original.

64. Ibid., 536.

65. Lincoln, "First Inaugural Address, March 4, 1861," in Fehrenbacher, *Lincoln: Speeches and Writings: 1859–1865*, 215, 224.

66. *Life and Writings*, III, 74–75, 79.

67. Ibid., 67.

Epilogue

1. *Frederick Douglass Papers*, 3: 521, headnote.

2. *Life and Writings*, III, 110.

3. Ibid., 250.

4. Ibid., 241–46.

5. Ibid., 246–48.

6. Ibid., 248–49.

7. *Life and Times*, 801.

8. Ronald C. White, Jr., *Lincoln's Greatest Speech: The Second Inaugural* (New York: Simon and Schuster, 2002), 41.

9. Lincoln, "Second Inaugural Address, March 4, 1865," in Fehrenbacher, *Lincoln: Speeches and Writings: 1859–1865*, 686–87.

10. *Life and Times*, 801–804.

11. Merrill D. Peterson, *Lincoln in American Memory* (New York: Oxford University Press, 1994), 55–60.

12. Quarles, *Frederick Douglass*, 277.
13. *Life and Times*, 854–55.
14. Ibid., IV, 309–10. In *Life and Times*, 801–802. Douglass states that he often quoted the "solemn words" of Lincoln's second Inaugural Address.
15. *Life and Writings*, IV, 309–11.
16. Ibid., III, 404.
17. Abraham Lincoln to Horace Greeley, August 22, 1862, in Fehrenbacher, *Lincoln: Speeches and Writings, 1858–1865*, 357–58.
18. Sundquist, *To Wake the Nations*, 114.
19. Foner, *The Story of American Freedom*, 92.
20. Fehrenbacher, *Lincoln: Speeches and Writings, 1858–1865*, 585.
21. *Life and Writings*, IV, 310–12.
22. *Life and Times*, 792.
23. Lincoln, "Fourth Lincoln-Douglas Debate, Charleston, Illinois, September 18, 1858," in Fehrenbacher, *Lincoln: Speeches and Writings: 1832–1858*, 636.
24. *Life and Writings*, IV, 312–13, 315.
25. James M. McPherson, *Abraham Lincoln and the Second American Revolution* (New York: Oxford University Press, 1991), 31, 45.
26. *Life and Writings*, IV, 316.
27. Ibid., 316–17.
28. Ibid., 317.
29. Benjamin Quarles, *Lincoln and the Negro* (New York: Oxford University Press, 1962), 83, 86.
30. John Hope Franklin, "Lincoln and Public Morality," in Franklin, *Race and History: Selected Essays 1938–1988* (Baton Rouge: Louisiana State University Press, 1989), 168. Other modern black scholars do not share Douglass's positive view of Lincoln. See, for example, Lerone Bennett Jr., *Forced into Glory: Abraham Lincoln's White Dream* (Chicago: Johnson Publishing Company, 2000). According to James M. McPherson, Douglass had "a more realistic appreciation of Lincoln's leadership in the war for the Union than do modern black critics." McPherson, "A New Birth of Freedom," in McPherson, *Drawn with the Sword: Reflections on the American Civil War* (New York: Oxford University Press, 1996), 182.
31. *Life and Writings*, IV, 314.
32. Ibid., 149.

SELECTED
BIBLIOGRAPHY

Adams, Francis D., and Barry Sanders. *Alienable Rights: The Exclusion of African Americans in a White Man's Land, 1619–2000*. New York: Harper Collins Publishers, 2003.

Andrews, William L. *"My Bondage and My Freedom and the American Literary Renaissance of the 1850s."* In *Critical Essays on Frederick Douglass*. Ed. William L. Andrews, 133–47. Boston: G. K. Hall & Co., 1991.

———. Introduction, *Frederick Douglass, My Bondage and My Freedom*. Edited with an introduction by William L. Andrews, xi–xxviii. Urbana: University of Illinois Press, 1987.

———. *To Tell a Free Story: The First Century of Afro-American Autobiography, 1760–1865*. Urbana: University of Illinois Press, 1986.

Andrews, William L., and William S. McFeely, eds. *Narrative of the Life of Frederick Douglass, An American Slave, Written By Himself*. Norton Critical Edition. New York: W. W. Norton & Co., 1997.

Aptheker, Herbert. *Abolitionism: A Revolutionary Movement*. Boston: Twayne Publishers, 1989.

———. *To Be Free: Studies in American Negro History*. New York: International Publishers, 1948.

Bacon, Jacqueline. "'Do You Understand Your Own Language?' Revolutionary Topoi in the Rhetoric of African-American Abolitionists." *Rhetoric Society Quarterly* 28 (1998), 55–75.

Baker, Houston A., Jr. *Long Black Song: Essays in Black American Literature and Culture*. Charlottesville: University of Virginia Press, 1972.

———. *The Journey Back: Issues in Black Literature and Criticism*. Chicago: University of Chicago Press, 1980.

Balkin, J. M., and Sanford Levinson. "The Canons of Constitutional Law." *Harvard Law Review* 111 (1998): 964–1024.

Barber, Sotirios A. *On What the Constitution Means*. Baltimore: Johns Hopkins University Press, 1984.

Barnes, Gilbert Hobbs. *The Antislavery Impulse, 1830–1844*. Gloucester, Massachusetts: Peter Smith, 1957.

Becker, Carl. *The Declaration of Independence: A Study in the History of Ideas*. 1922. New York: Vintage Books, 1958.

Bell, Bernard W. "The African-American Jeremiad and Frederick Douglass's Fourth of July 1852 Speech." In *The Fourth of July: Political Oratory and Literary Reactions, 1776–1876*. Ed. P. Goetsch and G. Hurm, 139–53. Tubingen: Gunter Narr Verlag, 1993.

Bellah, Robert N. "Civil Religion in America." *Daedalus* 96 (1967): 1–21.

Bennett, Lerone, Jr. *Before the Mayflower: A History of Black America*. Sixth revised edition Harmondsworth, England: Penguin Books, 1993.

Bercovitch, Sacvan. *The American Jeremiad*. Madison, W.I.: University of Wisconsin Press, 1978.

Berry, Mary Frances. *Black Resistance/White Law: A History of Constitutional Racism in America*. New York: Penguin Books, 1995.

Blassingame, John W., et al. eds. *The Frederick Douglass Papers*. Five Volumes. New Haven: Yale University Press, 1979–92.

Blassingame, John W. *Frederick Douglass: The Clarion Voice*. Washington, D.C. National Park Service, U.S. Department of the Interior, 1976.

———. Introduction. *Narrative of the Life of Frederick Douglass, An American Slave, Written by Himself*. Ed. John W. Blassingame, John R. McKivigan, and Peter P. Hinks, ix-xli. New Haven: Yale University Press, 2001.

Blight, David W. *Frederick Douglass' Civil War: Keeping Faith in Jubilee*. Baton Rouge: Louisiana State University Press, 1989.

Bormann, Ernest G., ed. *Forerunners of Black Power: The Rhetoric of Abolition*. Englewood Cliffs, N.J.: Prentice-Hall, Inc., 1971.

Boxill, Bernard R. "Douglass Against the Emigrationists." In *Frederick Douglass: A Critical Reader*. Edited by Lawson and Kirkland, 21–49. Walden, MA: Blackwell Publishers, 1999.

Burke, Ronald K. *Frederick Douglass: Crusading Orator for Human Rights*. New York: Garland Publishing, Inc., 1996.

Butterfield, Stephen. *Black Autobiography in America*. Amherst: University of Massachusetts Press, 1974.

Cain, William E., ed. *William Lloyd Garrison and the Fight Against Slavery: Selections from the Liberator*. Boston: Bedford Books of St. Martin's Press, 1995.

Campbell, Stanley W. *The Slave Catchers: Enforcement of the Fugitive Slave Law, 1850–1860*. Chapel Hill: University of North Carolina Press, 1970.

Chesebrough, David B. *Frederick Douglass: Oratory from Slavery*. Westport, CT: Greenwood Press, 1998.

Chesnutt, Charles W. *Frederick Douglass*. 1899. A Centenary Edition. Atlanta: Clark Atlanta University Press, 2001.

Colaiaco, James A. *Martin Luther King, Jr.: Apostle of Militant Nonviolence*. New York: St. Martin's Press, 1988; paperback edition, with preface, 1993.

Corwin, Edwin S. *The "Higher Law" Background of American Constitutional Law*. Ithaca: Cornell University Press, 1955.

Cover, Robert M. *Justice Accused: Antislavery and the Judicial Process*. New Haven: Yale University Press, 1975.

Crane, Gregg D. "Douglass's Natural Rights Constitutionalism." In *Approaches to Teaching Narrative of the Life of Frederick Douglass*. Ed. James C. Hall, 73–80.

Curry, Richard O. "Righteous Violence." In *The Abolitionists: Means, Ends, and Motivations*. Third Edition. Ed. Lawrence B. Goodheart and Hugh Hawkins, 136–43. Lexington, MA: D.C. Heath and Co., 1995.

Davis, Charles T., and Henry Louis Gates, Jr., eds. *The Slave's Narrative.* New York: Oxford University Press, 1985.

Dick, Robert C. *Black Protest: Issues and Tactics.* Westport, CT: Greenwood Press, 1974.

Diedrich, Maria. *Love Across Color Lines: Ottilie Assing and Frederick Douglass.* New York: Hill and Wang, 1999.

Dillon, Merton L. *The Abolitionists: The Growth of a Dissenting Minority.* Dekalb, IL: Northern Illinois University Press, 1974.

Donald, David. *Lincoln.* New York: Simon & Schuster, 1995.

Douglass, Frederick. *Autobiographies.* Edited with notes by Henry Louis Gates, Jr. New York: Library of America, 1994.

———. *My Bondage and My Freedom.* Edited with an Introduction by William L. Andrews. Urbana: University of Illinois Press, 1987.

———. *My Bondage and My Freedom.* New York: Dover Publications, Inc., 1855/1969.

———. *Narrative of the Life of Frederick Douglass, an American Slave, Written by Himself.* Edited with an introduction by David Blight. Boston: Bedford Books of St. Martin's Press, 1993.

———. *Narrative of the Life of Frederick Douglass, an American Slave, Written by Himself.* Edited with an introduction by Houston A. Baker, Jr. New York: Viking Penguin, 1982.

———. "The Heroic Slave." In Ronald T. Takaki, *Violence in the Black Imagination: Essays and Documents,* 37–77. New York: G. P. Putnam's Sons, 1972.

Du Bois, Eugene E. *The City of Frederick Douglass: Rochester's African-American People and Places.* Third edition. Landmark Society of Western New York, 1998.

Du Bois, W.E. B. *John Brown.* Edited and with an introduction by David Roediger. New York: The Modern Library, 2001.

Dumond, Dwight. *Antislavery: The Crusade for Freedom in America.* Ann Arbor: University of Michigan Press, 1961.

———. *Antislavery Origins of the Civil War in the United States.* Ann Arbor: University of Michigan Press, 1939.

Ehrlich, Walter. *They Have No Rights: Dred Scott's Struggle for Freedom.* Westport, CT: Greenwood Press, 1979.

Fabre, Geneviève. "African-American Commemoration Celebration in the Nineteenth Century." In *History and Memory in African-American Culture.* Ed. Geneviève Fabre and Robert O'Meally, 72–91. New York: Oxford University Press, 1994.

Fehrenbacher, Don E., ed. *Abraham Lincoln: Speeches and Writings, 1832–1858.* New York: Library of America, 1989.

———. *Abraham Lincoln: Speeches and Writings, 1859–1865.* New York: Library of America, 1989.

———. *The Dred Scott Case: Its Significance in American Law and Politics.* Oxford: Oxford University Press, 1978.

———. "The Dred Scott Case." In *Quarrels that Have Shaped the Constitution.* Ed. John A. Garraty, 87–99. New York: Harper & Row, Publishers, 1987.

———. "Dred Scott v. Sandford." In *Encyclopedia of the American Constitution.* Volume 2. Ed. Leonard W. Levy, Kenneth L. Karst, and Dennis J. Mahoney, 584–87. New York: Macmillan Publishing Company, 1986.

————. "Only His Stepchildren." In *Lincoln in Text and Context.* Ed. Don E. Fehrenbacher, 95–112. Stanford: Stanford University Press, 1987.

————. *The Slaveholding Republic: An Account of the United States Government's Relations to Slavery.* Completed and edited by Ward M. McAfee. Oxford: Oxford University Press, 2001.

————. "Slavery, the Framers, and the Living Constitution." In *Slavery and Its Consequences: The Constitution, Equality, and Race.* Ed. Robert A. Goldwin and Art Kaufman, 1–22. Washington, D.C.: American Enterprise Institute, 1988.

Filler, Louis. *The Crusade Against Slavery: 1830–1860.* New York: Harper Brothers, Publishers, 1960.

Finkelman, Paul. "The Centrality of Slavery in American Legal Development." In *Slavery and the Law.* Ed. Paul Finkelman, 3–26. Lanham, MD, Rowman & Littlefield Publishers, Inc., 2002.

————. *Dred Scott v. Sandford: A Brief History with Documents.* Boston: Bedford Books of St. Martin's Press, 1997.

————. "Slavery and the Constitutional Convention: Making a Covenant with Death." In *Beyond Confederation: Origins of the Constitution and American National Identity.* Ed. Richard Beeman, Stephen Botein, and Edward C. Carter II. 188–225. Chapel Hill: University of North Carolina Press, 1987.

Foner, Eric. *Free Soil, Free Labor, Free Men: The Ideology of the Republican Party before the Civil War.* New York: Oxford University Press, 1970.

Foner, Eric, and Olivia Mahoney. *A House Divided: America in the Age of Lincoln.* New York: W. W. Norton & Co., 1990.

Foner, Philip S. *Frederick Douglass: A Biography.* New York: Citadel Press, 1964.

————. *Frederick Douglass on Women's Rights.* New York: Da Capo Press, 1992.

————. ed. *The Life and Writings of Frederick Douglass.* Five Volumes. New York: International Publishers, 1950–75.

Forbes, Ella. "Every Man Fights for His Freedom: The Rhetoric of African-American Resistance in the Mid-Nineteenth Century." In *Understanding African American Rhetoric: Classical Origins to Contemporary Innovations.* Ed. Ronald L. Jackson and Elaine B. Richardson, 155–170. New York: Routledge, 2003.

Franklin, John Hope. *From Slavery to Freedom.* Fifth edition. New York: Alfred A. Knopf, 1980.

————. "The Moral Legacy of the Founding Fathers." In *Race and History: Selected Essays, 1938–1988.* Ed. John Hope Franklin, 153–62. Baton Rouge: Louisiana State University Press, 1989.

Freehling, William W. "The Founding Fathers and Slavery." In *American Negro Slavery: A Modern Reader.* Third edition. Ed. Allen Weinstein, Frank Otto Gatell, and David Sarasohn, 3–20. New York: Oxford University Press, 1979.

Friedman, Lawrence J. *Gregarious Saints: Self and Community in American Abolitionism, 1830–1870.* Cambridge: Cambridge University Press, 1982.

Fulkerson, R. Gerald. "Exile as Emergence: Frederick Douglass in Great Britain, 1845–1847." *Quarterly Journal of Speech* 60 (1974): 69–82.

————. "Frederick Douglass (1818–1895)." *African-American Orators: A Bio-Critical Sourcebook.* Edited by Richard W. Leeman, 82–97. Westport, CT: Greenwood Press, 1996.

Garvey, T. Gregory. "Frederick Douglass's Change of Opinion on the U.S. Constitution: Abolitionism and the 'Elements of Moral Power,'" *American Transcendental Quarterly* 9 (1999): 229–43.

Gates, Henry Louis, Jr. *Figures in Black: Words, Signs, and the 'Racial' Self.* New York: Oxford University Press, 1989.

———. Introduction. *Narrative of the Life of Frederick Douglass, An American Slave: Written By Himself.* New York: A Laurel Book, Bantam Doubleday Dell Publishing, Co., Inc., 1997.

Gerber, Scott Douglas. *To Secure These Rights: The Declaration of Independence and Constitutional Interpretation.* New York: New York University Press, 1995.

Gerteis, Louis S. *Morality and Utility in American Antislavery Reform.* Chapel Hill: University of North Carolina Press, 1987.

Glaude, Eddie S., Jr. *Exodus!: Religion, Race, and Nation in Early Nineteenth-Century Black America.* Chicago: University of Chicago Press, 2000.

Goldstein, Leslie Friedman. "Morality and Prudence in the Statesmanship of Frederick Douglass." *Polity* 16 (1984): 606–23.

———. "Violence as an Instrument for Social Change: The Views of Frederick Douglass (1817–1895)." *Journal of Negro History* 41 (January 1976): 61–72.

Goldwin, Robert A. *Why Blacks, Women, and Jews Are Not Mentioned in the Constitution and Other Unorthodox Views.* Washington, D.C.: The American Enterprise Institute, 1990.

Gregory, James Monroe. *Frederick Douglass, the Orator.* New York: Thomas Y. Cromwell, 1893.

Guelzo, Allen C. "Apple of Gold in a Picture of Silver: The Constitution and Liberty," in *The Lincoln Enigma.* Ed. by Gabor Boritt, 86–107. Oxford: Oxford University Press, 2001.

Harding, Vincent. *There Is a River: The Black Struggle for Freedom in America.* New York: Harcourt Brace Jovanovich, 1981.

Higginbotham, A. Leon. *Shades of Freedom: Racial Politics and Presumptions of the American Judicial Process.* New York: Oxford University Press, 1996.

Holland, Frederic May. *Frederick Douglass: The Colored Orator.* New York: Funk & Wagnall, 1891.

Holzer, Harold. *Lincoln at Cooper Union: The Speech that Made Abraham Lincoln President.* New York: Simon and Schuster, 2004.

Hopkins, Vincent C. *Dred Scott's Case.* New York: Fordham University Press, 1951.

Horton, James Oliver, and Lois E. Horton. "A Federal Assault: African Americans and the Impact of the Fugitive Slave Law of 1850," in *Slavery and the Law.* Ed. Paul Finkelman, 143–60. Lanham: MD: Rowman & Littlefield Publishers, Inc., 2002.

———. *Hard Road to Freedom: The Story of African America.* New Brunswick, N.J.: Rutgers University Press, 2001.

———. *In Hope of Liberty: Culture, Community and Protest Among Northern Free Blacks, 1700–1860.* New York: Oxford University Press, 1997.

Howard-Pitney, David. *The Afro-American Jeremiad: Appeals for Justice in America.* Philadelphia: Temple University Press, 1990.

————. "The Enduring Black Jeremiad: The American Jeremiad and Black Protest Rhetoric, From Frederick Douglass to W. E. B. Du Bois, 1841–1919." *American Quarterly* 38 (1986): 481–92.

Huggins, Nathan Irvin. *Slave and Citizen: The Life of Frederick Douglass.* New York: Longman, 1980.

Hyman, Harold, and William M. Wiecek. *Equal Justice Under Law: Constitutional Development: 1835–1875.* New York: Harper & Row, Publishers, 1982.

Jacobsohn, Gary J. *The Supreme Court and the Decline of Constitutional Aspiration.* Totowa, N.J.: Rowman & Littlefield Publishers, 1986.

Jaffa, Harry. *Crisis of the House Divided: An Interpretation of the Issues in the Lincoln-Douglas Debates.* Chicago: University of Chicago Press, 1982.

————. *A New Birth of Freedom: Abraham Lincoln and the Coming of the Civil War.* Lanham, MD: Rowman & Littlefield Publishers, Inc., 2000.

Jasinski, James. "Rearticulating History in Epideictic Discourse: Frederick Douglass's 'The Meaning of the Fourth of July to the Negro,'" in *Rhetoric and Political Culture in Nineteenth-Century America.* Ed. Thomas W. Benson, 71–89. East Lansing: Michigan State University Press, 1997.

Jordan, Winthrop. *White Over Black: American Attitudes Toward the Negro, 1550–1812.* Chapel Hill: University of North Carolina Press, 1968.

Kingston, Steve. *Frederick Douglass: Abolitionist, Liberator, Statesman.* New York: National Negro Congress, 1941.

Kraditor, Aileen S. *Means and Ends in American Abolitionism: Garrison and His Critics on Strategy and Tactics, 1834–1850.* New York: Pantheon Books, 1969.

Kutler, Stanley I., ed. *The Dred Scott Decision: Law or Politics?* Boston: Houghton Mifflin Company, 1967.

Lampe, Gregory P. *Frederick Douglass: Freedom's Voice, 1818–1845.* East Lansing: Michigan State University Press, 1998.

Lawson, Bill E., and Frank M. Kirkland, eds. *Frederick Douglass: A Critical Reader.* Walden, MA: Blackwell Publishers, 1999.

Levine, Robert S. *Martin Delany, Frederick Douglass, and the Politics of Representative Identity.* Chapel Hill: University of North Carolina Press, 1997.

Levinson, Sanford. *Constitutional Faith.* Princeton: Princeton University Press, 1988.

Levy, Leonard W. *Original Intent and the Framers' Constitution.* Chicago: Ivan R. Dee, 1988.

Levy, Leonard, Kenneth L. Karst, and Dennis J. Mahoney, eds. *Encyclopedia of the Constitution.* Four Volumes. New York: Macmillan Publishing Company, 1986.

Lieberman, Jethro K. *The Enduring Constitution: An Exploration of the First Two Hundred Years.* New York: Harper & Row, Publishers, 1987.

Litwack, Leon F. "The Emancipation of the Negro Abolitionist." In *The Antislavery Vanguard.* Ed. Martin Duberman, 137–55. Princeton: Princeton University Press, 1965.

————. *North of Slavery: The Negro in the Free States: 1790–1860.* Chicago: University of Chicago Press, 1961.

Lucaites, John Louis. "The Irony of 'Equality' in Black Abolitionist Discourse: The Case of Frederick Douglass's 'What to the Slave is the Fourth of July?,'" in *Rhetoric and Political Culture in Nineteenth-Century America.* Ed. Thomas W. Benson, 47–69. East Lansing: Michigan State University Press, 1997.

Lynd, Staughton. "The Abolitionist Critique of the United States Constitution. In *The Antislavery Vanguard: New Essays on the Abolitionists*. Ed.
Martin Duberman, 209–39. Princeton: Princeton University Press,
1965.

———. *Class Conflict, Slavery, and the United States Constitution*. Indianapolis:
Bobbs-Merrill Co., 1967.

Mabee, Carleton. *Black Freedom: The Nonviolent Abolitionists From 1830 Through
the Civil War.* London: Collier-Macmillan, 1970.

Mahoney, Dennis J. "The Declaration of Independence as a Constitutional
Document." In *The Framing and Ratification of the Constitution*. Ed. Leonard
W. Levy and Dennis J. Mahoney, 54–68. New York: Macmillan Publish-
ing Company, 1987.

———. "Preamble." In *Encyclopedia of the Constitution*. Volume 3. Ed. Leonard
W. Levy, Kenneth L. Karst, and Dennis J. Mahoney, 1435–36. New York:
Macmillan Publishing Company, 1986.

Maier, Pauline, ed. *The Declaration of Independence and the Constitution of the
United States*. New York: Bantam Books, 1998.

Martin, Waldo, Jr. "Frederick Douglass: Humanist as Race Leader." In *Black
Leaders of the Nineteenth Century*. Ed. Litwack and August Meier, 59–84. Urbana: University of Illinois Press, 1991.

———. *The Mind of Frederick Douglass*. Chapel Hill: University of North Carolina Press, 1984.

Martin, Howard. "The Fourth of July Oration." *The Quarterly Journal of Speech*
44 (1958): 393–401.

Mayer, Henry. *All on Fire: William Lloyd Garrison and the Abolition of Slavery.*
New York: St. Martin's Press, 1998.

McClure, Kevin R. "Frederick Douglass's Use of Comparison in his Fourth of
July Oration: A Textual Criticism." *Western Journal of Communication* 64
(2000), 425–44.

McFeely, William. *Frederick Douglass*. New York: W. W. Norton & Co.,
1991.

McKivigan, John R. "The Frederick Douglass-Gerrit Smith Friendship and
Political Abolitionism in the 1850s." In *Frederick Douglass: New Literary and
Historical Essays*. Ed. Eric J. Sundquist, 205–32. Cambridge: Cambridge
University Press, 1990.

McPherson, James M. *Abraham Lincoln and the Second American Revolution*. New
York: Oxford University Press, 1991.

———. *Ordeal by Fire, Volume I: The Coming of War.* Second edition. New York:
McGraw-Hill, Inc., 1993.

———. "Politics and Judicial Responsibility: *Dred Scott v. Sandford*." In *Great
Cases in Constitutional Law*. Ed. Robert P. George, 90–93. Princeton: Princeton University Press, 2000.

Meier, August. "Frederick Douglass's Vision for America: A Case Study in
Nineteenth-Century Protest." In *Freedom and Reform: Essays in Honor of
Henry Steele Commager*. Ed. Harold M. Hyman and Leonard W. Levy,
127–48. New York: Harper & Row, Publishers, 1967.

Miller, Kelly. "Frederick Douglass." In Kelly Miller, *Race Adjustment: Essays on
the Negro in America*. (1907). Reprinted with new title, *Race Adjustment: The
Everlasting Stain*, 211–20. New York: Arno Press, 1968.

Miller, Douglas T. *Frederick Douglass and the Fight for Freedom.* New York: Facts on File Publications, 1988.

Mills, Charles W. "Whose Fourth of July? Frederick Douglass and 'Original Intent.'" In *Frederick Douglass: A Critical Reader.* Ed. Lawson and Kirkland, 100–42.

Moses, Wilson Jeremiah. *Black Messiahs and Uncle Toms: Social and Literary Manipulations of a Religious Myth.* University Park: Pennsylvania State University Press, 1982.

Murphy, Walter F. "The Art of Constitutional Interpretation: A Preliminary Showing," in *Essays on the Constitution of the United States.* Ed. M. Judd Harmon. 130–59. Port Washington, NY: Kennikat Press, 1978.

Nieman, Donald G. *Promises to Keep: African-Americans and the Constitutional Order, 1776 to the Present.* New York: Oxford University Press, 1991.

Nye, Russel B. *William Lloyd Garrison and the Humanitarian Reformers.* Boston: Little, Brown and Company, 1955.

Oates, Stephen B. *Abraham Lincoln: The Man Behind the Myths.* New York: Harper & Row Publishers, 1984.

———. *To Purge This Land with Blood: A Biography of John Brown.* New York: Harper & Row Publishers, 1970.

———. *With Malice Toward None: A Life of Abraham Lincoln.* New York: Harper & Row Publishers, 1977.

Paludan, Phillip Shaw. "Hercules Unbound: Lincoln, Slavery, and the Intentions of the Framers." In *The Constitution, Law, and American Life: Critical Aspects of the Nineteenth-Century Experience.* Ed. Donald G. Nieman, 1–22. Athens: University of Georgia Press, 1992.

Pease, William H., and Jane H. Pease. Eds. *The Antislavery Argument.* Indianapolis: The Bobbs-Merrill Company, Inc., 1965.

Perry, Lewis. *Radical Abolitionism: Anarchy and the Government of God in Antislavery Thought.* Ithaca: Cornell University Press, 1973.

Peterson, Merrill D. *Lincoln in American Memory.* New York: Oxford University Press, 1994.

Potter, David M. *The Impending Crisis: 1848–1861.* Completed and edited by Don E. Fehrenbacher. New York: Harper & Row, Publishers, 1976.

Powell, H. Jefferson. "The Original Understanding of Original Intent." In *Interpreting the Constitution: The Debate over Original Intent.* Ed. Jack N. Rakove, 53–115. Boston: Northeastern University Press, 1990.

Preston, Dickson J. *Young Frederick Douglass: The Maryland Years.* Baltimore: Johns Hopkins University Press, 1980.

Quarles, Benjamin. *Black Abolitionists.* New York: Oxford University Press, 1969.

———. *Black Mosaic: Essays in Afro-American History and Historiography.* Amherst: University of Massachusetts Press, 1988.

———. *Frederick Douglass.* Washington, D.C.: Associated Publishers, Inc., 1948.

Raboteau, Albert J. "African-Americans, Exodus, and the American Israel," in *African-American Christianity: Essays in History.* Ed. Paul E. Johnson, 1–17. Berkeley: University of California Press, 1994.

Rael, Patrick. *Black Identity and Black Protest in the Antebellum North.* Chapel Hill: University of North Carolina Press, 2002.

Rossiter, Clinton. *Seedtime of the Republic: The Origin of the American Tradition of Political Liberty.* New York: Harcourt, Brace and Company, 1953.

Schrader, David E. "Natural Law in the Constitutional Thought of Frederick Douglass." In *Frederick Douglass: A Critical Reader.* Ed. Lawson and Kirkland, 85–99.

Schwartz, Bernard. *A History of the Supreme Court.* New York: Oxford University Press, 1993.

Sewell, Richard. *Ballots for Freedom: Antislavery Politics in the United States, 1837–1860.* New York: Oxford University Press, 1976.

Smith, Valerie. *Self-Discovery and Authority in Afro-American Narrative.* Cambridge: Harvard University Press, 1987.

Stephens, Gregory. "Frederick Douglass's Multiracial Abolitionism: 'Antagonistic Cooperation' and 'Redeemable Ideals' in the July 5 Speech." *Communication Studies* 48 (1997), 1–19.

———. *On Racial Frontiers: The New Culture of Frederick Douglass, Ralph Ellison, and Bob Marley.* Cambridge: Cambridge University Press, 1999.

Stewart, James Brewer. *Holy Warriors: The Abolitionists and American Slavery.* New York: Hill and Wang, 1976.

Storing, Herbert J. "Frederick Douglass." In *Toward a More Perfect Union: Writings of Herbert J. Storing.* Ed. Joseph M. Bessette. 151–75. Washington, D.C.: The American Enterprise Institute, 1995.

———. "Slavery and the Moral Foundations of the American Republic." In *The Moral Foundations of the American Republic.* Third edition. Ed. Robert H. Horwitz, 313–32. Charlottesville: University Press of Virginia, 1986.

Sundquist, Eric J., ed. *Frederick Douglass: New Literary and Historical Essays.* Cambridge: Cambridge University Press, 1990.

———. *To Wake the Nations: Race in the Making of American Literature.* Cambridge: Harvard University Press, 1993.

Sunstein, Cass R. "*Dred Scott v. Sandford* and Its Legacy," in *Great Cases in Constitutional Law.* Ed. Robert P. George, 64–89. Princeton: Princeton University Press, 2000.

Sweet, Leonard I. "The Fourth of July and Black Americans in the Nineteenth Century: Northern Leadership Opinion within the Context of the Black Experience." *Journal of Negro History* 61 (1976): 256–75.

Swisher, Carl B. *The Oliver Wendell Holmes Devise History of the Supreme Court of the United States.* Volume V: The Taney Period, 1836–64. New York; Macmillan Publishing Co., Inc., 1974.

Takaki, Ronald. *Violence in the Black Imagination: Essays and Documents.* New York: G. P. Putnam's Sons, 1972.

Thomas, John L. *The Liberator, William Lloyd Garrison: A Biography.* Boston: Little, Brown and Company, 1963.

Thurow, Glen E. "The Gettysburg Address and the Declaration of Independence," in *Abraham Lincoln, The Gettysburg Address, and American Constitutionalism.* Ed. Leo Paul S. de Alvarez, 55–75. Irving, TX: University of Dallas Press, 1976.

Tillery, Tyrone. "The Inevitability of the Douglass-Garrison Conflict." *Phylon* 37 (1976): 137–49.

Tushnet, Mark V. *The American Law of Slavery, 1810–1860: Considerations of Humanity and Interest.* Princeton: Princeton University Press, 1981.

Tuveson, Ernest Lee. *Redeemer Nation: The Idea of America's Millennial Role.* Chicago: University of Chicago Press, 1968.

Voss, Frederick S. *Majestic in His Wrath: A Pictorial Life of Frederick Douglass.* Washington, D.C.: Smithsonian Institution Press, 1995.

Walker, Peter F. *Moral Choices: Memory, Desire, and Imagination in Nineteenth-Century American Abolition.* Baton Rouge: Louisiana State University Press, 1978.

Walters, Ronald G. *The Antislavery Appeal: American Abolitionism after 1830.* New York: W. W. Norton & Company, 1978.

Warren, Charles. *The Supreme Court in United States History.* Revised edition. Volume Two: 1836–1918. Boston: Little, Brown, and Company, 1926.

Washington, Booker T. *Frederick Douglass.* 1906. New York: Argosy-Antiquarian Ltd., 1969.

West, Thomas G. *Vindicating the Founders: Race, Sex, Class, and Justice in the Origins of America.* Lanham, MD: Rowman & Littlefield, 1997.

White, Ronald C., Jr. *Lincoln's Greatest Speech: The Second Inaugural.* New York: Simon and Schuster, 2002.

Whitfield, George. "Frederick Douglass: Negro Abolitionist." *Today's Speech* 11 (1963), 6–8; 24.

Wiecek, William M. *The Sources of Antislavery Constitutionalism in America.* Ithaca: Cornell University Press, 1977.

Wills, Garry. *Lincoln at Gettysburg: The Words That Remade America.* New York: Simon & Schuster, 1992.

ACKNOWLEDGMENTS

I wish to express appreciation to my friends and colleagues in the New York University General Studies Program who read all or part of an early version of my work: Joyce Apsel, Walter Miller, Ron Rainey, and John Ross. I am grateful for their useful suggestions. I thank my family, including my father, Alfred Colaiaco, and Josephine and Maria Ruggeri, for their abiding support. The memory of my mother, Helen Colaiaco, continues to sustain me.

The staff at Palgrave Macmillan deserves recognition. I thank Airié Stuart for perceiving the merit of my book; Alessandra Bastagli for providing valuable editorial assistance in bringing the manuscript to final form; Donna Cherry for guiding my book through the production process; and Enid Stubin for her excellent copyediting.

My greatest debt is to my wife, Nancy Ruggeri Colaiaco, to whom this book is dedicated. Her readings of multiple drafts did much to improve my book. I am deeply grateful for her insights, encouragement, and love. Needless to say, although this book has profited from the readings of others, I alone bear responsibility for its contents.

James A. Colaiaco
Rockville Centre, New York

INDEX